Choctaws at the Crossroads

The Political Economy of Class and Culture in the Oklahoma Timber Region

SANDRA FAIMAN-SILVA

University of Nebraska Press
Lincoln & London

First Bison Books printing: 2000
Most recent printing indicated by the last digit below:
10   9   8   7   6   5   4   3   2   1

Library of Congress Cataloging-in-Publication data. Faiman-
Silva, Sandra L. Choctaws at the crossroads : the political economy of class and culture in the Oklahoma timber region / Sandra
Faiman-Silva. p. cm. Includes bibliographical references
and index. ISBN 0-8032-2001-4 (cl.: alk. paper) ISBN 0-8032-6902-1
(pa.: alk. paper) 1. Choctaw Indians – Economic conditions.
2. Choctaw Indians – Social conditions. E99.C8F35 1998
305.897'3 – DC21 97-2349 CIP

Portions of chapter 7 appeared previously in Sandra L. Faiman-
Silva, "Tribal Land to Private Land: A Century of Oklahoma
Choctaw Timberland Alienation from the 1880s to the 1980s,"
Journal of Forest History 32.4 (1988): 191–204.

Portions of chapters 8, 10, 12, and 14 appeared previously in
Sandra Faiman-Silva, "Decolonizing the Choctaw Nation:
Choctaw Political Economy in the Twentieth Century," *American Indian Culture and Research Journal* 17.2 (1993): 43–73. Copyright Regents of the University of California.

Portions of chapter 12 appeared previously in Sandra Faiman-
Silva, "Multinational Corporate Development in the American
Hinterland: The Case of the Oklahoma Choctaws" in *The Politi-
cal Economy of North American Indians*, ed. John H. Moore (Nor-
man: University of Oklahoma Press, 1993), 214–39. Copyright
University of Oklahoma Press.

For Ishmael, Luke, and Ben

What you gonna do 'bout these hardworking men
Whole families and women and kids pouring in
Looking for land and there's land to be found
But lumber is king in a lumbering town. . . .

Woody Guthrie "Lumber Is King"

CONTENTS

ILLUSTRATIONS

TABLES

Acknowledgments

This book, which began in the early 1980s as a doctoral research project, has been many years in the making. In the course of writing, revising, and updating, it has matured like the family I raised along with it. During that decade and a half, Choctaw change processes have been clarified both for me and for the Choctaws themselves, who have emerged quite drastically changed, empowered, and economically on a surer footing than they were when, as a not-so-young graduate student, I went to the field in 1980 with my former husband, Dr. George Silva, who served as a Public Health Service physician at the Talihina Indian Hospital, now called the Choctaw Nation Indian Hospital.

Many voices can be heard in the story that follows. Several subjects of this study have passed away, leaving children and grandchildren to remember the times of hardship recounted and shared with me. Many families moved from abject poverty into the middle class and now live in modern mutual-help homes. Some still work for Weyerhaeuser and in the food-processing industry.

I want to thank the many people who have assisted with this research, particularly the fifty Choctaw families who permitted me to come into their homes, visit, and interview, and who provided me with invaluable insights into their daily lives and their unique survival strategies under often difficult circumstances. Several individuals were especially helpful in providing essential contacts, insights, and their time so that I could gain a better understanding of Choctaw communities and the quandaries they face. They include Leslie James, Juanita Jefferson, Charlie Jones, Shirley Lowman, and Grant Wilson.

I would also like to extend my appreciation to Mary Fitzgerald, Talihina's town librarian, who enabled me to pursue library work in a remote village of rural Oklahoma. Minnie Voyles was an energetic and enthusiastic supporter of not only my work but also her tribe and community. My friends Etta Mae James and Ella (Zucker) Shattuck have a special place in my heart and my memories of fifteen years of sharing life in Talihina, Oklahoma.

Members of the International Association of Machinists and Aerospace Workers, Local Lodge W15 (formerly International Woodworkers of America [IWA] Local 5–15), particularly Wayne Ray and Tribal Council member Billy Paul Baker, shared their insights, time, and wisdom and allowed me to witness the last remnants of a historic timbering tradition in southeastern Oklahoma. This book honors these men and women and the communities they represent.

A great source of theoretical encouragement in the early 1980s was the work of the Anthropology Resource Center, which was in the forefront of exploring the genocidal effects of multinational corporate penetration into indigenous communities throughout the world. The work of this organization, among others, has inspired me to examine an American community in depth, and the lives of Native Americans, to expose the conditions of exploitation under which they live.

I also wish to thank my graduate advisor, Maureen J. Giovannini, for her guidance throughout several phases of research and writing. Her assistance in developing and organizing the themes of my research were extremely helpful. John Moore, too, deserves a special note of appreciation for his extremely helpful comments on an earlier version of the manuscript and his ongoing encouragement and support of my work. Thomas Hall and other anonymous reviewers were also particularly helpful in refining my theoretical analysis.

My three sons, Ishmael, Luke, and Ben, deserve a special note of appreciation for their patience throughout. Ishmael and Luke, who grew up with this manuscript, and Benjamin, who was born in the Choctaw Nation, have been very accepting of all of my preoccupations. And my friend Mary Brunette, although not an anthropologist, has offered sensitive suggestions and support through several years of this project.

This research project is based on work supported by the National Science Foundation under doctoral dissertation research grant no. BNS-8022456. Any opinions, findings, and conclusions or recommendations expressed in this publication are those of the author and do not necessarily reflect the views of the National Science Foundation. I wish to express my appreciation to the Foundation for making this research undertaking possible by supporting this study.

This book is dedicated to the Choctaw *okla*, the Choctaw people, who fill the following pages with their words, work, and wisdom, and whose road I hope is recounted with respect.

Introduction

Anthropologists researching Native American communities occupy an uncertain position. Historically, our discipline's link with colonialism, imperialism, and cultural dominance has brought distrust of our work and anthropology's agenda, problems raised in internal disciplinary debates since the 1960s (see Hymes 1969; Gough 1968; Asad 1975; Harrison, ed., 1991; Mohanty 1991). Native American spokespeople, perhaps none more forcefully than Vine Deloria Jr., have also targeted anthropologists, calling us the "curse" of American Indians (1969:78). The Inter-American Commission on Human Rights of the Indian Law Resource Center has declared, "Indian leaders today are adamant that they will speak for themselves, and that missionaries, anthropologists, government officials, lawyers and charitable organizations will not speak on their behalf without express authorization of the Indians themselves" (reported in *Akwesasne Notes* 23.4 [1992]: 5).

Today anthropologists are critically examining the very meaning of what we do and how we do it. The core perspectives of our discipline, and so-called critically informed perspectives such as neo-Marxism, world-systems analysis, and even participant-observation fieldwork itself (see Harrison 1991; D'Amico-Samuels 1991; Ulin 1991), have been subject to intense self-scrutiny. Feminist anthropologists have demanded that we acknowledge our own embeddedness in the oppressive systems we describe and analyze. Postmodernists point out that we must allow the voices of the "other," that is, those subjects of our ostensibly "objective" inquiry, to engage us in mutual inquiry and debate. Native consultants – called "informants" in earlier anthropological jargon – have become collaborators in research, both in the formulation of questions to be addressed and in data gathering and analysis (see Borofsky 1993; Mohanty 1991; D'Amico-Samuels 1991).

Our critical perspective must develop a mature critical understanding of the intersection of race, class, gender, and ethnicity, argues Harrison (1991:3). In short, we must decolonize anthropology by eliminating andro-centric, Eurocentric, canonical frames of discourse and develop collabora-tive, genuinely critically informed, praxis-oriented, and deconstructive texts that empower us, our subjects, and our audience.

This book seeks to contribute critically informed insights into historically contextualized political-economic processes, offered by an outside, inter-ested, and, I hope, compassionate observer. Analyses are meant to explore and illuminate complex social forces, albeit from a non-native anthropolo-gist's viewpoint.

Much of the data for the current study of the Choctaw Nation was gath-ered in the old style of anthropological fieldwork. As participant-observer, interviewer, and investigator, I worked alone in a wide range of field sites, from county courthouses to clear-cuts and to rural homes lacking electricity and running water. My research brought me from boardrooms to living rooms; from local church and neighborhood communities to the local head-quarters of the Weyerhaeuser Corporation, Inc., and the Woodworkers Union, Local W15. I sought to be a "good listener," sensitive to the nuances of Choctaw rural life through close observation and reasoned inquiry.

The story I weave is complex and dialectical, historical, structural, and ideological. It is a lens through which I would like to think crucial under-standings can be gleaned about cultural process, ethnicity, and class conflict. I explore the beginnings of Choctaw/Euro-American contact to understand in detail how the Choctaws became embedded in a world economy domi-nated by Eurocentric political, economic, and cultural ways. I ask what forces combined to produce a new tribal cultural reality, exemplified today by a highly polished corporatelike entity headed by a powerful exemplar of the U.S. "Horatio Alger" myth of success: Choctaw chief Hollis E. Roberts.

My research was framed in the tradition of Laura Nader (1969) of "study-ing up" as well as down, weaving the threads and unfolding the creases of complex lifeways connected locally, regionally, and nationally, both histori-cally and in the present. My perspective has also been informed by depen-dency, neo-Marxist, and world-systems inquiry. Like that of Marxists, who also have been frequently castigated as gadflies, the work of anthropologists is synthetic, dialectical, and critical, offering insights into the complex work-ings of culture systems, both synchronically and diachronically. It is through this lens that I have attempted to understand Choctaw persistence and change by exploring the relationship among ethnicity, class, gender, and Native American tribalism historically and structurally (see Valentine 1975; Cohen 1978; Bee and Gingerich 1977; Worsley 1970; Albers and James 1986; Castile 1993; Muga 1984, 1988; see also Barth, ed., 1969; Hall 1996; Fernández Kelly 1989).

The Choctaw Nation, encompassing a region of ten and a half counties in extreme southeastern Oklahoma, is home to approximately sixteen thousand Choctaws. Formerly a tribal reservation of 6.8 million acres including more than 2 million acres of prime timberland, the Choctaw reservation was allotted beginning in 1903 as a result of the 1887 Dawes Severalty or Allotment Act. The tribe currently owns about sixty-five thousand acres, most in tracts of five acres or less. Relatively rich in natural resources, particularly timber, southeastern Oklahoma is the state's poorest region economically. And like many people in the Third World, southeastern Oklahoma's poor people live in an environment of wealth from which they only marginally benefit. More than one-third of Choctaws living in the timber region were unemployed in 1987 (*Bishinik* 5/87:2).

Choctaw history recounts events frequently heard in indigenous/Euro-American contact relations that transformed societies rooted in reciprocal egalitarianism to class-based and often racially stratified communities fully submerged in mainstream U.S. culture. In the Choctaw story, the intersection of indigenous and exogenous forces precipitated Choctaw social change along three intersecting lines: political, economic, and cultural, bringing together a complex array of actors and agents, fields and forces that brought the Choctaws to near-extinction in the early twentieth century.

The Choctaw story is not unique. Since the 1960s anthropologists, development scholars, political economists, and historians have documented global processes of land alienation, marginalization, and underdevelopment of some population sectors at the hands of others. World-systems inquiry has explored how the rise of capitalism in the mid-fifteenth century brought about a globally interdependent economy characterized by inequalities between so-called core sectors and peripheral or marginal economic regions. The world-systems perspective seeks to explain the relations between core developed economies and peripheral, underdeveloped regions in the context of colonialism, imperialism, and development, relations that are shown to be unequal in how core and peripheral sectors access resources, political power, and decision making (see Wallerstein 1976, 1980, 1984; Girvan 1970; Gilpin 1975; Seddon, ed., 1978:28; La Clau 1977; Bonilla and Girling 1973; Foster-Carter 1978; Frank 1969; Cardoso and Faletto 1979; Laite 1981; Goodman and Redclift 1982; Cook and Binford 1986; Hall 1988, 1995, 1996; Ward 1993; Ward, ed., 1990; Dunaway 1996).

World-system "incorporation," according to Thomas Hall (1995:4), is an interactive process of subsumption and transformation of peripheral sectors by core or metropolitan sectors interested in accessing local land, labor, and natural resources. The relationship between core and periphery, analysts argue, is inherently unequal and hierarchical: the core concentrates power, wealth, and knowledge, while the periphery is typically oriented toward production for use. Local responses to incorporation range from accommodation or assimilation to resistance and annihilation, argues Hall (1996:4; see also Nagel and Snipp 1993; Dunaway 1996). Shelton Davis (1977) has shown that Brazil's so-called economic miracle of corporate development led to the virtual annihilation of many Brazilian tribes, the rise of a landless urban class, and widespread destruction of the fragile Amazon forest. In his study of a formerly subsistence-based Panamanian village, Stephen Gudeman (1978), linking micro- and macroanalytical perspectives, has analyzed the transformation from subsistence production to wage labor in a government-owned sugar plantation system. June Nash (1979) has examined the oppressive system of labor exploitation in Bolivia's tin-mining industry to show how Indian peasants have kept alive their own cultural values and traditions while nurturing a sense of class consciousness. Wilma Dunaway (1996) traces Appalachian Cherokee accommodation, transformation, and resistance to capitalist incorporation in the eighteenth century.

Dependency and world-systems theories were originally developed by Latin American political and economic scholars in the 1950s and 1960s to account for Latin America's underdevelopment in spite of vast inputs of money and technology from the United States and the failure of techniques called "import substitution" aimed to eliminate Third World poverty and underdevelopment (see Frank 1969; La Clau 1977; O'Brien 1975:7; Booth 1975:51). André Gunder Frank, an early formulator of dependency theory, proposed several explanations of underdevelopment that constitute the framework of dependency theory today. He argued that three "contradictions" of capitalism fostered and perpetuated underdevelopment in peripheral societies: (1) "the contradiction of expropriation/appropriation of economic surplus," which results in "economic development for the few and underdevelopment for the many" (Booth 1975:67–68); (2) polarization between metropolitan centers and satellite peripheries promoting "economic development and structural underdevelopment"; and (3) the "contradiction of continuity in change," which for Frank implied that capitalist expansion throughout space and time is replicated structurally and is not unique to any particular region (Frank 1969:12–15; Booth 1975:69; O'Brien 1975:22). Frank's perspective gave rise to other global critiques of industrial capitalism, colonialism, and imperialism, in the works of Immanuel Wallerstein (1976, 1984), Peter Worsley (1984), Eric Wolf (1982), and John Clammer (ed., 1978; 1987), to cite a few.

In the present study I draw on macro- and microframeworks to analyze Choctaw history and cultural change. Anthropology's unique microanalytical focus, Carol Smith (1983) notes, provides an important critical perspective to examine local and regional embeddedness in larger global political economies (see also Anders 1980; Hall 1987, 1988, 1995, 1996). Using data from western Guatemala, Smith (1983:347) argues that in regional or peripheral studies, "the pattern of class, political and economic differentiation caused by the growth of the capitalist world economy can be seen in microcosm." Actors from the many layers of society – center, periphery, and semiperiphery – intersect in dynamic and culturally contingent histories, giving rise to complex and varied social outcomes and class struggles. It is through critically and historically informed analysis of local and regional sociocultural contexts that observers can trace the global rise of capitalism and indigenous transformations.

Studies of rural capitalist penetration into Latin America, South Asia, and Africa have illuminated patterns of unequal development produced by external control of resources and decision making in peripheral sectors. The core concentrates technology, capital resources, and political know-how, while the periphery contains underutilized raw materials, a reservoir of laborers, and an abundance of poverty. As J. Iain Prattis (1980:311) argues, "marginal regions are not just deterministic consequences of industrial capitalism; they constitute a vital cornerstone of the entire economic system" (see also Wallerstein 1976; G. Smith 1985; Chevalier 1983; Bernstein 1988; Cook and Binford 1986; Binford and Cook 1991). Colonizers sought land, natural resources, and cheap labor for industrializing European states. Subordinate indigenous enclaves served as cheap, readily available labor forces;

lands they occupied were veritable gold mines for colonial economic opportunities; and relationships were established whereby the resources of the colonized served the interests of the colonizer (see Wolf 1982; Wallerstein 1976; Memmi 1965; Cornell 1988:151).

In this emerging "capitalist world economy," as Wallerstein (1976:17) argues, state-based political forces served the interests of market expansion, by providing macroincentives such as military protection, financial backing, pacification mechanisms (missionaries, schools), and external change agents (government agencies, settlers) to subdue and eventually subordinate indigenous enclave populations. Three components essential to global economy formation came together in the capitalist expansion process, according to Wallerstein (1976:29): "territorial expansion of Europe," effective labor control mechanisms, and "strong state machineries" to control administratively the relationship between center and periphery.

Much has been written about the capitalist global expansion process since the era of European exploration and Columbus's rediscovery of the New World. Scholars generally agree that global expansion has given rise to political-economic relationships that are international, transformative, and unequal (see Wallerstein 1976, 1980, 1984, 1989; Frank 1969; Wolf 1983; Clapham 1985:6–7; Terray 1972; Hindess and Hirst 1975; Long 1975; Godelier 1977). "Within this system, the capitalist core regions tend to benefit significantly from international transactions while the peripheral regions become underdeveloped" (White 1983:xvi). The center–periphery articulation fosters the marginalization of hinterland populations – often minorities, rural poor, or immigrants – and their transformation into wage laborers, whose surplus value enriches the centrally placed capitalist enterprise.

The resulting relationship between center and periphery is structurally unequal, dialectical, and transformative. Once-independent or semi-autonomous subsistence producers are subsumed under external market-oriented economic relations through dependency relationships, transforming not only physical environments but also social relations and subsistence patterns in the process. Hinterland producers, sometimes indigenous ethnic enclaves, articulate with capitalist sectors as a semiperipheral labor force, combining subsistence activities such as food, craft, and commodity production with wage labor, and as commodity consumers in market transactions (see Godelier 1972; Terray 1972; Dupré and Rey 1978; Bloch, ed., 1975; Foster-Carter 1978; Prattis 1987; see also Wallerstein 1976; Seddon, ed.,

1978:28; La Clau 1977; Bonilla and Girling 1973; Frank 1969; Cardoso and Faletto 1979; Laite 1981; Goodman and Redclift 1982; Cook and Binford 1986). Central American scholars have documented how land, resource, and human exploitation of that region over five centuries gave rise to a rigidly stratified society where less than 10 percent of the population controls 80 percent of strategic resources, 80 percent of rural peasants have insufficient land to provide for their families' food needs, and three quarters of children are malnourished (see Barry 1987).

With the rediscovery in the 1960s of A. V. Chayanov's research on Russian peasants (Chayanov 1966 [1925]; Sahlins 1972; see also Cook and Binford 1986), debate ensued over how various "modes of production," such as precapitalist or peasant, relate to or "articulate with" capitalist modes of production: whether as autonomous, independent "precapitalist" subsistence producers, "*behaviorally inclined* toward simple reproduction," or as "product[s] of an *objectively imposed* set of structural conditions" (Binford and Cook 1991:76 [emphasis in original]; see also Chevalier 1983; C. Smith 1983; G. Smith 1985; Baber 1987:61ff.; Bernstein 1988). French Marxist anthropologists, informed by Althusser and Balibar's *Reading Capital* (1979) and seeking alternative explanations to competing formalist/substantivist and neoclassical economic approaches, synthesized French structuralism with "articulation of modes of production" analyses to explore both the articulation of precapitalist and capitalist modes of production and "the survival of pre- and non-capitalist relations of production as a structured feature of capitalism" (Prattis 1987:25, 29; see Godelier 1972; Terray 1972; Dupré and Rey 1978; Bloch, ed., 1975; Foster-Carter 1978; see Prattis 1987:27–32 for a discussion of the "French school").

Studies of rural U.S. communities (see Colclough 1988; Weinberg 1987; Lovejoy and Krannich 1982) reveal the effects of center–periphery articulation: metropolitan-directed rural development activities often promote underdevelopment and domestic dependency rather than local economic sustainability or growth. Similarities with Third World underdevelopment are clear. Manufacturing and processing industries (e.g., textiles, light manufacturing, food processing) and resource extraction enterprises (e.g., coal, oil, and gas extraction and timber) have been particularly attracted to poverty belts in the Deep South and Southwest, where natural resources, cheap and often nonunionized labor, and favorable taxation policies are readily available (see Lovejoy and Krannich 1982; Colclough 1988).

Some anthropologists, historians, and political economists, such as Joseph Jorgensen (1978), Eric Wolf (1982), Duane Champagne (1989), Stephen Cornell (1988), and Thomas Hall (1988, 1995, 1996), have analyzed U.S. Native American communities in the context of exogenous penetration to critically examine culture contact, land expropriation, political demise, and indigenous cultural transformation. Jorgensen (1971, 1978, 1986b) applied Frank's metropolitan-satellite model to the history of Native Americans and concluded that "Indian underdevelopment is the product of the full integration of United States Indians into the United States political economy – albeit as super-exploited victims of that society" (1971:84). In a case study of the Utes of Colorado and Utah, Jorgensen found that they had been systematically alienated from their land through forced sales to white ranchers, which were fully approved by government agencies charged with protecting Ute interests. The result was to leave the Utes as a destitute population without a viable subsistence base. Government solutions to Ute problems were purely cosmetic: welfare subsidies, health care, and education, with little attention paid to recreating a viable subsistence base for a once self-sufficient people (Jorgensen 1971:90, 109). Jorgensen concluded that rural poverty was not due to rural isolation but to "the way in which . . . urban centers of finance, political influence, and power have grown at the expense of rural areas" (1971:85).

Like Third World enclaves, Native American communities are sources of valuable natural resources, such as coal, natural gas, uranium, timber, or cattle grazing land (see Jorgensen et al. 1978; Ismaelillo and Wright, eds., 1982:107–10; *Cultural Survival Quarterly* 17.3 [fall 1993]: 29–30; Champagne 1989:90–94; C. Smith 1982). Some communities provide sites or labor or both for hazardous industries such as chemical finishing or contaminated waste disposal (see Jorgensen et al. 1978; Hernandez 1994:40–42; LaDuke 1994:43–48; Dawson 1992:389–97). Native Americans also have experienced "boom and bust" cycles, border boom towns, elevated cancer rates, increased rates of intoxication, and diminished health status as by-products of development initiatives in their communities (see Jorgensen et al. 1978; Olson and Wilson 1986:186–87). Alice Littlefield (1991) has explored the similarities between Native American political-economic development vis-à-vis U.S. private enterprise and colonialism and dependency situations elsewhere, showing how U.S. policies work to proletarianize Native Americans, thus serving private-sector interests. Champagne (1989) has investigated Native American culture contact in the context of three effects: what he termed geopolitical or internal colonialism, market incorporation, and cultural-normative transformation. His analysis shows the multifaceted and diverse ways indigenous transformation is effected, politically, economically, and culturally. Richard White (1983) has also used a multiconceptual model to apply insights gleaned from dependency frameworks to investigate three Native American groups: Navajos, Mississippi Choctaws, and Pawnees. He has examined how environmental, political, and cultural transformation occurred in the process of indigenous incorporation into the Euro-American market economy.

The present study of southeastern Oklahoma's timber region Choctaws explores the process of Choctaw peripheralization into a marginal labor force serving the interests of those at the center of commerce and decision making: multinational corporations and nation-state power wielders. Choctaws today occupy what Jorgensen (1978:3) calls a "domestic dependent" niche, serving as a laboring class in a satellite area dominated by a multinational timber company, Weyerhaeuser Corporation. Choctaw cultural transformation began even prior to removal, as a result of the introduction of guns, livestock, intermarriage, and missionizing and the gradual submission to Euro-American cultural values and market relations (see White 1983). The result has been a complex restructuring of Choctaw society and culture into a sometimes racially and increasingly class-stratified society, with the peripheralization of some segments and the transformation into bourgeoisie of others.

Southeastern Oklahoma, like the Deep South, has attracted industries seeking nonunionized unskilled workers, particularly industries related to resource extraction and chicken processing. Weyerhaeuser Corporation and Tyson Foods, Inc., both multinational corporations with extensive portfolios, have found the Choctaw Nation a vast resource of extractable cheap labor, as later pages reveal. Their production strategies have brought at best marginal economic gains for local populations.

Tracing Choctaw cultural transformation and incorporation into the Euro-American political economy is complex, necessitating inquiry along several interrelated axes of analysis: political, economic, and cultural. The current study builds on Cornell's (1988:12–15) and Hall's (1988:25) models of indigenous incorporation into Euro-American society, as well as Champagne's (1989) and White's (1983) discussions of Mississippi-era Choctaw social change. I explore persisting themes in the integration of Choctaws into the Euro-American political economy to show the dialectical aspects of indigenous incorporation from the colonial era to the present. I frame my analysis politically and culturally in the context of transformation from "nation" to "tribe" and finally to "ethnic minority." Economically, Choctaw transformation occurred as a transition from a mixed hunting/foraging/trading mode of production permitting economic self-sufficiency to a class-based relationship rooted in a capitalist mode of production. Choctaw political self-determination was stripped in the process, at least temporarily, when the Choctaws lost their "nationhood status," emerging as a rural marginal ethnic enclave. In the late twentieth century Choctaw transformation to a rural proletariat/bourgeoisie is nearly complete, as the Choctaws chart their own path toward political, economic, and cultural self-determination.

The Choctaw story provides a particularly valuable regional longitudinal study in microcosm (see C. Smith 1983). Traceable are the nation's indigenous roots in its ancestral Mississippi homeland, the clash of cultures when white entry – first benign, later more insidious – gradually transformed the "hearts and minds" of some Choctaw segments, mainly newly emergent, entrepreneurially oriented mixed-blood elites and intermarried whites, into formidable agents of change.

The dialectical and multifaceted contact and change process is explored using categories borrowed from world-systems, underdevelopment, neo-Marxist, and other theoretical frameworks. Choctaw responses to contact and change are shown to be diverse and complex, depending on political, economic, cultural, and environmental factors. Contact and change gave rise to new social formations and new class relationships, within a context of embeddedness in an enlarged sphere of political-economic hegemony.

To examine Choctaw history and contemporary culture, it has been necessary to combine traditional anthropological research methods with globally focused, dialectically informed models of social change. I have attempted to combine anthropology's traditional microanalytic focus with broader perspectives that are historically and structurally informed (see C. Smith 1983). I examine indigenous cultural realities in the immediate protocontact period to contextualize indigenous Choctaw cultural reality. I then analyze the contact situation in the context of changing indigenous and exogenous political and economic relationships, internal and external change agents, and the heterogeneous indigenous responses to culture contact and change in the nineteenth and twentieth centuries.

Introduction

What I propose, building on Cornell's (1988:151–53) and Hall's (1988:25) Indian assimilation/incorporation models, is that Choctaws throughout the contact era, like many Native American tribes, have responded heterogeneously to exogenous change forces along the entire spectrum of what Cornell calls integrative/segregative and reformative/transformative axes. While some Choctaws largely assimilated mainstream U.S. cultural traits and ideologies, other segments responded with greater degrees of resistance, segregation, and isolationism. Factional divisions rooted in racial and kinship idioms emerged as sometimes racially stratified class divisions in the contact era and persisted into the 1980s. I show that historical and contemporary Choctaw tribal political and economic strategies at the macrolevel represent reasoned survival strategies of a subordinated group seeking to accommodate to a new social reality of market embeddedness while preserving at least some remnants of indigenous cultural belief and practice.

Today the Choctaw Nation is highly unified under the leadership of a chief reelected in 1995 with over 80 percent of the tribal vote. Under his leadership, earlier tribal traditions are being modified and new cultural traditions evolve as the Choctaws forge a late twentieth-century tribal reality. Choctaw cultural persistence today is an effort to maximize economic opportunities within the dominant U.S. economy while retaining traditional remnants as assimilated tribalists. As the current study argues, however, the future is uncertain for the Choctaws, just as it is for Native Americans generally.

This book has captured a piece of Choctaw life at a time when some of the last remnants of partially embedded Choctaw communities remain. Many timber region Choctaw families in the early 1980s still relied on a mixed-subsistence household strategy, combining commodity production, transfer payments, and wage labor. Choctaw residence enclaves retained the flavor of kin-based indigenous Choctaw communities, with locally focused cultural activities rooted in neighborhoods, shared religious rituals, community celebrations, and informal exchange networks. By placing the contemporary cultural reality of these local timber region communities into the wider context of the political-economic reality of Choctaw tribal cultural persistence, we can explore how the Choctaw tribe has responded to full embeddedness in mainstream U.S. culture.

The Choctaw story brings to bear virtually every significant force in Native American cultural change: factionalism, intermarriage, the church, secular schools, land cessions, forced tribal relocation, post–Civil War treaty making, tribal termination, allotment, near tribal demise, tribal reconstitution, charismatic leadership, and organized gaming. This study raises a looming question: Will Choctaw culture survive, or will the Choctaws emerge as just another segment of rural southeastern Oklahoman society, as a rural bourgeoisie or proletariat largely devoid of cultural or subcultural distinctiveness? This question is particularly salient in light of the leadership of the tribe's popular chief, whose perspective seems to be that the tribe as such is largely superfluous and that his role is as tribal "business manager," not culture conservator.

Using field data, I analyze the complex relationship among players in the drama of production, reproduction, and capitalist development in southeastern Oklahoma, seeking answers to how Choctaws work toward balancing economic and cultural interests with larger political-economic forces. The mediating variable of Choctaw culture stands in the balance as the Choctaws work to enter the U.S. economic mainstream, the cornerstone of their entrepreneurial effort being the Choctaw Nation Bingo Palace in Durant, Oklahoma, which opened in 1985.

Once the decision was made to investigate the Choctaw Nation timber region political economy, fortuitous circumstances facilitated settlement in the region to undertake fieldwork. My former husband, a Public Health Service physician, was stationed at the Talihina Indian Hospital (now the Choctaw Nation Indian Hospital), which serves the entire Choctaw Nation population. This hospital, located at the northern edge of the timber region in Talihina, with a population of fifteen hundred, became my residence while I undertook my fieldwork activities over a period of two years, between 1980 and 1982.

Rural U.S. communities, unlike small-scale isolated, homogeneous cultures, interact with the wider society to a greater degree than many societies that anthropologists have historically examined. Therefore a more comprehensive, multifaceted method – combining participant observation fieldwork and formal interviewing techniques, supplemented by library, archival, and county data analysis – was found to be absolutely essential to obtaining data crucial to questions under investigation. Time had to be divided among several investigative foci, including researching landownership patterns at county courthouses in the Choctaw Nation, archival research at the Oklahoma Historical Society's Indian Archives in Oklahoma City, and historical research at various libraries. Formal interviews were conducted with tribal officials, as well as officials from the International Woodworkers of America (now the International Association of Machinists and Aerospace Workers, Local Lodge W15), Weyerhaeuser Corporation, and the Bureau of Indian Affairs, to obtain diverse points of view on problems relating to my research goals. By transcending traditional anthropological methods of small-scale community analysis, I addressed broader questions than those historically viewed as the concern of anthropologists. An important result of this multifaceted analysis has been to examine not only Choctaw culture but also the wider society in which Choctaws are embedded.

Throughout this book, narrative segments drawn from fieldwork data draw the reader into a dialectical process of historical and structural comparison. Chapter 1 introduces the reader to indigenous Choctaw culture and the multistranded process of Choctaw social change. Choctaw political leadership, economic subsistence activities, incipient Euro-American trade, and the process of early Euro-American colonization are discussed. Chapter 2 introduces the reader to the model of Choctaw transformation, showing the complex intersection of change forces along political, economic, and sociocultural axes. The emergence of a racially stratified two-class system, comprising full-blood Choctaws on the one hand and blended mixed-blood/white families on the other, is shown to have significantly altered the course of Choctaw history and culture. In chapter 3, two crucial change agents in Mississippi and Indian Territory Choctaw communities are analyzed: missions and secular schools. The roles of various institutional, infrastructural, and human factors that shaped Choctaw cultural transformation from indigenous "nation" to peripheral "tribe" are examined.

Chapter 4 introduces the reader to the postremoval Choctaw Nation and critically examines the pre–Civil War era. This is shown to be a period when the Choctaws reestablished various tribal institutions in their new homeland in the context of a racially stratified two-class structure. Chapter 5 discusses the Choctaws' post–Civil War transition from nation to tribe and their transformation into an "internal colony" of the United States. The Choctaws, although seeking to assert sovereign rights over their land and resources, could not stop the formidable tide of white encroachment. Chapter 6 examines the early twentieth-century postallotment era, when the Choctaws faced tribal termination, land allotment, and political demise. The machinations of agents of U.S. interests, including private corporate and government officials, are discussed.

Chapter 7 explores the rise of a multinational corporate presence in the southeastern Oklahoma timber region, with the entry of two family-owned timber giants, Dierks Forests, Inc., and Weyerhaeuser Corporation. The local private timber industry's rise to prominence is examined structurally and dialectically in relation to the original Choctaw landowners. Chapter 8 provides a demographic overview of southeastern Oklahoma, particularly McCurtain and Pushmataha Counties, which are the focus of this ethnographic study. Choctaw poverty is placed within a broader context of economic embeddedness in an externally controlled economy.

In chapters 9 and 10 the reader is introduced to the Choctaws up close, as we investigate how rural Choctaws maintain and reproduce their means of production, formally and informally, beginning with an analysis of the Choctaw study sample in chapter 9. In chapter 10 Choctaw informal production and distribution strategies are described through portraits of selected Choctaw households.

Chapter 11 begins a macroanalysis of the relation of Choctaw households to the timber region economy as a semiperipheral labor force. The chapter examines how Choctaws glean a living through a combination of wage labor, petty commodity production, and unearned income sources. Chapter 12 explores the relationship between Choctaws and two local corporate giants, Weyerhaeuser and Tyson Foods, and examines corporate profit-maximizing production strategies, including the use of nonunionized contracted labor. In chapter 13 the macroanalysis focuses on the highly profitable strategies Weyerhaeuser and Tyson Foods use to maximize profits and minimize costs. I investigate direct and indirect corporate profit-making strategies, including tax incentives, public welfare subsidies, and other forms of "corporate welfare."

In chapter 14 the discussion returns to the Choctaws, to explore how the Choctaws have redefined "tribalism" in the late twentieth century and emerged as a rural ethnic minority competing – many say highly successfully – in the marketplace. Choctaws are redefining tribalism and charting new territory as a rural U.S. ethnic minority community seeking to retain at least a remnant of its indigenous past. The final chapter brings together the multistranded threads of inquiry to critically explore Choctaw persistence and change as they enter the twenty-first century. As noted, Choctaws have redefined their own ethnicity, accommodating to U.S. capitalism as entrepreneurs themselves and embracing a rural lifestyle with a radically redefined sense of their tribal ethnicity and identity.

This study of timber region Choctaws investigates a particular segment of southeastern Oklahoma Choctaws, who have experienced over the past two decades profound changes in their relationship to the local political economy and to the tribal entity. This segment has been affected most profoundly by the region's uneven development, promoted earlier by Dierks and currently by Weyerhaeuser and Tyson Foods. Each industry has historically used and continues to use many local citizens – not just Choctaws – as the economic foundation for their respective enterprises in ways that exploit local citizens. This study explores class, racial, and gender hierarchies in the U.S. political economy that affect every citizen, whether white, black, Native American, immigrant, or other. The Choctaws are part of a larger political economy rooted in racial, class, and gender asymmetries.

This study is not intended to detract from the many successes of the Choctaw people, nor do I aim to be a spokesperson for Choctaw people. Instead, I intend to reveal conditions that have contributed to the quandary of poverty many Choctaws face who cannot make a decent living in an environment of abundance, not because they don't want to, but because of the structure of exploitation that has developed in southeastern Oklahoma over the past one and a half centuries, which can be best understood as a by-product of capitalism. This study illustrates a problem that is not unique to the Choctaw Nation but is replicated in many rural poor U.S. communities in which a valuable resource has been alienated from its original owners and has become a strategic component of the production strategy brought by an intrusive corporate enterprise.

This study also explores Native American ethnicity, ethnic formation, persistence, and change. Choctaw ethnicity, like Native American ethnicity in general, is in transition as the twenty-first century approaches. Ethnicity remains a negotiated feature of tribal life with an uncertain future, bound as it has perennially been with wider U.S. political, economic, and cultural realities.

CHOCTAWS AT THE CROSSROADS

ONE

Choctaw Indigenous Ways

Choctaw Nation, 1982. The July day was typically hot. The elderly couple – he in denim overalls, she in a housedress, each with hoe in hand – tended the eighth-acre patch of garden located next to their austere cabin: corn, squash, peppers, chives, muscadine, and herbs neatly arranged. They paused to greet me and invited me into their simply furnished home. A well pump in the yard and absence of the ubiquitous television set signaled the lack of indoor plumbing and electricity. The dwelling was dark and cool, simply furnished with a couch, chair, kitchen table and chairs, and many photos proudly displaying children and grandchildren, some in baseball uniforms, others in graduation gowns. She spoke little English; he was bilingual. Both were full-bloods, having raised a family of eight children in this very dwelling.

One daughter lives next door in a modern "mutual help" Indian home, and several other children live in a small family neighborhood on a twenty-acre tract, the remnants of the wife's tribal allotment. Typical of ancient Choctaw matrilineal inheritance traditions, her allotment was subdivided to provide two-acre house sites for her children. Seven "mutual help" Indian homes were built through a government assistance program instituted in 1969 under the Housing and Urban Development (HUD) program to improve substandard living conditions among Native American families.

This scene, starkly reminiscent of eighteenth- and nineteenth-century accounts by early travelers such as Gideon Lincecum (see Wood 1985), Henry Benson (1860), and Horatio Cushman (1899, 1962 [1899]), shows that not much has changed for this Choctaw family on first glance. However, much has changed since the Choctaws made their first European contacts in the sixteenth century, left Mississippi in 1831 in the Trail of Tears, lost their vast Indian Territory tribal estate in the early twentieth century, and reemerged under a newly constituted tribal structure in 1971.

Subsistence gardening, foraging, and hunting are no longer the primarily livelihood-sustaining activities of Oklahoma Choctaws, as they were until nearly World War II. Today the Oklahoma Choctaw Nation vista is broken by Weyerhaeuser Corporation clear-cuts and monocropped loblolly pine forests in various stages of maturity, artificially planted as part of Weyerhaeuser's scientific tree cultivation industry. Weyerhaeuser trucks frequently pass, and in the springtime workers are seen planting tiny seedlings on barren clear-cuts. Choctaws, once owners of a vast tribal estate of 6.8 million acres, are today a marginally distinct local minority, constituting less than 15 percent of the total population. Whites constitute 80 percent of the region's inhabitants, along with about 5 percent African Americans, descendants of former slaves.

The Choctaw story is well documented by Henry Benson (1860), Angie Debo (1934, 1972 [1940]), John R. Swanton (1931), Horatio Cushman (1962 [1899]), Arthur DeRosier (1967, 1970), and more recently Richard White (1983) and Duane Champagne (1989), each adding to a comprehensive history and critical analysis of one of the most oft-studied of North American tribes. In reexamining the Choctaw story, we must grapple with the romance of many of these earlier accounts, infused as they are with themes of tribal simplicity, austerity, and "naturalness" of an ancient past unfettered by aggrandizement, private property concerns, competition, or hegemonic discourse. We must struggle with a historic reality of colonization, imperialism, oppression, and expropriation, all of which define Choctaw history in both Mississippi and Oklahoma, just as these processes defined Euro-American contacts throughout Native North America (see Robbins 1994; Meyer 1994; Jorgensen 1978). We must finally explore what it means to be Choctaw today, a meaning redefined since the early 1980s as the tribe has been economically and politically energized under the leadership of their current chief, Hollis Roberts.

CHOCTAW COLONY, INTERNAL COLONY, PERIPHERY

Choctaws made their first European contacts in 1540, when Hernando DeSoto, supported by an armed cavalry, battled the Choctaws near present-day Mobile, Alabama, killing over fifteen hundred tribalists (DeRosier 1970:14–15). This was only the beginning of a history of contact and tribal transformation that would bring the Choctaws through several stages: from autonomous tribal entity, to partial articulation with a metropolitan center, and finally to full incorporation into world capitalism as a peripheral enclave: a marginalized rural ethnic minority. Contact was a global phenomenon, transforming the Choctaw region from subsistence to full market embeddedness, from producers for use to participants in a global political economy as rural proletarians.

Over more than two centuries Native American nations would become what C. Matthew Snipp (1986a, 1986b, 1988:2) aptly terms "captive-nations," and others have called "colonies," "hinterlands," "peripheries," or "dependent enclaves," of emerging global capitalism. Indian land, including the Mississippi Choctaw homeland, was valuable to the expanding eighteenth- and nineteenth-century Atlantic seaboard economy, and indigenous political and economic rights stood weakly against global capitalism's aggrandizing production and market interests. The Choctaws, an independent political entity at contact – a nation – would soon become a "colony," later an "internal colony," and finally a "periphery" of the Euro-American political economy.

The making of a world economy was a dialectical process of political and economic incorporation and transformation, "the historical process by which noncapitalist zones are absorbed into the capitalist world-system" (Dunaway 1996:456; see also Wallerstein 1976, 1980; Hall 1996:445–56, 1995, 1988; Dos Santos 1970). Colonization linked preindustrial or noncapitalist indigenous groups with metropolitan-based entrepreneurially driven capitalist producers in unequal, dependent relationships. Robert Bee and Ronald Gingerich (1977:71), citing Robert Blauner, write:

The colony exists subordinated to, and dependent upon, the mother country. Typically the colonizers exploit the land, the raw materials, the labor, and other resources of the colonized nation; in addition a formal recognition is given to the difference in power, autonomy, and political status, and the various agencies are set up to maintain this subordination.

Rural Native American communities, like colonized peoples throughout Europe's colonial sphere, became "dependent enclave[s]" (Wallerstein 1976, 1980, 1989), politically disempowered and culturally degraded (Mohawk 1991:500; see also White 1983; Jorgensen 1978; Anders 1980). In the inherently unequal core/periphery relationship, notes Theotônio Dos Santos (1970:231),

the economy of certain countries is conditioned by the development and expansion of another economy to which the former is subjected. . . . The relation assume[s] the

3

form of dependence when some countries (the dominant ones) can expand and can be self-sustaining, while other countries (the dependent ones) can do this only as a reflection of that expansion.

Native North Americans, Snipp argues (1988:3, 1986a, 1986b), experienced internal colonization in two phases: First, indigenous sovereign nations were degraded into "sovereign wards" of U.S. political authority, retaining only limited political power as semiautonomous tribes. In the second phase, the core region's political and economic agendas were linked: U.S. political clout was used to aggrandize local indigenous resources and exploit cheap unskilled labor (see Wilkins 1993:398). The "internal colony" – what Wilma Dunaway (1996:455) calls a "frontier" and dependency and world-systems theorists (Wallerstein 1976; see also Hall 1988:25) term the "periphery" or "dependent periphery" – is thereby subsumed within the core region politically, economically, and culturally.

This dynamic process, as the following discussion of the Choctaws shows, structurally and culturally transforms the periphery. The core sector's agenda is mercantilist, capitalist, and aggrandizing (Robbins 1994:62). Peripheral indigenes are destabilized and marginalized, as their land and surplus labor are expropriated, and they are insidiously incorporated into the metropolitan political economy as a peripheral enclave proletariat (see Dunaway 1996:455–58; Hall 1995; Flora et al. 1992:37–44).

Frontier incorporation is dynamic. Local populations – despite economic and political disadvantages – react to, respond to, and even resist domination. "Indigenous people," Dunaway (1996:455) argues, citing Taylor and Pease (1994), "are not passive receptacles of Western political, economic and cultural domination." Indigenous populations negotiate, subvert, attack, and accommodate outside forces, to preserve their own cultural, political, and economic integrity. The frontier is the locus of center/periphery contact, combat, and change. New political realities emerge as sovereign nations contest prior rights and emerging global powers assert political and economic hegemony. Meanings of sovereignty, self-determination, nation, tribe, and ethnicity are negotiated, contested, maintained, and sometimes annihilated as power is brokered between contesting factions.

CHOCTAW CONTACT AND CHANGE

Between 1540 and tribal termination in 1906, the making of a Choctaw internal colony occurred through a dialectical process linking independent

Choctaw political, economic, and cultural structures with those of intrusive colonizing agents in asymmetrical encounters, transforming a formerly viable tribe into a tool of colonial interests. As a colony, Choctaws were subsumed economically by colonizers seeking land, natural resources, and cheap labor, initially for mother countries and later for the emerging U.S. mercantile and industrial economy. In the final phase of peripheralization, the Choctaws experienced nearly complete land alienation, tribal political termination, and eventual transformation into rural proletarians – wage laborers – inadequately provisioned to sustain themselves as subsistence producers and obliged to enter the wage labor sector as unskilled laborers. This marked full Choctaw dependence and marginalization as a regional rural ethnic enclave.

Native Americans, including the Choctaws, were early on useful as commodity producers, trading animal pelts and food to hungry settlers. They proved useless as a servile labor force for the early plantation-based agricultural economy, however, owing to disease and native resistance to servitude (see White 1983; Dunaway 1994). Colonists coveted indigenous land and natural resources, expropriable only by removing the human obstacles to colonization through negotiation, "civilization," and more commonly, annihilation.

Native/European contact, as elsewhere, had four possible outcomes, according to Joane Nagel and C. Matthew Snipp (1993:203–4):

annihilation, . . . destruction of one group by the other . . . ; *assimilation*, . . . the absorption of an ethnic minority group into the dominant culture, . . . *amalgamation*, . . . the mutual adaptation and mixing of ethnic populations . . . , often described as a 'melting pot' . . . [and] *accommodation*, . . . the maintenance of ethnic distinctiveness among different groups, resulting in cultural pluralism.

New World Native/European encounters displayed the entire range of possible outcomes, from total annihilation to partial and in some instances complete assimilation. The outcome of contact between often unwilling and resistant players is inevitably transformative. This "ethnic reorganization," according to Nagel and Snipp (1993:205), "is best understood as a strategy by which ethnic minority groups attempt to cope with the forces of change."

As throughout regions of European colonization, colonists gradually developed institutional mechanisms – "colonial structures" – to effect colonization agendas, giving rise to "colonial relations" intended to undermine

Choctaw political, economic, and cultural autonomy and penetrate the very core of Choctaw tribal viability. According to Dunaway (1994:237), "Incorporation necessitated a reorientation of preexisting subsistence patterns and the creation of new economic activities geared toward commodity production, market exchanges and the creation of surplus." Politically, indigenous self-rule must be eliminated by redefining the tribal entity, from "native nation" to "domestic dependent" ethnicity. Political decisions were made externally by agents of the U.S. government, rather than internally by Choctaw leaders. Culturally, indigenes were to be "civilized" and proletarianized to Euro-American values, norms, and practices (see Bee and Gingerich 1977:71; Dunaway 1994; Bailey and Flores 1973).

Euro-Americans had three hegemonic agendas in their indigenous encounters, according to Stephen Cornell (1988:56–62): to expropriate indigenous resources (mainly land in North America), transform indigenous cultures by "civilizing" Indians, and gain political control by dismantling indigenous nations. The two cultures first met "nation to nation," albeit as unequal contestants. Choctaws in the process became subsumed under U.S. authority as what Chief Justice John Marshall in his 1831 Supreme Court decision, *Cherokee Nation* v. *State of Georgia* (30 U.S. [5 Pet.] 1), aptly called a "domestic dependent nation," as "a ward to his guardian . . . completely under the sovereignty and dominion of the U.S." (Berkhofer 1978:163–64; see also Satz 1975:45; Mills 1919:11–15; Mohawk 1991:496). Choctaws struggled to retain legitimate national sovereignty and cultural integrity, while the United States implemented its own imperialist agenda of "separation and assimilation": separation from land and assimilation into mainstream U.S. society (see Strong and Van Winkle 1993:12). The Choctaws were economic pawns to U.S. imperialism, notes Louis Smith (1988:11); their indigenous culture was expendable. The result was cultural genocide, tribal ghettoization, and political-economic marginalization.

Euro-American contact brought a profound new order to the Choctaws, a nation formerly organized around an indigenous cultural reality rooted in kinship, rank, mixed subsistence, and intertribal trade. The transformed Choctaw nation was characterized by marked differences in wealth, market-oriented production, centralized leadership, and eventual land allotment and U.S. citizenship. In the process, Choctaw "nationhood" was radically transformed and redefined to accommodate to this new relationship as an enclave population subsumed under a formidable multinational power, the

United States of America. National sovereignty gave way to what Pauline Turner Strong and Barrik Van Winkle (1993:14) describe as "limited political sovereignty under federal trusteeship," an ambiguous existence at best.

The Choctaw story is complex, dialectical, multidimensional, and often ambiguous, as forces for culture persistence confront forces for change within contexts as variable as ethnicity, class, the wielding of power, and economic production. As we critically examine the Choctaw contact situation in the late eighteenth and early nineteenth centuries, we open a window into the beginnings of the dialectics of competing class interests in Choctaw/Euro-American relations. Although the story is a familiar one in Native American history, the wrinkles and folds of the Choctaw case reveal just how systems of social equality gave way to social hierarchy and Euro-American hegemony through the several phases of contact: as colony, internal colony, and finally rural periphery, in Native North America. The Choctaw response, rooted in indigenous pragmatism, shows how Native American survival strategies work to accommodate to new social, economic, and political realities while striving to retain something that is uniquely Indian (see Wilkins 1993; D. Smith 1994).

Choctaw Nation, 1982. Assistant Chief: "We have always had chiefs, and I will say the majority of the people would not hesitate to come see the chief or call him about anything. It's not that they look at him as knowing all or can do all, but for advice and assistance that's who they come to. It's always been that way, to my understanding, one way or another. In the older days, if the man of the family was killed or something, the widow and her children would look to the chief and he would make sure they had food or a horse or lodging."

CHOCTAW INDIGENOUS WAYS

Kinship was the defining idiom of Choctaw indigenous culture, delineating loyalties, leadership, and subsistence aggregates (see Champagne 1989:52–53). Choctaws lived in loosely aggregated, geographically dispersed kinbased bands in their sixteenth- and seventeenth-century lower Mississippi Valley homeland and relied on a mixed hunting/foraging/horticulture subsistence economy, with a gender-based division of labor. Centralized leadership appeared weak, and decision making was localized in the hands of influential war and peace (or village) chiefs drawn from ranked matrilineal clans.

7

By the 1750s Choctaws inhabited three districts (formerly five or possibly six), upon which kinship, political, and even subcultural divisions appeared to have been based (see Champagne 1989: 37–38, 52–53; White 1983:37–38). Districts were most likely by-products of ancient Choctaw matrilineal moieties, called the *Inhulahta*, or "esteemed people," and the *Imoklasha* or *Kashapa okla*, the "people of the other side." Moieties were subdivided into several nontotemic, exogamous, matrilineal "kindred" clans, called *iksa*. Intra-*iksa* marriage was strictly prohibited until increased white contact along with intermarriage eliminated this practice, probably by the 1820s (Swanton 1931:76–78, 81; Searcey 1985:35).

Choctaw settlements and dispersed homesteads appeared as a "patchwork of woodland, cultivated land and abandoned fields" along the courses of rivers and streams (White 1983:24). Swanton (1931:95) estimated that there were forty to fifty "towns" or settlements inhabited at any one time. A 1772 compilation and mapping of the Choctaw Nation named as many as sixty Choctaw towns (McKee 1971:115; see also Swanton 1931:95). Map 1.1 shows the Mississippi Choctaw homeland in the 1820s, noting a sample of towns in its three districts: Upper Towns (northeast), Lower Towns (northwest), and Sixtowns (southeast). The map also shows current county boundaries. The Choctaw population, estimated at from twenty thousand to thirty thousand during the late precontact period, appeared to have remained stable until forced removal in the 1830s (Hodge 1912:289; McKee 1971:117; White 1983:5).

Local Choctaw leadership was apparently fluid and flexible, with individuals competing for loyal followers among their kin base. Local subchiefs, headmen, or clan elders, sometimes called mingoes and later "captains," had jurisdiction over village and neighborhood settlements (Spaulding 1974:34; Hudson n.d.; Swanton 1918:54–55; McKee and Schlenker 1980:16; White 1983:38). Principal chiefs drawn from the district's senior matrilineal *iksa* (clan) governed tribal districts. Chiefly status, according to White (1983: 39ff.), was akin to a "big man" system, rooted in kin loyalties and chiefly generosity. Choice of leaders was based on a combination of heredity, popularity, and personal merit (Swanton 1918:54–55; 1931:92; Hudson n.d.). Chiefs were foremost focal "point men" around whom loyal kinfolk rallied and through whom communal wealth was redistributed in cycles of feasting and council gatherings (see Noley 1985a; Peregrine 1991:200–201).

Women participated in Choctaw politics indirectly through their ma-

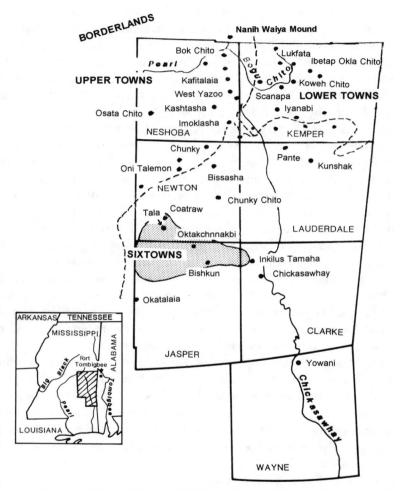

Map 1.1. Preremoval lower Mississippi Valley Choctaw homeland, 1820s. *Sources*: Adapted from map 2, "Choctaw Towns and Districts," in Richard White, *The Roots of Dependency, Subsistence, Environment, and Social Change among the Choctaws, Pawnees, and Navajos* (Lincoln: University of Nebraska Press, 1983), by permission of the University of Nebraska Press; and figure 4, "The Old Choctaw Country, Mississippi," in Jesse O. McKee and Jon A. Schlenker, *The Choctaws: Cultural Evolution of a Native American Tribe* (Jackson: University Press of Mississippi, 1980).

trilineally linked brothers and maternal uncles. Although women did not vote or sit at council meetings (Swanton 1931:99), their brothers represented them in political decision making. Women's political influence through *iksa* affiliations appeared substantial, however, prompting an earlier observer to conclude, "It is said that if the women wanted a certain chief he was almost certain of election" (Swanton 1931:101). Matrilineal clan ties were also evident in seating arrangements at political and religious gatherings, where women and their children sat at one fire with their clansmen, while husbands sat at another with their own kin (Swanton 1931:77).

As among other Mississippian cultures, Choctaw clans were ranked (White 1983:39–40; see also Swanton 1931:95; Debo 1934:21). Ranking was based on both individual merit and *iksa*. Cushman (1899:197) reported that males were ranked according to war and civil honors into four categories: *mingoes*, or peace and war chiefs; "beloved men," or leading warriors; common warriors; and "those who have not struck a blow or who have killed only a woman or a child" (see also Spaulding 1974:34–35; McKee and Schlenker 1980:40–41; Noley 1985a:59–60; White 1983:39). Ranking on the basis of war deeds, gender, and age was evident in seating arrangements at ritual and political gatherings, where elder males and esteemed warriors were seated around an inner circle, while more junior and less accomplished warriors sat in an outer circle (Cushman 1899:147–48; Spaulding 1974:36).

The indigenous Choctaw hunting/foraging/horticultural subsistence cycle, well adapted to the local environment, fluctuated with increased Euro-American contact, game depletion, and other ecological changes, according to White (1983:13–14, 28–29). Until the late eighteenth century, mixed subsistence based on a complementary gender-based division of labor provided the tribe with a reliable livelihood base. When agricultural crops failed owing to drought, Choctaws increased hunting and foraging activities accordingly. The varied subsistence base, combined with indigenous traditions rooted in reciprocal exchange and chiefly redistribution, promoted economic leveling and gender equality and insured all tribal members adequate access to resources (White 1983:42–46).

Choctaws, like indigenous peoples elsewhere, did not conceive of land as private property. Garden land was held in common and subject to "usufruct" or use rights. Individuals or families retained farming rights so long as they used a tract to farm or garden. Hunting territories were subject to common use and did not appear to be assigned individually. Tribal members respected the rights of others to use the public domain and would not seek access to a piece of land until abandoned by a previous tenant (Swanton 1931:103; White 1983:20).

Choctaws inhabited log or adobe cabins covered with mud and bark. The one—room cabins, built by the men, were windowless and had dirt floors. A central fireplace provided heat and served as a cooking hearth. The room was simply furnished, with raised beds along the outer walls and few other furnishings, such as earthenware and reed cooking utensils and perhaps a chair or two (Swanton 1918:57—58; McKee and Schlenker 1980:19—20).

The Choctaw division of labor was based on gender and age. Women and children performed most cultivating, harvesting, and food preparation, although in later times entire families might join together on larger plots for cultivation and harvesting. Crops were grown on small plots in close proximity to the home, according to earlier accounts. Eighteenth-century accounts describe considerable land under cultivation, some in "large plantations, or country farms" (DeRosier 1970:10). Maize, the most important crop, was the focus of celebrations and rituals, including the Green Corn Dance, marking the corn harvest, and a new fire ceremony. Maize contributed an estimated two-thirds of the Choctaw subsistence diet, with game, fish, and forage contributing the rest, according to White (1983:24). Prior to white contact Choctaws reportedly traded surplus maize to neighboring tribes. Swanton (1931:46) reported that Chickasaws almost yearly obtained supplies from Choctaws to supplement their own inadequate harvests. In addition to corn, Choctaws grew a variety of indigenous crops, including beans, squash, sunflowers, sweet potatoes, and tobacco, which they consumed themselves and also traded to neighboring tribes. Following its introduction by Euro-Americans, cotton was also cultivated (Adair 1930 [1775]: 435—37; Cushman 1899:194, 197—98, 214—16; Hodge 1912:288; Swanton 1918:59; 1928:691; 1931:46—47, 55—58, 84, 91; Campbell 1959:11, 16; Spaulding 1974:26—27, 29; McKee and Schlenker 1980:17—18; see also Wells 1985:29—30; Searcey 1985; Noley 1985a; White 1983:20).

Gathering, another important dietary food source, was also performed mainly by women, assisted by children and the elderly, who procured an extremely wide variety of plants, fruits, roots, and nuts, along with medicinal items and other seasonally available produce. Fruits and nuts, including berries, grapes, acorns, chestnuts, and pecans, were stored in the home in baskets and other receptacles for later use (Campbell 1959:15).

By matrilineal descent and inheritance rules, Choctaw women owned rights to their farms. Swanton (1931:104) reported that when a wife died, her property went to her surviving children, who were cared for by her kinsmen until they could provide for themselves. The father, on the other hand, had responsibilities to his sister's children, although historical accounts do not clearly define the degree to which Choctaw males performed these obligations to their matrilineal kin (Eggan 1937:41).

Men supplied game, constructed homes, and made tools and other household implements. They also served as political leaders and were charged with protecting the community and its citizens from undesirable enemies. Bows and arrows were used to hunt larger animals, including bear, deer, and bison. Smaller animals, often hunted by young boys, included turkey, squirrel, rabbit, and beaver. Products of the hunt not only supplied important foods but were also used to make clothing, shoes, and ornamentation. Animal by-products served as bone implements for cooking and hunting; as oils for tanning leather, cooking, or personal grooming; and even as agricultural implements. Choctaw women were responsible for tanning hides and making clothing. Choctaws shared their hunting grounds with neighboring tribes, particularly the Chickasaws, and appeared to have been less protective of hunting territory than they were of their agricultural lands, which were reserved for their exclusive use (Swanton 1931:46; Debo 1934:11, 18; see also Searcey 1985; McKee and Schlenker 1980:18–19).

The Choctaw exogamous clan system and gender-based division of labor contained safeguards against clan or lineage monopoly, and against patriarchal gender dominance, by segregating economic and political spheres along gender and clan lines. Ties of blood (consanguinity) and marriage (affinity) intersected along political and economic axes: the husband controlled the political sphere, while the wife controlled access to land and it material by-products. The sexual division of labor reaffirmed a wife's access to land, since she was responsible for the agricultural work on the family estate. The husband and his clan, on the other hand, accrued political rights, responsibilities, and power in the wider social sphere of community government and decision making at local, regional, and national levels (Eggan 1937:41; Swanton 1931:95; McKee and Schlenker 1980:41). This delicate balance was further protected both by democratically based Choctaw consensus-building and the gender-based clan political structure described earlier.

Choctaw Nation, 1982. It is Saturday night. Families have gathered at this small Presbyterian church for a Third Saturday Sing. Everyone brings something to share, covered dishes containing *tan'fula* (corn hominy), pinto beans, macaroni and cheese, Indian fry bread, jellies, watermelon, or dessert. This evening, to mark his and his wife's fiftieth wedding anniversary, the church elder has slaughtered a pig, which he carefully roasts outside. Members from throughout the church's ten-county circuit have come to join the festivities, as many do each Saturday night. Many will spend the night, young folk and old, singing religious songs in traditional Choctaw dialect, some long ago translated into English by early missionaries. Traditional Choctaw is preferred, as are the customs and rituals that have bound these enclaves together for so many generations. The church is located just across the highway from a small neighborhood enclave, from which much of its membership is drawn. Older members helped build this church with their own hands. Some lived in years past in the tiny outbuildings that encircle the church like a womb, creating a feeling of intimate, although austere, community, rooted in traditions of reciprocity, sharing, and respect.

CULTURE CONTACT AND TRANSFORMATION

Throughout the eighteenth century localized Choctaw clans and subclans dealt individually and opportunistically with French and British settlers, mainly traders seeking animal pelts in exchange for useful items of trade. Choctaw headmen "saw commerce as an extension of reciprocity, not as hard bargaining for personal advantage" (White 1983:57, 64–65). They built exchange networks with Europeans based on prior indigenous intra- and intertribal trade practices rooted in generosity and reciprocity (see also Albers 1993; Klein 1993; Champagne 1989:53). Dozens of local headmen, both peace and war chiefs, garnered followers among loyal constituents by serving as foci for commodity redistribution to their loyal followers, often controlling access to guns and other increasingly valuable European commodities. Headmen garnered prestige and status to the degree to which they could deliver valued trade items to their constituents (see White 1983:44–46, III–12; Cushman 1962 [1899]: 197).

Choctaw transformation to capitalism and incorporation into the Euro-American political economy was, as Dunaway (1996:456), citing Marx, notes among the Appalachian Cherokees, "an historical dialectical process that involves both *social structure* and *human agency* . . . determined by hegemonic forces in the capitalist world system. . . . the impacted people act, react and resist. . . . The outcome is *dialectical*" (emphasis in original). Choctaws en-

tered the European trade nexus opportunistically, as part of their own survival strategy, gradually relying on European trade, first with French traders
in the eighteenth century and later British settlers, selling animal pelts, antlers, horn, nuts, and beeswax in exchange for knives, guns, fishhooks, cloth,
blankets, glass beads, needles and thread, and other desirable items (Swanton 1918:55–57; Noley 1985b:103; Campbell 1959:19; L. Smith 1988:53–54).
Choctaws cautiously welcomed new trade goods and markets for their own
items, and by the mid-eighteenth century many Choctaws relied on newly
introduced agricultural and hunting technologies, as well as cotton
clothing, textiles, and iron cooking implements, all labor-saving devices for
Choctaw subsistence producers (see Swanton 1918; Debo 1934:26; Cushman
1962 [1899]: 194; DeRosier 1970:16).

Euro-Americans throughout the colonial and early national periods
worked to promote their own assimilationist and aggrandizing economic,
social, and political agendas: to gain access to valued indigenous commodities, insure alliances, and pacify and "civilize" Native Americans (Wells
1987:25–28; see also Klein 1993; Dunaway 1994, 1996; Meyer 1994). Tribal
trade allegiances varied with locality, depending on the success or failure of
French or British contacts at the time, and upon Euro-American political-
economic ambitions (White 1983:52ff., 64–68; L. Smith 1988:11–12; Dunaway
1994:220–21). "In this competition for territory and the deerskin trade the
Southeastern Indians became pawns" to Euro-American colonizing interests, noted Louis Smith (1988:11). Chiefs and *mingoes*, sometimes called captains or "medal chiefs" by Euro-Americans, were frequently paid royalties,
gifts, or annuities by British and French officials to secure their loyalty in
trade partnerships.

Trade was one tool for Choctaw incorporation, "transform[ing] . . . this
external arena into a peripheral fringe of the capitalist world-system" (Dunaway 1996:458; see also Klein 1993:141–43). Colonizer and colonized each had
drastically different trade agendas, however. Choctaws viewed trade as an
opportunity to obtain useful commodities and increase the prestige of key
individuals – headmen and "medal chiefs" – who controlled trading networks. The Euro-American trade agenda, particularly when the region became attractive not for pelts but as a prime cotton-producing area, was far
more grand: to bring Choctaw land, resources, and labor into the nascent
U.S. market economy.

Choctaw material needs, as subsistence-oriented producers, were initially limited; Euro-American appetites, however, would prove insatiable. "By the time of the American Revolution," states Samuel Wells (1987:37), "the white trader had become a ubiquitous feature in Indian Country." The Southeast's European population in the century between 1690 and 1790 grew from an estimated fifty thousand to one million, with approximately half a million African slaves by 1790 (Kehoe 1992:191). In 1785 the U.S. government entered into its first formal treaty with the Choctaws and several neighboring tribes, the Treaty of Hopewell, which established permanent boundaries and created formal mechanisms for trade and association with the tribe.

Eighteenth-century colonists were interested mainly in the southern Appalachian region (see Dunaway 1996:459); however, attention turned in the nineteenth century to the lower Mississippi Valley region, the emerging economic heartland of a nascent global economy. The year 1800 appeared to be a watershed in the Mississippi Valley region's global incorporation process, beginning a period of ever-increasing white entry, not as transitory sojourners, like the French, but as permanent colonists and settlers attracted to "4,150,000 acres . . . in the delta region – the richest cotton lands in the South" (Wright 1928:104; see also Swanton 1928:1–2; DeRosier 1970:32). White entry became an irreversible tide bringing land- and resource-hungry migrants. Wells (1987:40, 22) estimates that "scores" of white traders lived in the lower Mississippi Valley region by the early 1800s, having entered relatively freely with tribal consent and generally permitted to marry Indian women.

Political circumstances in 1800 abetted the Euro-American imperialist and hegemonic colonizing agendas. Thomas Jefferson became president in that year, professing to protect tribal sovereignty and self-determination. He soon became not a champion of Native Americans but rather a defender of the rights of the dominant society to usurp tribal land by any means necessary. As DeRosier (1970:15) states,

The primary motive of all of the colonizers was economic. Mercantilism, the economic doctrine of the day, taught among other things, that the nation with the most favorable balance of trade would control the destiny of Europe. The greatest country would be the one with access to strategic raw materials – materials that could be shipped to the mother country, transformed into finished products, and then resold in the colonies and on the continent at a substantial profit.

Cotton was a key element in mercantilism. Eli Whitney's invention of the cotton gin in 1793, along with advances in textile manufacturing equipment, brought greatly increased demand for raw cotton throughout Europe and the United States. American cotton plantations, centered mainly in the eastern seaboard states of Virginia and the Carolinas, slowly moved to the southern Mississippi River Valley region as large-scale agriculturists sought to increase cotton production to meet growing demands. As cotton manufacture was refined, the slave trade grew to provide cheap laborers for the enlarged cotton plantations (Bailey 1973:164–65).

The cotton economy stimulated economic growth in the United States and western Europe by providing markets for both raw materials and finished products, linking old and new worlds in a nexus of trade and enterprise. The slave/cotton production system, according to Ronald Bailey (1973:165), accounted for nearly 50 percent of British trade at the end of the seventeenth century. Cotton production also permitted phenomenal industrial and mercantile growth in the United States. Quoting Bruchey, Bailey writes:

American earnings from the sale of cotton abroad permitted the importation of capital necessary to sustain the pace of growth, and at the same time helped supply the means by which significantly specialized geographic regions were enabled to exchange their respective surpluses with each other. This tendency to concentrate resources on particular kinds of economic activity . . . enabled the economy as a whole to function with a higher degree of efficiency and speed the pace of its growth. (Bailey 1973:166–67)

The lower Mississippi Valley, ideally suited to large-scale cotton production, was crucial to expansion-minded cotton producers. Whites, to gain access to the fertile region, had to either somehow remove indigenous tribes living there or rewrite existing treaties granting tribes rights to this land in perpetuity.

Choctaw Nation, 1982. Weyerhaeuser Company Spokesperson: "When we first came [to Oklahoma in 1969] we would back off if someone said they owned the land. . . . Then suddenly came this large multiplying thing. All people made claims on the land and what they said was forty or one hundred acres suddenly came up to be two or three thousand acres we were losing. It was because of that they decided to try to establish some very firm property lines."

TRANSFORMING "NATION" TO "TRIBE"

According to Strong and Van Winkle (1993:12), the term "tribe" first appeared formally in U.S./Indian discourse in the commerce clause of the U.S. Constitution, replacing the word "nation." This was not merely a minor linguistic aberration, as they note, but marked a dramatic transformation in the very substance of Indian national self-determination. Indian "nationhood" meant political sovereignty, economic autonomy, and independent self-determination. Once Native Americans were viewed not as "nations" but as "tribes," their sovereign status was recast as "quasi-independent" conquered nations: "domestic dependent tribes." Tribes *were* an aberration: culturally and racially "primitive," socially and politically disorganized.

Manifest Destiny, the doctrine that argued that the dominant society enjoyed, by the force of its own ethnic, political, and economic superiority, the right to realize its will and dominate inferior "races," became under Thomas Jefferson's influence a useful tool to expropriate native land and transform Native American "nations" into "tribes." Arguing that Indians must be "civilized," assimilated, and confined to small plots to free their surplus land for white occupancy, Jefferson's views enjoyed strong popular support, particularly among those interested in developing the lower Mississippi Valley cotton industry. Jefferson proposed various forms of bribery to force eastern tribes to remove west. A common tactic was to bankrupt Indians using the "Indian factory system." Trading posts, called "factories," were established by the government among the Indians, ostensibly to provide needed trade goods and prevent exploitation by unscrupulous traders. This system was manipulated and corrupted, whereby Indians were encouraged to incur excessive debts at the trading posts. When debts became so large that they could not be repaid, the tribe was forced to sell livestock, land, and sometimes even give up women and children to cancel the debt (Ferguson 1985:218, 220; DeRosier 1970:27–28; Wells 1987:27–28; 116–17; 130–32; White 1983:96; Kelley 1991:74; Dunaway 1996:460–61). In response to tactics of intimidation, extortion, and indifference, the Choctaws between 1801 and 1820 ceded approximately half of their trans-Mississippi tribal estate to whites (McKee and Schlenker 1980:50–59).

Jefferson soon introduced a new solution to the "Indian problem": wholesale removal westward of entire tribes. This policy was designed to ghettoize indigenous tribes in remote regions deemed of little value to U.S. political and economic interests. Indian Territory, now the state of Oklahoma, was earmarked as an appropriate tribal enclave region for dozens of tribes, including the Five Civilized Tribes (the Choctaws, Chickasaws, Cherokees, Creeks, and Seminoles) as well as many from Kansas, Nebraska, the upper Midwest, and Great Plains.

The removal policy was refined and proposals for its implementation made throughout the first three decades of the nineteenth century. John C. Calhoun, in 1817–20 secretary of war under President James Monroe (the War Department still supervised Indian affairs at the time), chose the Choctaws to be the first Mississippi tribe with whom the government would attempt to negotiate a removal treaty, ostensibly because they exhibited a greater degree of assimilation to white values, attitudes, and practices than did many of their neighbors, and because their successful removal would set an example for the removal of other tribes (DeRosier 1970:46).

Andrew Jackson won his presidency bid in 1829 with overwhelming support of southern and western states for his pro-removal and "states' rights" platforms (Satz 1975:18–30; McLoughlin 1985:401; Young 1958). In that same year the state of Mississippi passed legislation called "An Act to Extend the Laws of the State of Mississippi over the persons and property of the Indians resident within its limits," which "repealed all the rights, privileges, immunities and franchises of the Indians and announced that Mississippi law governed all persons within the limits of the state" (DeRosier 1967:346–47).

Choctaws were factionally divided over removal. Traditionalists stood resolutely against removal, while many progressives joined a pro-removal faction reconciled to what they viewed as inevitable (White 1983:140; Wright 1928:106–9; Morrison 1987:15–16; Debo 1934:49–50; 52; White 1983:140). Full-bloods elected two of their own leaders – Moshulatubbee, chief of the Lower Towns District, and Nitvkechi, chief of the Sixtowns District – to represent them against Greenwood LeFlore, the mixed-blood leader who had been elected chief of the entire Choctaw Nation several months previously. Nitvkechi and Upper Towns District chief Hummingbird, both full-bloods, refused to recognize Sam Garland, a mixed-blood, as chief of the Sixtowns District, and neither signed the Removal Treaty of Dancing Rabbit Creek. The three signatories, LeFlore, Folsom, and Garland, were all mixed-bloods (Wright 1928:107; Hudson 1939:9–10).

The two segments for and against removal variously allied with missionaries; Methodists defended the LeFlore faction, and Presbyterians, although not so vocal, appeared to ally with the full-bloods (Wright 1928:107n). Both factions met, armed with followers, in early August 1830, although the fear of bloodshed appeared to avert violence. This conflict showed deep tribal divisions among conservative and progressive factions, divisions that split the tribe racially and culturally. Conservative full-bloods in particular forcefully opposed removal. The tribe ultimately accepted removal, although many blamed LeFlore and his faction for the course that history had taken. In the end LeFlore did not migrate to Indian Territory but accepted a Mississippi allotment from the government (Foreman 1934:21–23, 26, 28, 39; Morrison 1987:14–16; Debo 1934:53–54).

The Choctaws, numbering close to fifteen thousand, along with an estimated one thousand slaves (Jeltz 1945:16), were removed from Mississippi during 1831–33 in three separate government-supervised migrations. An estimated twenty-five hundred Choctaws died on the 350-mile trek, in which they were forced to migrate during a devastating blizzard in the winter of 1830–31 and experienced a cholera epidemic during the summer of 1832. Many Choctaws did not even have shoes to wear on their forced march, known today as the "Trail of Tears," a term coined by a Choctaw chief at the time who aptly named the fateful trek of his people a "Trail of Tears and Death" (Poulin 1981:76; Wright 1928).

The Choctaws' indigenous mode of production, rooted in kinship idioms, reciprocity, and gender complementarity, emphasized production for use of shared resources rather than individual resource ownership or production for exchange. As an autonomous nation, the Choctaws adapted effectively to their rich Mississippi River environment. Once European and later Euro-American entrepreneurs discovered the abundant Choctaw homeland, Choctaws had to struggle to retain not only their ancestral lands but their entire way of life.

Initially, Choctaws accommodated to newcomers by adopting useful intrusive technologies and opportunistically entering trade networks, thereby broadening their own subsistence options. Choctaws, perhaps naively, believed that concessions on their part, coupled with strategic alliances, would eventually be met with white accommodation. They failed, however, to fully perceive the voracious "appetites of land hungry cotton-minded whites" (DeRosier 1967:345). Nor could the Choctaws anticipate the extremes to which whites would go to open Indian lands to whites, or the effects white infiltration would have on their indigenous ways.

Euro-American hegemonic interests slowly prevailed, transforming an autonomous nation into a colony of U.S. private-sector interests. As the following chapter explores, political, economic, and cultural factors intersected to foster Choctaw change and accommodation to what would become a radically transformed relationship with outsiders, not as nation to nation, but as marginalized enclave to dominant colonizer.

TWO

Choctaw Seeds of Change

Choctaw Nation, 1982. Assistant Chief: "Somewhere along through the years we have really lost most of the traditional ceremonies and way of living. We still are Indian and we still have something of the old. . . . We still speak a different language than whites or blacks. . . . Traditional beliefs, legends, and ceremonies are almost nonexistent. There is some attempt being made now, and successfully, to bring back certain dances, and things are being revived. The people doing it have had to go to Mississippi to learn the dances, to learn what we did years ago and why we did it."

Choctaw incorporation as a rural peripheral sector of the U.S. and global political economy began even prior to their forced removal to Indian Territory in 1831. Indigenous incorporation within nation-states, Thomas Hall argues (1987:4), is "shaped by local social structure and local actions . . . transform[ing] an autonomous group into an ethnic group." Peripheral economic incorporation into a global system, according to Christopher Chase-Dunn and Hall (1991:7), gives rise to "a stratified set of relations of dominance and dependence between 'developed' and 'developing' countries . . . operating according to a logic of 'capital imperialism,' in which core regions accumulate resources by exploiting peripheral regions." Within what Chase-Dunn and Hall (1991:19) call the *core/periphery hierarchy*, domination is political, economic, and ideological.

The previous chapter discussed how endogenous elements, including decentralized bands, opportunistic trade initiatives, and desire for trade commodities, brought Choctaws increasingly into the Euro-American cultural sphere. External agents – missions, schools, government bureaucracies, traders, and entrepreneurs – also were formidable agents of change. This web of interrelated political, economic, and cultural variables dialectically intersected over time to produce a dynamic, often conflictive struggle between colonizing agents and Choctaw indigenes.

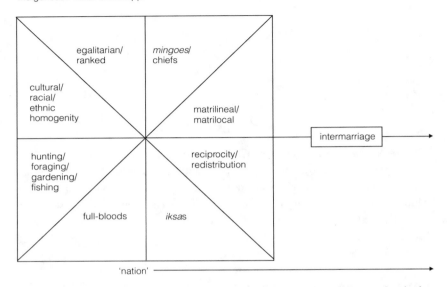

Indigenous Phase: Mississippi

Figure 2.1. Phases of Choctaw contact and culture change: internal/external articulation model.

CHOCTAW-WHITE CONTACT AND RACIAL/CLASS STRATIFICATION
Choctaws experienced the full thrust of U.S. political, economic, and cultural imperialism in a variety of contexts. These ranged from the breakup of hereditary political leadership and attempts to introduce Christianity and secular schools, on the one hand, to coercive post–Civil War treaties, the entry of the railroads, and eventual tribal land allotment and the demise of tribal government, on the other. As more and more whites gained access to tribal wealth, political clout, and cultural influence – as Indian agents and missionaries and through intermarriage – class divisions intensified over issues of leadership, treaty making, missionizing, and removal. What ensued was a process of class differentiation, frequently along racial lines, which solidified into a "racial/class" structure, with traditionalists, mainly full-bloods, seeking to preserve traditional Choctaw ways, while progressives, including intermarried whites and their mixed-blood descendants, became powerful culture brokers – mediators between divergent Choctaw and Euro-American cultural traditions (Morrison 1987:12; see also Wells 1987).

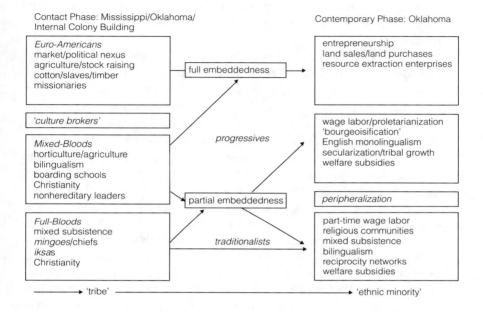

Contact Phase: Mississippi/Oklahoma/
Internal Colony Building

Contemporary Phase: Oklahoma

| *Euro-Americans* |
| market/political nexus |
| agriculture/stock raising |
| cotton/slaves/timber |
| missionaries |

full embeddedness

| entrepreneurship |
| land sales/land purchases |
| resource extraction enterprises |

| *'culture brokers'* |

progressives

| wage labor/proletarianization |
| 'bourgeoisification' |
| English monolingualism |
| secularization/tribal growth |
| welfare subsidies |

| *Mixed-Bloods* |
| horticulture/agriculture |
| bilingualism |
| boarding schools |
| Christianity |
| nonhereditary leaders |

partial embeddedness

| *peripheralization* |

| *Full-Bloods* |
| mixed subsistence |
| *mingoes*/chiefs |
| *iksa*s |
| Christianity |

traditionalists

| part-time wage labor |
| religious communities |
| mixed subsistence |
| bilingualism |
| reciprocity networks |
| welfare subsidies |

'tribe' — — — — — — — — — — — — — — — — — → 'ethnic minority'

Figure 2.1, adapted from Cornell (1988:14, 101–5), Snipp (1986a, 1986b, 1988), and Hall (1987:7, 1988:25), diagrams the phases of Choctaw contact and culture change from "nation" to "tribe" and finally to "ethnic minority," showing the dialectics of Choctaw economic, national, and racial-ethnic interrelationships. The figure traces three periods of Choctaw history: the *indigenous period*; the *contact phase* of colonization, when the Choctaws became an internal colony; and the *contemporary phase* of political, economic, and cultural peripheralization, when the Choctaws became a marginalized ethnic minority and peripheral labor force. This diagram is a heuristic devise to explore Choctaw transformation from autonomy to incorporation and finally to peripheralization as a rural secondary labor force and ethnic minority subculture. Terminology is borrowed from various sources, including world-systems and dependency frameworks that are contextualized politically, economically, and culturally (see Wallerstein 1976, 1980; Frank 1969; Jorgensen 1978; Hall 1988, 1995, 1996; Chase-Dunn and Hall 1991; Dunaway 1996). Whereas such terms as "internal colony" and "peripheralization" con-

23

note economic relations between core and periphery or colony and center, they also connote asymmetrical political realities and cultural dominance relationships.

Core/periphery contacts are dialectical and multidimensional, often bringing new definitions of tribal membership, altered family and household structures, transformed indigenous cultural features, and sometimes even cultural extinction or annihilation. Native Americans, as prior sovereign nations, responded to contact and change in unique and diverse ways along the spectrum from accommodation to annihilation. "Ethnic reorganization" or cultural blending processes (Dunaway 1996:457) are, according to Nagel and Snipp (1993:204), "strateg[ies] by which ethnic minority groups attempt to cope with forces of change." Unique among U.S. ethnic groups, both because of their particular status as domestic sovereign entities and as bearers of autonomous indigenous cultural traditions, Native Americans generally and Choctaws specifically provide insights into phenomena of culture change and persistence and of ethnic reorganization, which have become increasingly common as ethnic groups in Europe, the Middle East, Africa, and the Western Hemisphere seek to assert cultural viability within dominant nation-states, often resorting to violent interethnic confrontations (see Tishkov 1993; Tambiah 1993).

Choctaw culture change over the three eras is complex and multidimensional, giving rise to ever more diverse and increasingly stratified segments (see Hall 1988:26). Choctaw embeddedness in Eurocentric market-oriented society increased over time through social contacts, intermarriage, and market and trade encounters. Some Choctaw segments, such as progressives, however, were more directly embedded in the mainstream political economy, while others, such as traditionalists, mainly full-bloods, were only partially embedded while retaining many indigenous features. In the multistranded contact encounters, Choctaw sovereignty persisted only for a time among particular tribal segments in limited arenas, while majority cultural dominance increased in other arenas, abetted by greater economic dependence, intermarriage, and the intrusive culture's hegemonic political power.

The indigenous phase, as figure 2.1 shows, is marked by homogeneity in several aspects, including mixed subsistence, *iksas* (clans), decentralized chiefly leadership, full-blood status, egalitarian resource distribution, and complementary, gender-based division of labor. The second phase, in both Mississippi and Indian Territory, brings increased cultural heterogeneity as indigenous and Euro-American cultural patterns intersect and three socially and racially stratified classes emerge. In this phase of "market articulation" (see Hall 1988:24) or "internal colony building," indigenous patterns persisted into the postremoval era among some Choctaw segments, who tenaciously clung to former kinship networks and mixed subsistence patterns. This is true particularly among Mississippi Sixtowns migrants who reestablished traditional Choctaw settlements in the interior Indian Territory timber region in what is now Oklahoma's McCurtain and Pushmataha Counties, as later discussions will reveal.

Choctaw progressives, mainly mixed-bloods, modified indigenous cultural practices in the preremoval phase, and some migrated to the Mississippi borderland region, adopted agriculture, animal husbandry, and increasingly participated in market exchanges, to be discussed shortly.

THE POLITICAL ECONOMY OF CHANGE

The Choctaw nation at contact was characterized by fractionated and decentralized kin-based production units, headed by numerous categories of leading men, from *mingoes* to chiefs, as described in chapter 1. Chiefs garnered substantial power over both resource distribution and followers, power that increased as Choctaws embraced Euro-American attitudes toward private property and individual aggrandizement. Controlling the increasingly important nexus of trade in pelts, guns, and agricultural commodities enhanced one's status as "big man or generous man," argues Alan Klein (1993:153; 148–49; see also White 1983:40–46, 55–56, 78–79; Albers 1993:100–102; Dunaway 1996:465–67). Chiefly wielding of power in the early contact era, White (1983:64) claims, did not give rise to true social classes, however, "since chiefs never controlled the means of production in agriculture, and did not long retain their monopoly of the gun." Nor did chiefs exercise patriarchal authority over women, who wielded considerable direct economic power and indirect political influence in kin-based political and economic spheres.[1]

Tribal political divisions were brought about both by internal factional and Euro-American interests. British, French, and Spanish colonists competing for regional access used intertribal antagonisms and internal conflicts

---

1. See Sacks 1979: esp.65–95 for a relevant discussion of women's status differences in egalitarian as opposed to ranked and stratified societies.

between competing Choctaw chiefs, headmen, and neighborhood kin groups to preserve their own regional power bases (see L. Smith 1988:11–12; Albers 1993:101–12; Klein 1993:143–47; Dunaway 1994:220–22, 1996:464–67). Titles and chiefly "medals" were arbitrarily bestowed and annuities randomly paid to "headmen" by Euro-Americans irrespective of clan rank to protect Choctaw loyalty and solidify Euro-American access to land and trade opportunities.

In the little more than a decade between 1763 and 1776 the new mixture of trade, liquor and war brought by the English corroded those parts of Choctaw society that rested on the old order hunting economy. . . .
. . . By the 1770s the medal chiefs, more than ever before, had become chiefs simply because Europeans had given them medals. Their traditional functions were in shambles; their real power was often virtually nonexistent. (White 1983:78–82, 98; see also Klein 1993:153)

As Dunaway notes among the Cherokees (1994:222–25), Euro-Americans encouraged Choctaws to dispense with localized leadership traditions rooted in *iksa*-based hereditary captaincies in favor of more centralized chiefly roles, thereby strengthening the chiefly power of certain individuals. U.S. government agents preferred to deal with larger constituencies: tribal entities rather than band or *iksa*. Not only was it easier to negotiate with a smaller number of more influential leaders, but Euro-Americans anticipated that such individuals would be more easily co-optable (White 1983:112).

Along with increased trading contacts and an ever more depleted land and resource base, Choctaws faced more direct encroachment by Euro-American settlers in the late eighteenth and early nineteenth centuries. White men frequently married Choctaw women and became a permanent tribal constituency, producing a new generation of mixed-blood offspring (Wells 1987).

Intermarriage was not new to the Choctaws, nor did it appear unusual. Captive women and children were frequently taken by southeastern tribes, and ongoing relations among neighbors such as the Natchez and Creeks undoubtedly brought at least some voluntary romantic liaisons, which may have provided the cultural basis for acceptance of white male liaisons. Choctaw women apparently accommodated to male sexual advances – intertribal or interethnic, but historical documents are unclear as to whether and to what degree women entered freely into such liaisons. Framed within the familiar indigenous idiom, Choctaws did not appear to systematically resist Euro-American intermarriage, particularly with trappers and hunters who adopted rural lifestyles similar to their own.[2]

Bloodedness is a problematic concept, implying racial rather than cultural membership criteria. As Cornell argues (1988:238n), "The full-blood/mixed-blood terminology . . . implies a biological distinction and is therefore misleading. The difference has far more to do with culture than biology, referring generally to the perceived extent to which an individual's life is organized and lived in Indian versus non-Indian ways." Choctaw/Euro-American intermarriage had a profound cultural impact, opening a wedge to cultural exchange and the softening of intercultural differences between Euro-Americans and indigenes. As Klein (1993:152) notes, among Plains tribes, with intermarriage, "more than any other area we can see the potential for racial and cultural differences to be ameliorated."

RACIAL, CLASS, AND GENDER DIVISIONS

Euro-American economic, political, and social encroachments combined with intermarriage brought what Patricia Albers and William R. James (1986:9–10) describe as competing "ethnic ideologies" built on class, behavioral, and ideological differences. The political, economic, and ideological agendas of intermarried whites and mixed-bloods came to differ radically from traditionalists, both mixed- and full-blood, a process depicted above in figure 2.1. Intermarried whites, fully embedded in Euro-American ideology and value systems, introduced Euro-American values emphasizing private property, patriarchal privilege, industry, and market trade into what was formerly a reciprocity-based egalitarian society. Mixed-bloods and intermarried whites gained added leverage as mediators and culture brokers, fluent in European languages and more sympathetic to the cultural realities of the new social order. Progressives, frequently linked genealogically, culturally, and ideologically to the majority Euro-American culture, became "forces for social change." Whites and mixed-bloods had added leverage,

2. See Wells 1987; Baird 1972:14; Cornell 1988:238n; but see also Sacks 1979; Mohanty 1991:17–19. The role of women in the indigenous transformations to capitalism needs to be further examined, as Ward (1993) notes. Mohanty (1991:17) asserts that "sexual encounters between white men and native women often took the form of rape." Existing historic accounts fail to address the fact that Choctaw women undoubtedly were frequently coerced into romantic liaisons, both by neighboring tribalists and white intruders.

since Indian agents often preferred to deal with tribal representatives fluent in the majority culture's language and practices (see Albers and James 1986:1; Valentine 1975; Castile 1993).

Politically, decentralized indigenous groupings rooted in *iksa* and clan were eroded in favor of centralized chiefly statuses, often held by influential mixed-bloods. According to Gibson (1973:80–81; see also Morrison 1987:16), this class began to form a sort of Choctaw aristocracy, eroding the tribal clanship system on which tribal leadership was based. "More and more the avenue to tribal leadership shifted from clan association based on wisdom and bravery to mixed-blood parentage based on accommodation to the emerging new order" (see also White 1983:114–17; Champagne 1989:54–55; Morrison 1987:12; Wells 1987).

Slowly these factions emerged into full-blown social classes, dividing the tribe economically and culturally. "There were now," according to White (1983:109), "identifiable rich families and identifiable poor families. . . . Conflict between the pastoralists and hunters occurred especially in the early years of the transition when cattle owners were whites or mixed-bloods and the hunters, most often hungry and desperate, were full-bloods." Choctaw transformation to capitalism shows how capitalist and patriarchal agendas interconnect in hinterland development. Gender and racial asymmetry were by-products of the Choctaw transition, just as they have been in other marginalized milieus globally (see Shelton and Agger 1993:30; Cook 1990; Harris 1990; Collins 1990; Collins and Gimenez, eds., 1990; Scott 1986). Entrepreneurial white males were instrumental in introducing new technologies, means of production, and market relations, radically altering household production strategies and challenging women's household and community status.

Intermarriage also infused Euro-American patriarchal norms and values into the egalitarian Choctaw social fabric, marginalizing women economically and politically. Choctaw women were unwitting and perhaps unwilling conduits through whom white men accessed legitimate or quasi-legitimate tribal leadership roles and tribal property. In the process, women's legitimate economic, political, and social roles in Choctaw society were transformed, particularly as land moved from communal to private ownership. Patriarchal ideologies stripped Choctaw women of rights to family property and complementary labor and subordinated their status in the household and wider community. Men, frequently intermarried whites, increasingly controlled family and tribal means of production in land, thereby deteriorating women's economic and political power (see Sacks 1979; Cook 1990; Dunn, Almquist, and Chafetz 1993).

Class and gender differentiation were aggravated in the late colonial era when some Choctaws began to migrate into what White (1983:98–99) called the Choctaw "borderlands," seeking new hunting and agriculture territories (see map 1.1). Many mixed-blood and intermarried white borderland migrants introduced cattle raising and later cotton cultivation, transforming indigenous subsistence patterns rooted in production for use into full-blown market-oriented agricultural enterprise. This subsistence shift, prompted by resource depletion, warfare, and disease and combined with white entry, radically transformed Choctaw land and resource use patterns as well as cultural attitudes toward resource use and exchange. According to White, "Livestock did not enter just the lands of the Choctaws; it entered their culture as well and made pastoralists of many who had been hunters" (White 1983:103–5; see also L. Smith 1988:53–54). Livestock and land were gradually being transformed from collective to private property, benefiting not the tribal whole but individual Choctaws, often mixed-bloods and intermarried whites.

These technological innovations profoundly affected Choctaw women's status and power. Whereas traditional production strategies placed women as equal coparticipants in a complementary division of labor, new technological innovations such as commoditized livestock ranching and slave-based agriculture were managed mainly by male heads of household. Dana Dunn, Elizabeth Almquist, and Janet Chafetz (1993:81) note that since men typically control new technologies – agricultural or industrial – the transition to capitalism promoted gender stratification, an argument put forth by Ester Boserup (1970). As women's access to economic resources deteriorates, their influence in household and community decision making also diminishes, while the status, power, and prestige of males is enhanced. In the Choctaw case, mixed-blood males were particularly advantaged in these economic transitions (see also Collins 1990; Collins and Gimenez, eds., 1990; Scott 1986; Ward 1993:50–51; Harris 1990).

Ranching, livestock raising, and increasingly agriculture were particularly evident in two of the three Mississippi Choctaw districts, Upper Towns and Lower Towns, both inhabited by many mixed-blood families (see figure 2.1, above). The Sixtowns District, more wooded and less amenable to livestock raising, retained its emphasis on mixed hunting/foraging/horticultural subsistence (White 1983:108). Champagne (1989:54) estimates that in the 1820s more than 90 percent of Choctaws remained small-scale agriculturists oriented to subsistence production. A small but influential class of "entrepreneurial planters," however, lived a wholly different lifestyle. While the average Choctaw hunter/forager subsistence producer had approximately 5 to 20 acres under cultivation, mostly in corn, the Choctaw elite of mainly mixed-blood and intermarried white families, such as Greenwood and Benjamin LeFlore, David Folsom, John Pitchlynn, and Joel Nail, had anywhere from 100 to 250 acres under cultivation, and most owned slaves (White 1983:133–34; Jeltz 1945:9; Wells 1987).

Although only a small percentage of Choctaws participated in market-oriented agricultural production in the 1820s, this progressive segment increasingly dominated the tribe's internal and external political affairs. "Taken together, the full-blood and mixed-blood market farmers formed a critical transitional segment of the nation, one that increasingly dominated local as well as national positions of authority" (White 1983:134). Philosophically, the new faction embraced values emphasizing entrepreneurship, individual aggrandizement, industry, frugality, temperance, monogamy, patrilineal descent, and eventually Christianity and secular education. They viewed their aggrandizing activities as beneficial and their less successful countrymen as lazy (White 1983:117–18, 137–38; Champagne 1989:54).

The entrepreneurial class swelled precipitously in the late eighteenth and early nineteenth centuries through intermarriage, which occurred frequently between European and Euro-American males, often traders, and Choctaw women, who together produced hundreds of mixed-blood offspring. Whites carried their Euro-American surnames into the ranks of Choctaw leadership during subsequent decades in both Mississippi and Indian Territory (see Morrison 1987:12–14; Wells 1987; Hudson n.d., 1931; Gunning n.d.). Prominent white traders and early cattle-ranching families included Louis Durant, Nathaniel Folsom, Isaac Pitchlynn, Louis and Michael LeFlore, and Pierre Juzan Sr. (see Wells 1987:42, 44, 49–54, 68–72; White 1983:104), names that recur frequently in the ranks of Choctaw leaders in decades to come. As Kehoe (1992:182) notes, the children of such unions "were full members of their mother's towns, entitled to the same rights and privileges as any other Indian" (see also Baird 1972:14).

Intermarried whites were adept traders, familiar with Euro-American ag-

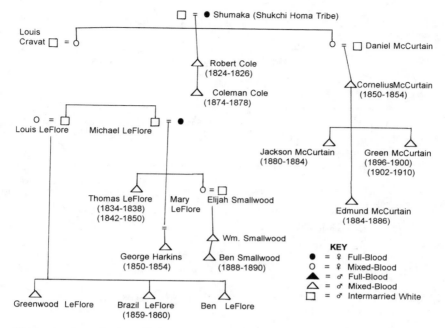

Figure 2.2. Genealogies, Mississippi Northwest Upper Towns District, Indian Territory Apukshunnubbee District.

ricultural techniques, fluent in English (and French before 1783), and frequently bilingual. They easily entered into amiable, often intimate relations with their Choctaw neighbors (see Wells 1987:4, 80). Family genealogies of prominent Choctaw mixed-blood or blended families from each of the three Mississippi districts and corresponding Indian Territory districts are shown in figures 2.2, 2.3, and 2.4.

With ever-increasing cultural and social contacts, Choctaw factions, formerly *iksa* based, crystallized around emerging tribal class divisions. Frequently racially cast, factional divisions were mirrored in many Native American communities struggling with similar contact-era upheavals and even persist in the twentieth century on many reservations (see Schusky 1994; Meyer 1994). Choctaw factional antagonisms surfaced over a variety of issues, including disputes over land cession, tribal removal, and assimilation. Traditionalists frequently resisted integration into Euro-American political, economic, and cultural spheres, whether it be cash crop production,

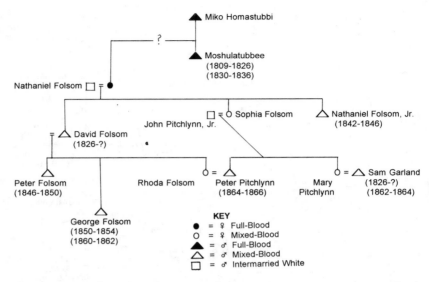

Figure 2.3. Genealogies, Mississippi Northeast Lower Towns District, Indian Territory Moshulatubbee District.

Christianity, or secular schools. Traditionalists also resisted efforts to dispense with indigenous cultural features, such as hereditary chieftainships, *iksas*, matrilineality, and communal rituals.

Assimilationist factions, on the other hand, mainly mixed-bloods, tied genealogically and culturally to whites, adopted what Cornell (1988:153–54) labels an "integrative/transformative" posture in the contact situation. This faction adopted Eurocentric cultural traits and values and encouraged Choctaw cultural transformation and accommodation to a new social order (see Wells 1987:2–4; see also Meyer 1994:31ff., 103–7).

Critical to Choctaw leadership were positions taken on important local issues including land cession, tribal removal, and accommodation to the new Euro-American-dominated political-economic order. Undoubtedly, the most pressing issues facing Choctaws, with the most far-reaching implications, were land cession and tribal removal to Indian Territory. Traditionally oriented tribalists feared total loss of their indigenous lifestyle and land resources, while the entrepreneurially oriented class sought to retain their lucrative land and livestock holdings as long as possible, which had been largely individualized and privatized in the Choctaw constitution of 1826.

32

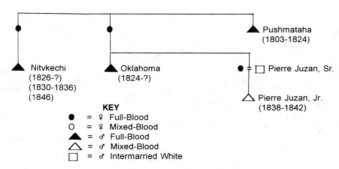

Figure 2.4. Genealogies, Mississippi Southwest Sixtowns District, Indian Territory Pushmataha District.

Mixed-bloods led the opposition to land cession during the period 1800–1830, since they stood to lose substantially if forced to relinquish their valuable grazing and agricultural lands in the borderland regions (White 1983:114–17). The hunting faction, mainly full-bloods, was attracted by the chance to access vast tracts of apparently virgin hunting territory west of the Mississippi River. Mixed-bloods, continuing to oppose any cession treaties, emerged as leaders following the 1820 Treaty of Doaks Stand, in which the Choctaws finally agreed to cede six million acres of land for western territories. Traditionalists, however, became increasingly more suspicious of progressives, whom they accused of selling out to white secessionists.

Facing ever-increasing pressure to vacate their Mississippi homeland, Choctaw progressives in 1826 led the tribe in formulating a new political agenda combining resistance to removal with a pragmatic assimilationist focus. Progressives drafted a constitution in 1826 that dispensed with many ancient Choctaw practices, including hereditary chiefs, traditional burial practices, infanticide, polygyny, and matrilineal inheritance. An abrupt transition from full-blood to mixed-blood representation in all three Mississippi districts occurred in that year when all three districts elected mixed-blood leaders: Sam Garland in Sixtowns, Greenwood LeFlore in Upper Towns, and David Folsom in Lower Towns. The council also adopted a written code of laws for the first time (White 1983:126–27; Debo 1934:49). Only five full-bloods have served as district or principal chief since 1830, including the current tribal chief, Hollis Roberts. More than twenty who served were children or grandchildren of white men.

Chiefly genealogical connections, diagramed in figures 2.2, 2.3, and 2.4

Map 2.1. Old Choctaw Nation districts and important towns, Indian Territory, 1830s. *Source*: Based on map 38, "Choctaw Nation: Political Divisions," in John W. Morris, Charles R. Goins, and Edwin C. McReynolds, *Historical Atlas of Oklahoma*, 2d ed. (Norman: University of Oklahoma Press, 1976), by permission of the University of Oklahoma Press.

above, show how Choctaw political power was both tightly controlled by leading Choctaw blended families and held overwhelmingly and increasingly by entrepreneurial-minded progressives, mainly mixed-bloods, both prior to and following Indian Territory resettlement. Typically, migrants from Mississippi settled together in their new homeland, establishing settlements in three Indian Territory districts: Pushmataha, Moshulatubbee, and Apuckshunnubbee, shown in map 2.1.

Prominent Upper Towns families, including the Folsoms, Pitchlynns, and Garlands, settled in the Moshulatubbee District. Members of the Cole, LeFlore, McCurtain, and Smallwood families, from Mississippi Lower Towns, migrated to the Apuckshunnubbee District. Many Apuckshunnubbee District settlers also came from Greenwood LeFlore's Upper Towns District in Mississippi, including six hundred settlers, known as the "Thomas LeFlore Company," who arrived in 1832 and settled west of Eagletown in what is today McCurtain County (Wright 1921:117).

The Choctaw families that were relocated to the Pushmataha District, many former residents of the Sixtowns District, did not become fully dominated by mixed-blood leadership until after removal. That district retained full-blood leadership intermittently until 1846, through the hereditary line of Pushmataha, the Sixtowns District chief from 1803 to 1824, as shown in figure 2.4. Pushmataha's nephew Nitvkechi was district chief three times. In Sixtowns, traditional subsistence practices had persisted, and market embeddedness had remained more attenuated, a legacy that appeared to have been carried to Indian Territory. Pierre Juzan Jr., Pushmataha District chief from 1838 to 1842 and a descendant of a prominent French family, traced genealogical links to Pushmataha and Nitvkechi (Wells 1987:84–86). Following removal, this district was intermittently presided over by members of the Folsom family, including Isaac and George Folsom, who retained tight control of the Moshulatubbee District as well (see Wells 1987; Hudson n.d., 1939; Gunning n.d.).

The immediate preremoval era in the 1820s marked a crucial stage in the Euro-American domination process, transforming Choctaws from nation to marginalized tribe. Euro-Americans used a variety of strategies to penetrate Choctaw society, including intermarriage and co-opting indigenous "medal" chiefs. Increased market participation and ideological conversion further intensified Choctaw racial and class divisions. Mixed-bloods and intermarried whites served as culture brokers, controlling tribal resources, information, and decision making. Indigenous cultural features were slowly eroding as a mixed-blood aristocracy took over much of Choctaw leadership in the immediate preremoval phase. Although individuals served as formidable change agents, the institutions they brought, particularly Christian churches and secular schools, had an even greater impact on Choctaw indigenous culture in the postremoval phase, as the Choctaw Nation assimilated the Euro-American market ideology.

Choctaw women were unwitting change agents, both as culture mediators in blended households and in their radically changed relationship to household wealth, political power, and decision making under patriarchal relations of production. Some Choctaw women, as throughout regions of hinterland development globally, saw their relations to household means of production deteriorate as households relied on male-controlled production strategies and market trade. Women, however, continued to play an important role in many rural households as unwaged subsistence and commodity producers into the contemporary era, as later discussions will explore.

Euro-American hegemonic interests slowly prevailed, transforming an autonomous nation rooted in indigenous kin networks into a colony of U.S. private-sector interests. The next chapter explores the role of two formidable change agents, churches and schools, in transforming nineteenth-century Choctaw culture.

THREE

Postcontact Change Agents:
Tribal, Religious, and Secular

The Choctaw homeland in Indian Territory, nearly 6.8 million acres, was bounded on the north by the Canadian and Arkansas Rivers and on the south by the Red River (see map 2.1). The region was characterized by two distinct topographies: upland hills and lowland valleys. The uplands contained Kiamichi and Sugar Loaf Mountains, part of the Ouachita Mountain range, extending westward from Arkansas. Its highest Oklahoma elevation, Rich Mountain, stood approximately 2,850 feet above sea level. The uplands marked the central divide of the Choctaw Nation, with the Poteau River to the north flowing into the Arkansas River, while the Kiamichi River drained into the Red River to the south. The region consisted generally of rocky, hilly, rough terrain, with sandstone and slate outcroppings. Approximately 90 percent of the Choctaw Nation was covered with timber in the 1830s, originally blackjack and post oak, with some black hickory, cottonwood, elm, walnut, and bois d'arc (Benson 1806:42; Morrison 1987:4–6).

North and south of the central uplands, prairie land and lowland valleys of the Red, Arkansas, and Canadian Rivers offered a different vista. Much of this region was grassland containing rich alluvial soils well suited to cattle ranching and corn and cotton cultivation. Euro-Americans had already settled along the Red River in what was previously called Arkansas Territory, building farms and homesteads (Morrison 1978:66).

Choctaw contact and change was a complex transformative process of adaptation, adoption, resistance, and accommodation: a cultural survival strategy, the substance of which was a dialectic between internal and external change agents (Nagel and Snipp 1993:206–7, 221). Colonization required that the Choctaws adapt to or adopt Euro-American values, behaviors, and cultural practices in concert with U.S. transformative agendas. Littlefield

(1993:43–45) and Forbes (1990:97–99) argue that the U.S. mission was not to "assimilate" Native Americans so much as it was to "proletarianize": to transform a formerly independent, self-sufficient mode of production into compliant wage labor, "separated from their means of production" through land grabbing, allotment, and manual training appropriate to their place in the new social order. Jack Forbes (1990:99) notes that colonial proletarian-ization involved radical cultural transformation where nonwhites "came to comprise not merely a working-class but a colonized proletariat with caste as opposed to national characteristics," inferiorized, emasculated, and "en-veloped" into the dominant culture. The question loomed, How could the Choctaws retain some semblance of cultural integrity in the contact and change situation, as external change agents worked to undermine the Choc-taw way of life?

The stages of Choctaw transformation, including forced removal to In-dian Territory, eventual land expropriation, and proletarianization, oc-curred as a dialectical process between a semiautonomous Choctaw tribe and agents of U.S. interests. Protestant denominational churches, secular schools, U.S. government agencies, and later the Bureau of Indian Affairs and private corporate interests all worked, sometimes independently and sometimes together, to undermine Choctaw autonomy and tribal integrity and forward their own agendas, whether religious, political, or economic.

Local Choctaw leaders – frequently mixed-bloods – brokered the transi-tion to modernity, linked as they were with U.S. agents of cultural change. In the process, similar to many Native/U.S. encounters, such as that among the White Earth Anishinaabeg described by Meyer (1994), internal factional antagonisms emerged, frequently along progressive/conservative axes, which were often racially and class configured (see Meyer 1994:99, 173–75).

CHANGE AGENTS: MISSIONS AND SCHOOLS

The Choctaws, once they reached Indian Territory in 1831, began imme-diately to recreate residence patterns, communities, and institutions remi-niscent of life in Mississippi. Two change agents – missions and schools – played an active role in fostering Choctaw cultural change, further pro-moting Euro-American class interests and transforming a homogeneous culture into a rural enclave of U.S. society by the twentieth century (Mor-rison 1987:15; McLoughlin 1985:399–400). Euro-American missionaries rep-resenting several denominations – mainly Presbyterian and Congregational, but also Methodist and Baptist – accompanied the Choctaws on their westward trek. As in Mississippi, missionaries expressed the popular view that only by Christianizing and educating Indians in Euro-American ways, particularly sedentary agriculture, could indigenous people be fully "civilized" into U.S. society. As William McLoughlin (1985:398) states,

> The missionary's role was to provide the schooling and the moral training to "wean" the Indians from their savage customs so that they, or their children, would blend easily into the cultural institutions of Euro-American society. In short, the melting pot idea of assimilation was to be promoted by mission schools for the Native Americans in the same way that public schools would assimilate incoming aliens from the non-English nations of Europe. To Christianize was to Americanize.

Christian missionizing among the Choctaws began in earnest in 1817 when the American Board of Indian Missions established its first mission station at Eliot in the Upper Towns District and sent a Presbyterian missionary, Cyrus Kingsbury, to "civilize" and "Christianize" the "pagan aborigines" (Spaulding 1974:4; Morrison 1978:18; 23–24; see also Hedley 1993:189). In 1820 another New Englander, Cyrus Byington, led a party of twenty-three missionaries, workers, and ministers to Mississippi; in that year a second mission station was constructed at Mayhew, in the Lower Towns District, and Byington became its first resident missionary. David Folsom, a mixed-blood Choctaw, and John Pitchlynn, an intermarried white, were influential in lobbying for this and other missionary projects, writing letters to the American Board, assisting in selection of mission sites, and working on behalf of mission projects (Morrison 1978:21, 23–25; Conlan 1926:342–44). Mission schools were frequently situated close to white and mixed-blood homesteads, as for example that established in 1820 in the home of Charles Juzan. Mixed-bloods often petitioned the Choctaw Council for schools in their districts (Wells 1987:162–63).

The American Board of Indian Missions quickly established a network of mission stations, which included educational and religious buildings, farmland, and residential dwellings, creating in effect self-sufficient villages. The aim of the American Board was "to teach common school learning and the useful arts of life and Christianity; [and] so gradually to make the whole tribe English in language, civilized in habits, and Christian in religion" (Morrison 1978:23). Both secular and religious agendas were incorporated into the early mission-sponsored educational curriculum, within the framework of an ideology promoting Christian conversion and Euro-American "civilizing."

Choctaw Nation, 1982. "You must come to our church sings to learn about Choctaw culture," I was told. "This is where we really live our lives as Choctaws." Church sings can be found nearly every night of the week somewhere in the Choctaw Nation. Church members attend faithfully, many traveling fifty miles along remote dirt roads to attend a Saturday night sing. Sometimes popular evangelical preachers or gospel singers are hired to perform, attracting an even bigger audience than usual. During the summer, churches sponsor week-long "church schools" attended by children of all ages.

During the 1820s Methodist, Baptist, and Cumberland Presbyterian missionaries joined the American Board's Presbyterian and Congregational Choctaw missionizing efforts. Methodist missionaries arrived in 1825, and in 1827 succeeded in converting Greenwood LeFlore, district chief of the Upper Towns. Methodists reportedly had four thousand converts by 1830, many of whom were mixed-blood families. Methodists also sponsored "Sunday schools" or "camp meetings," where adults and children would congregate on weekends, attending religious and secular educational sessions to learn to read, perform computations, and comprehend Christian teachings. By 1830 every corner of the Choctaw Nation was ministered to by approximately forty missionaries working in thirteen mission stations and thirty-three schools (Morrison 1978:24, 29; Spaulding 1974:106; Debo 1934:42, 45, 68–69).

Baptists employed yet another technique to Christianize and educate Choctaws: mission-sponsored boarding schools. Choctaw Academy, a boarding school formerly called Johnson's Academy, was constructed in 1818 on land owned by an active member of the Kentucky Baptist Society, Richard M. Johnson, a U.S. senator in the 1820s and a prominent supporter of Andrew Jackson and John C. Calhoun. Johnson, who lobbied for Indian education funding throughout his tenures as a state and federal government official, benefited from a so-called Indian Civilization Fund created in 1819 to provide tuition for Indian students to attend boarding schools, including his own Johnson's Academy. Beginning in 1825, funds were allocated specifically to educate Choctaw youth at Johnson's Academy, renamed Choctaw Academy, as a result of a provision written into article 2 of the 1825 treaty between the Choctaws and the U.S. government. Subsequently, through contacts with Peter Pitchlynn of the Lower Towns District, Choctaw youth were sent to the Choctaw Academy, an estimated twenty by Pitchlynn himself in 1825. Members of all the prominent mixed-blood families, including the Folsoms, Pitchlynns, Juzons, Harkins, Durants, and LeFlores, among others, sent their sons to Choctaw Academy (Morrison 1978:33–38; Kidwell 1987:53, 64).

Choctaw Nation, 1982. Elderly Choctaws told of dehumanizing and frightful experiences at Indian boarding schools, where their hair was cut and they were forced to speak English. They dreaded being taken from their parents, kinfolk, neighbors, and familiar rural community settings to live with strangers for many months.

Choctaw Nation, 1993. Wheelock Academy graduates gathered for a historic reunion on the impressive grounds of the now dilapidated and deteriorating – and strangely out of place – building. Many spoke nostalgically of time spent at Wheelock, a girls' boarding school founded in 1832 in southern McCurtain County, not far from Wright City, Weyerhaeuser's Oklahoma headquarters. Children from impoverished families were assured decent meals, clothing, and a warm place to sleep. Students were taught the three *R*s, sewing, cooking, and other domestic skills. Many went on to college, and some left the Choctaw Nation during the 1950s in government-sponsored relocation programs. Graduates talked of efforts to rehabilitate the historic structure, but were discouraged that neither the tribe nor the county historical society would commit sufficient funds to rehabilitate the grand main building.

Denominational missionizing and educational work among Native Americans was unambiguously endorsed by U.S. government officials, particularly John C. Calhoun and Andrew Jackson, and backed by widespread popular support throughout the United States, as part of the effort to transform indigenous tribal members into U.S. citizens. Intermarried whites and mixed-bloods also endorsed missionizing, viewing their work pragmatically as a way to access Euro-American cultural skills, opportunities, and resources. Many, such as mixed-blood David Folsom, encouraged missionaries to enter the Choctaw Nation and frequently served as liaisons between Missionaries and the Choctaw people.

Mission reports . . . always stated that requests came from "the Indians," or "the Choctaws" in this case. What was not reported was that almost invariably the so-called "Indians" were from a minority faction who were of mixed Indian and white blood and usually included some all-white or intermarried citizens of the Indian Nation. In the case of the Choctaws, the petitioners for mission schools in 1818 bore names such as Pitchlynn, LeFlore, and Folsom, who were either intermarried whites or Indians with white fathers and Choctaw mothers. Full blood names such as Pushmataha, Moshulatubbee, or Apukshunubbee were notably missing from the reports requesting that missionaries be sent. (Morrison 1978:19–20)

David Folsom, the mixed-blood son of the white trader Nathaniel Folsom, became a spokesperson and ally of the missionaries, translated texts into Choctaw, opened mission schools, and urged Choctaws to adopt the ways of whites. Folsom in 1822 admonished fellow Choctaws to

strive to the utmost to acquire the manners, the knowledge and language of the missionaries. It is true your fathers have possessed this land, notwithstanding their ignorance of these things, but this you cannot be expected to do unless you become civilized. . . . It is therefore indispensably necessary that the rising generation shall be educated and learn the ways of the white people. (Conlan 1926:343)

Folsom was pivotal in bringing both Christianity and secular educational institutions to his people in their Mississippi phase, and he continued his efforts in Indian Territory.

Not only were the Folsoms and Pitchlynns influential in lobbying for missionary access to the Choctaw Nation, but both also had prominent ties to Choctaw leadership. David Folsom became the first elected chief of the Lower Towns District in 1826, and his brother, Nathaniel Jr., was elected district chief of the Moshulatubbee District in Indian Territory in 1842. David's sons, Peter and George, each served as district chief following resettlement in Indian Territory. The genealogical charts in figures 2.2, 2.3, and 2.4 show the various connections among these prominent mixed-blood Choctaw families in Mississippi and Indian Territory.

Undoubtedly, much of the impetus for Choctaw missionary work was educational. As Clara Sue Kidwell notes, "pragmatically-minded Choctaws . . . were not as interested in Christian salvation as they were in education. . . . The desire of Choctaw leaders [was] to learn the ways of white men" (Kidwell 1987:54; see also Morrison 1978:31). As Richard White (1983:117) argues, for Choctaw progressives the church was a powerful change agent, reinforcing Euro-American values they themselves had come to adopt.

Mixed-bloods, including Folsom, LeFlore, and Pitchlynn, along with intermarried whites, lobbied to establish neighborhood schools or promoted local and boarding schools for Choctaw children. Peter Pitchlynn, the mixed-blood Choctaw, favored boarding schools, saying that "the only way to learn the white man's culture was to live in a white environment" (Morrison 1978:37). In 1830 approximately 260 Choctaw children were enrolled in schools in the nation, with an additional 89 boys enrolled in Choctaw Academy (Debo 1934:45).

Indian education financing, although initially carried out by various denominational sects, quickly became a component of U.S. policy designed to transform Choctaws from tribalists into "civilized" U.S. citizens. Tribal annuity payments as well as donations from wealthy Choctaws – "usually prosperous mixed-bloods" (Morrison 1978:27) – also were used to fund educational activities in the preremoval era. In addition, Choctaw tribal councils allocated funds for Indian education at Choctaw Academy from tribal annuity payments.

In the immediate pre- and postremoval era progressives and traditionalists disagreed over missionizing and secular schools. Traditionalists viewed missionizing activity with suspicion, as "subversive to tribal interest." Some distrusted missionary motives, while others complained about educational quality, particularly at schools sponsored by the American Board of Indian Missions (Benson 1860:37–38; Kidwell 1987:60, 66–67). Traditionalists linked church agendas with dangerous and undesirable change forces including assimilation and white domination. Missionaries openly opposed such diverse indigenous practices as polygamy, ball playing, matrilineal descent, collective landownership, and even female gardening, viewing these practices as contrary to Euro-American standards of propriety, or simply as "sinful" (McLoughlin 1985:398–400).

At removal, traditionalist ambivalence escalated, and two prominent full-blood district chiefs, Moshulatubbee and Nitvkechi, drafted a letter to the U.S. government seeking to prohibit missionaries from moving west (Morrison 1978:40, 1987:15; see also McLoughlin 1985:399). Another petition to the American Board missionary Cyrus Kingsbury, signed by Robert, John, and Israel Folsom, Benjamin Wright, and several others, asked missionaries to accompany them westward (Spaulding 1974:111). Leading proponents of missionaries and removal included Greenwood LeFlore and John Garland, both mixed-blood leaders. LeFlore, as noted above, never left Mississippi and instead accepted an allotment in the former Choctaw Nation.

Choctaw Nation, 1982. The Choctaw church elder, as in earlier days, is a cross between a "big man" and a Latin American cargo holder. As church deacon, he is responsible for virtually every aspect of Choctaw church life. He gives generously: land for a cemetery, food for a celebration, labor, counsel, and wisdom. He organizes work crews to repair and maintain church buildings and grounds. He serves as lay preacher and pastoral counselor, conducting church services when itinerant preachers are absent. Like *mingoes* of the past, he heads a network of kinfolk – siblings, in-laws, children, grandchildren – a loyal and energetic flock with whom he shares his wisdom, labor, and love.

INDIAN TERRITORY MISSIONIZING

Progressive factions began immediately to work with missionaries to promote missionary and educational work in Indian Territory. Most early schools and mission settlements were located in the southeastern and southwestern districts, Apuckshunnubbee and Pushmataha, near Choctaw migration entry points along the Mountain Fork River, near present-day Eagletown, or west of Fort Smith, Arkansas, shown in map 3.1. By 1832 four supply stations were established near Eagletown, and the first American Board–sponsored church, Nanih Hacha (Mountain River) was organized (Morrison 1978:66–67). An estimated fourteen hundred Choctaws lived within five miles, and as many as three thousand within twenty-five miles of the Nanih Hacha Church (Spaulding 1974:118; see also Morrison 1978:67; Foreman 1932).

The first Choctaw Nation mission school was established at Bethabara, near Eagletown, in the home of an American Board missionary, Loring S. Williams, whose wife served as teacher. Another missionary, Alfred (Allen) Wright, a Choctaw full-blood, established a mission station at Wheelock in 1832, eighty of whose members were former parishioners in Mississippi (Morrison 1978:67). Wheelock Station, "a 'very comfortable establishment . . . in one of the most healthy and favorable situations in that part of the country,'" became a center of religious and secular activity, operating as many as a dozen schools under American Board supervision (Morrison 1978:72). Cyrus Kingsbury arrived in Indian Territory in 1835 and reported that thirteen schools operated under American Board auspices, along with four churches, totaling 221 members (Spaulding 1974:133).

Missionary work in the Moshulatubbee District was slower to come, according to Henry C. Benson (1860:39), an American Board teacher who

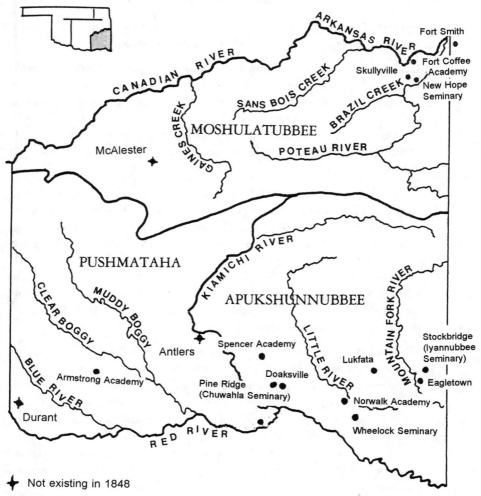

✦ Not existing in 1848

Map 3.1. Choctaw Nation districts and Choctaw schools, 1848. *Source*: James D. Morrison, *Schools for the Choctaws* (Durant OK: Southeastern Oklahoma State University, Choctaw Bilingual Education Program, 1978), xi.

traveled in Indian Territory in the 1830s and 1840s. By 1843 only one American Board–sponsored school was located in that district, along with two or three Baptist-sponsored schools (Morrison 1978:73). This slowness was due to the distrust of missionaries of that district's full-blood chief, Moshulatubbee, and his followers who had settled there, and it reflected a continuing full-blood resistance to missionizing and educative activities. Benson (1860:102, 103–5), noting the racial/class divisions, wrote:

Half-breeds were not in favor with the masses of the people. Though shrewd and intelligent, they were regarded with suspicion. The unadulterated Choctaw was thought to be purest and best; and hence full-bloods were considered the most true, patriotic and reliable . . . they could not vote for a man who had a fair complexion and blue eyes. . . . While the chiefs were all illiterate and full-blooded Indians, the United States interpreter and the trustees of the schools were all educated half-breeds.

Church leaders and schoolteachers during the early years in Indian Territory were mainly white missionaries, although by about 1860 Choctaw preachers had taken over nearly all of the Choctaw neighborhood churches (Debo 1934:229). Schools were supervised by district chiefs and a board of trustees appointed by them. Christian mission societies provided teachers to broaden Choctaw knowledge of English, arithmetic, writing, and of course, Christian theology. During the 1830s Choctaws supported five schools, with an enrollment of 101, as well as district schools, maintained by tribal and annuity payments (Debo 1934:60; 1978 73–76).

Choctaw Nation, 1982. Each church denomination sponsors an annual camp meeting, often a week-long gathering where all participate in church business meetings, communal meals, religious reverie, song, and play. Extended families come from distant homesteads to camp together, sharing a church cabin for cooking and meals, sleeping in campers and tents. Brothers and sisters prepare traditional dishes of pork, pinto beans, muscadine, and corn *tan'fula*. Siblings, cousins, and friends play together, paying respect to the gathering's solemnity when appropriate. Through the idiom of kinship and sharing, Choctaws remain connected to their communal and religious past.

Camp meetings were always extremely popular among Choctaws, held for religious activities, tribal meetings, council sessions, and even to disburse tribal annuity payments, and for stickball competitions (Debo 1934:78). Choctaw families gathered at a church ground or school, built a brush arbor or other shelter, and camped for several days around the designated spot. Missionaries, native lay preachers, or church elders provided instruction in Choctaw and English (see Bryce 1928:381, 362; Spaulding 1974:153–55). Families traveled long distances to attend these gatherings, reminiscent of earlier tribal meetings and community ceremonials. During the day, prayer meetings, business sessions, sings, and informal gatherings were held. Saturdays were devoted to teaching adults and children arithmetic, reading, and writing; Sunday was devoted to instruction in Christian theology. Food was prepared communally in large pots and included pork, beef, and yams as well as the traditional corn dish, *tan'fula*. Traditionally, men and women sat on opposite sides at church meetings, a practice that has continued into the contemporary era. Camp meetings appeared to be particularly popular in full-blood settlements, attended by an estimated six hundred to seven hundred children and adults during the 1840s (see Bryce 1928:381–82; Benson 1860:34–35, 120; Debo 1934:229; Spaulding 1974:154, 279; Morrison 1978:81, 1987:24).

Various Protestant denominations also introduced weekly "Saturday and sabbath schools" or "Sunday schools," in which families would camp on church grounds for weekly educational and religious instruction modeled on the traditional camp meeting. Neighborhood schools grew out of the camp meeting and sabbath school tradition, where families living near a church attended mission-sponsored religious and secular educational programs. Neighborhoods were encouraged to provide housing, construct a school building, and offer a small stipend to resident teachers (Morrison 1978:81). By 1860 five hundred Choctaw children attended neighborhood schools, with another four hundred attending boarding schools in the region, all conducted in English (Debo 1934:61–63).

In the Choctaw laboratory of the nineteenth century, seeds of change were sewn in political, economic, and cultural arenas. Choctaws were subsumed within the U.S. political economy ideologically and materially, structurally and relationally. The U.S. imperialist agenda was hegemonic: not only must Choctaws' land and resources be expropriated but their "hearts and minds" as well, either by voluntary accommodation or forced submission.

Although white influence in tribal affairs declined between 1831 and the Civil War, mixed-blood leaders carried on their own assimilationist agendas by controlling Choctaw Nation leadership positions and promoting Christianity, mercantilism, and secular education. Churches, along with church-sponsored and secular schools, served as agents of assimilation to "civilize" unruly and "backward" Choctaws to Euro-American ways. With U.S. and global interests solidly behind them, forces for change were unstoppable. As the following chapter explores, assimilationist and traditionalist factions each continued to press for their own interests; pre–Civil War strife, the post–Civil War treaty, the coming of railroads, and the inevitable tide of white immigration, however, brought the Choctaws to their final challenge: could tribal sovereignty and geographic cohesiveness be maintained in the face of ever-increasing Euro-American encroachment?

FOUR

Choctaw Self-Determination and
Tribal Class Divisions

Choctaw Nation, 1982. Assistant chief: "What makes these people [rural timber region Choctaws] different is that they are Indian and they still have something of the old. They speak a different language than the whites or the blacks would. Most in that area [the timber region] probably when they're with themselves, English is their second language. That makes them different. They are probably not as aware of opportunities that might be there for them as the whites and blacks would be, such as educational grants or financial aid, to secure a loan, or to buy a new washing machine, or possibly to add a room onto the house or get a car loan. . . . They are just not aware. They are not quite as apt to go to town to seek out how to do that."

The Choctaws, following forced removal from their Mississippi-area homeland, faced the Herculean task of preserving tribal viability while accommodating to a new political-economic order. The Indian Territory Choctaw Nation, intent on reconstituting itself as a viable sovereign nation, worked to strengthen tribal governance and nurture cultural traditions, combining prior indigenous aspects with the present assimilationist reality. Ongoing links to U.S. society and culture were solidified through extratribal institutions, including missions and secular schools, previously described. U.S. government agencies also worked to carry out their assimilationist and transformative agendas in Indian Territory. Eventually the Choctaws would experience their nation's political demise and near-extermination as they struggled to accommodate to ever-changing political economic realities.

Cultural contact is pervaded with ambiguities; social benefits bring personal and cultural costs. Seemingly benign structural or attitudinal modifications may have far-reaching implications for indigenous cultural integrity and viability. Intermarriage was just such an element, one that benignly entered the fabric of Choctaw life in the eighteenth century and served as a

49

powerful change-facilitating factor since that time. Intermarriage not only tested Choctaw definitions of basic cultural institutions, such as descent, inheritance, and political leadership, but also brought into existence new tribal elements: a culturally and racially blended elite. Using Nagel and Snipp's terminology (1993:104), ethnic group boundaries were necessarily expanded to accommodate new definitions of cultural membership. Powerful mixed-heritage individuals and families fostered radical modifications of indigenous Choctaw life and the tribe's relationship with the external world politically, economically, and culturally.

WHITE PRESENCE, CHOCTAW RESPONSE

Whites accompanied the Choctaws to Indian Territory as government agents, missionaries, and businessmen and were entitled to citizenship through marriage. Just as in Mississippi, many white men, including missionaries, government agents, and traders, married Choctaw women and lived in the nation with virtually all of the privileges of Choctaw citizenship. Choctaws regulated white entry by establishing as early as 1836 that all gainfully employed whites had to obtain permits (Knight 1953:79; Folsom 1869:72). Legislation regulating intermarriage enacted in 1849 stipulated that a white man must marry an Indian woman or be expelled from the nation (Folsom 1869:499; Debo 1934:77).

The tribe retained usufruct-based land-use principles, whereby tribal land was held collectively rather than in fee simple (i.e., without restrictions on transfer of ownership), as in private landownership systems. Individuals could occupy a tract of any size, and improvements built on it became the property of that individual. The land itself, however, remained tribal property, and only the improvements could be sold by the original occupant. When abandoned, the land reverted back to the tribe. Recognizing that communal land tenure had to be supported by law, the tribe enacted legislation calling for the penalty of death to any Choctaw citizen who conveyed tribal land to a noncitizen (Benson 1860:32–33; Edwards 1932:399; Graebner 1945:237–38; Debo 1934:68).

Land use reflected the varied Choctaw topography and divergent household subsistence and entrepreneurial strategies, ranging from subsistence farming to large-scale agricultural enterprises using slave labor. Individuals were not restricted in the amount of land they could cultivate, until a law passed in 1883 limited the size of pasture to one square mile. Prior to 1883 individuals could fence any amount of land so long as it was under their continuous use or cultivation. This allowed some enterprising Choctaws, mainly mixed-bloods and enterprising whites, to lay claim to large tracts for farming, ranching, and other entrepreneurial endeavors.

Descent and inheritance rules both underwent changes in response to Euro-American influences. Women and men often owned annuities and stock separately, according to Benson (1860:32), although strict matrilineal inheritance rules became subject to bilateral and in some cases patrilineal inheritance (Edwards 1932:400–402). Rather than being passed to one's descendants through the maternal line of uncles, property was inherited directly from fathers to their offspring (McKee and Schlenker 1980:100).

CHOCTAW RACIAL/CLASS DIVISIONS

Postremoval residence patterns and usufruct-based land tenure gave rise to two separate Choctaw classes, perpetuating earlier racial/class divisions already evident prior to removal. One class, composed largely of full-bloods, inhabited the heavily forested, hilly, marginal uplands and practiced subsistence horticulture on farms of one to twenty acres. According to Hudson (1932:295), "a number of [Choctaw settlers] who liked to hunt drifted northward into the mountainous district where wild game deer, bear, turkeys, etc. abounded." In the 1840s full-blood settlements, linked by newly forged "trailways" or wagon roads (Hudson 1932; 1934), were established at the present-day towns of Smithville on Buffalo Creek, Bethel, Nashoba, Octavia, and Battiest, as settlers drifted north and northeast from the vicinity of Eagletown into the Kiamitia (now Kiamichi) Mountains. A full-blood settlement sprang up at Hochatown, near Bethel, and church-based communities were established at Mount Zion as early as 1848, as well as at Good Spring and Big Lick, near Smithville. These settlers were only peripherally involved in the wider cash economy, producing mainly for domestic consumption rather than trade. Many Choctaw descendants still inhabit these communities, bearing names familiar from Choctaw history (Hudson 1932, 1934; Meserve 1936).

Full-blood subsistence and residence patterns were similar to those in the preremoval era. The region was rich in timber, although soil was rocky and the terrain too mountainous to easily cultivate or graze cattle. "Farmland being scarce, families located a mile or two apart along the river which flowed between Little River Mountain and Kiamitia Mountain. As they moved to the north they built a wagon road through these valleys following the river" (Hudson 1934:297). These rural folk did not generally own slaves, since their homesteads could be worked satisfactorily with family labor (Graebner 1945:241; but see Benson 1860:34).

Each household owned on average several ponies, about eight head of cattle, and ten to twenty hogs and raised about one hundred bushels of corn (Benson 1860:32–34; Debo 1934:113; McKee and Schlenker 1980:100). Their principal foods were corn, sweet potatoes, squash, peas, pumpkins, melons, beans, and meat, including game and domesticated cattle, supplemented with wild substitutes when staple crops failed, particularly acorns ground to a meal and wild potatoes. They also planted cotton for sale or to be woven into cloth. Crops, often planted in shallow mounds, were frequently plagued by droughts, and the tribal government assisted tribalists at such times by providing foodstuffs until they could recoup their losses. The 1850s were especially difficult owing to several years of drought, and Indian commissioner reports indicated that rural Choctaws were hit especially hard. Many Choctaws practiced a sort of migratory farming in the sparsely populated hilly regions, abandoning their simply constructed homesteads for more productive land when the soil lost its fertility or when homesteads were in disrepair (U.S. Commissioner of Indian Affairs 1854–58 [hereinafter cited as U.S. Commissioner]; Edwards 1932;406–8, 411–412; Graebner 1945:239, 245–47; Baum 1940).

Rural full-bloods participated only minimally in the wider urban-based cash economy, and their access to money was limited, because they neither participated in wage labor nor grew sufficient surplus crops to sell (Cushman 1962 [1899]: 190; Debo 1934:114). Rural full-bloods had minimal contact with larger regional settlements, with only a few rudely constructed roads and "a multitude of paths" (Benson 1860:120) linking rural settlements. "There were no Indian towns or villages in the Nation and but little inclination manifested by the people for settling in clusters or dense communities," according to Benson, who toured the Choctaw Nation in the 1830s. Towns of fifty to one hundred individuals, such as Skullyville and Doaksville, grew around Choctaw Indian Agency headquarters, with "a few cabins, a dry-goods store, and a blacksmith shop . . . in the vicinity of the Choctaw agency" (Benson 1860:32).

A second class, mainly mixed-bloods, occupied the lowlands along the

Red and Arkansas Rivers, where they undertook large-scale cattle ranching and crop cultivation using slave labor (see Hudson 1934:295; Jeltz 1945:24–25, 32–33). These enterprising Choctaws, bearing the names of prominent intermarried whites such as Cole, McCurtain, Pitchlynn, Jones, and Folsom, established large plantations, some more than five hundred acres, owned several hundred head of livestock, and maintained mining, ranching, and trading interests. They gradually built up towns and established huge estates along the Red River's rich bottomlands in the southern Choctaw Nation.

Following the deaths of Nitvkechi and Moshulatubbee, leadership moved firmly into the hands of this "mixed-blood aristocracy" (Morrison 1987:16), a forward-looking class who sponsored religious and educational advancements and promoted their own mercantile interests, including ranching, cotton and corn cultivation, mining, and trade (Edwards 1932:410; Debo 1934:110–11; Gunning n.d.:19; Hudson 1934:295; Jeltz 1945:25–33; Graebner 1945:236, 242–43; Debo 1934:60; 110–13). As Morrison argues (1987:17), "the slaveholding mixed-bloods were indeed an aristocracy, and they dominated Choctaw society just as the slaveholding aristocracy dominated the society of the whole South."

Prominent among the Choctaw elite were John McKinney, a lawyer who was elected Moshulatvbbi District chief in 1838; James Fletcher, a Methodist minister elected Apuckshunnubbee District chief that same year; and Pierre Juzan, son of a Frenchman, who had been educated at Armstrong Academy. Others included Thomas LeFlore, George W. Harkins, Peter Pitchlynn, David Folsom, and Wilson N. Jones, who all served as district and principal chiefs. Each established highly successful slave-based agriculture and cattle ranching enterprises. Wilson N. Jones, claimed by many to have been the wealthiest Choctaw citizen, built up a 17,600-acre agricultural estate on five plantations, with five thousand cattle and more than five hundred slaves; he owned a cotton gin and retail stores at Caddo and Doaksville, steamboats, mining interests, and a lavish plantation residence called Lake West (*Daily Oklahoman* 5/12/35: sec. D; Benson 1860:104–5; Hudson 1934:295; Jeltz 1945:33; Debo 1934:60; 110; Foreman, ed., 1930:259–61).

Another slave owner and Choctaw statesman was Peter Pitchlynn, who had brought slaves from Mississippi, purchased with annuities paid under the Treaty of Dancing Rabbit Creek (Meserve 1942:14; Jeltz 1945:33–34).

Table 4.1. Choctaw census in selected counties, 1867

	County	Indians	Intermarried whites	Black freedmen
Northern counties	Cedar	900	0	33
	Gaines	541	3	33
	Jacks Fork	1,009	2	53
	Nashoba	648	1	35
	Sugar Loaf	710	5	3
	Wade	498	2	0
Southern counties	Blue	1,609	17	258
	Kiamitia	1,606	13	245
	Red River	872	2	273
	Towson	1,119	9	265
	Total*	14,237	104	1,756

Source: McKee and Schlenker 1980:91.

*Includes other counties not listed.

Many slave owners purchased slaves at the time of removal with government annuity funds; some, such as Pitchlynn and Sam Garland, were paid with slaves for land taken in the removal treaty (Meserve 1942:14). In all, Choctaws brought 248 slaves from Mississippi, and by 1860 Choctaws reportedly owned 2,500 slaves (Debo 1934:69; McKee and Schlenker 1980:90–91). Choctaw slave owners developed a lavish lifestyle reminiscent of the southern cotton plantation culture they left behind in Mississippi, and they reportedly produced substantial surpluses in cotton and corn within a decade after their arrival. Surpluses were exported outside the nation or purchased by government agents for military use (Graebner 1945:234–35; see also U.S. Commissioner 1836+).

Slave-owning Choctaws concentrated mainly in the counties along the Red River marking the nation's southern border, as shown in table 4.1, which compares Choctaw, intermarried white, and freedmen populations in selected Choctaw Nation counties in 1867. Northern timber region counties contained very few whites and far fewer freedmen than did those along the Red River, where the large farms were located, revealing two distinct residence patterns (McKee and Schlenker 1980:90–91).

The few Choctaw Nation towns prior to railroad entry in the 1870s were mainly centers of U.S. government agency operations, cross-country avenues of trade, or the nascent export agriculture and cattle-ranching economies. Boggy Depot, situated on an important east-west transcontinental route, was a typical larger regional village, inhabited largely by mixed-bloods and whites who operated grist mills and trading posts and performed various treaty-mandated services. Boggy Depot became a thriving community during the 1860s. "Main Street . . . bore the appearance of prosperity . . . with pretentious residences, neat cottages, a hotel, several large two-story buildings, and several smaller buildings, of which one was a bakery and another an apothecary's shop" (Wright 1927:10). In 1873 a large grist mill and cotton gin were built, attracting individuals from a radius of seventy-five miles who came to have their corn ground (Wright 1927:9, 12).

Following railroad construction as a result of the post–Civil War Treaty of 1866, towns such as Boggy Depot declined in importance, while new centers of travel and trade emerged, as shown in map 4.1. Boggy Depot, located about twelve miles west of the Missouri, Kansas, and Texas right of way, was virtually abandoned after the rail route's completion and today contains only a small general store and post office (Wright 1927:14).

Factional antagonisms continued to surface in the postremoval era, reflecting conflicting views on land use, territorial status, and tribal self-determination. The 1850s, called the "fiery fifties," was an era of heightened factionalism around several issues, particularly slavery, territorial government, and mixed-blood/full-blood antagonisms. Slavery precipitated conflict between slave-owning Choctaws and their long-standing ally the American Board of Commissioners of Foreign Missions (ABCFM), headquartered in Hartford, Connecticut, which was pro-abolitionist and viewed Choctaw pro-slavery policies skeptically (Kingsbury Papers, folder 8, item 51, "A.B.C.M. and the Choctaw Nation"). As a result, the ABCFM formally terminated its affiliation with the Choctaws in 1859, and much of its work was taken over by the Presbyterian Board of Foreign Missions (Spaulding 1974:243). Several prominent American Board missionaries, including Cyrus Kingsbury and Cyrus Byington, transferred their work to the Presbyterian Board (Hiemstra 1949–50:34).

Mixed- and full-blood tribal divisions were evident both geographically and culturally in the trans-Mississippi Choctaw nation. Assimilationist-minded mixed-blood Choctaws settled in the rich alluvial plains of the Red and Canadian Rivers, particularly in the southwestern and southeastern Choctaw nation districts. The northern interior Moshulatubbee District remained

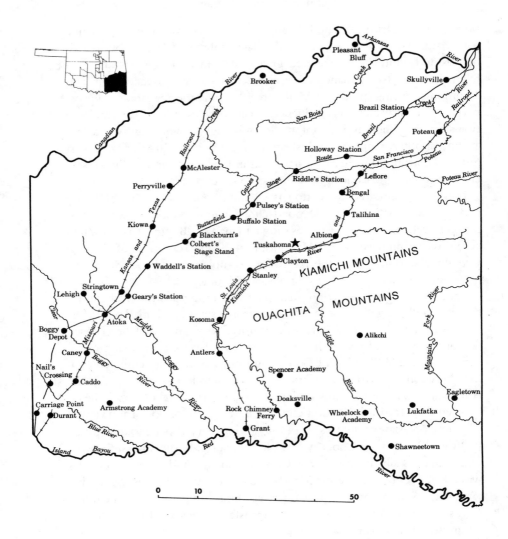

Map 4.1. Choctaw Nation, important places, showing emergence of towns along railroad routes after 1871. *Source*: Based on map 39, "Choctaw Nation: Important Places," in John W. Morris, Charles R. Goins, and Edwin C. McReynolds, *Historical Atlas of Oklahoma*, 2d ed. (Norman: University of Oklahoma Press, 1976), by permission of the University of Oklahoma Press.

under the influence of a full-blood faction disinterested in adopting Euro-American technology or values, religious or secular. While the traditionalists subsisted on mixed foraging, hunting, and gardening in the upland hills; mixed-bloods frequently built substantial farms using slave labor.

Before the Civil War, progressive mixed-bloods such as Peter P. Pitchlynn, Peter and Nathaniel Folsom, Cornelius McCurtain, and Robert M. Jones managed tribal affairs at district and national levels. Leaders worked to reconcile their own mercantilist entrepreneurial class interests with traditionally oriented factions seeking to preserve tribal unity, autonomy, and collective landownership. Tribal leaders solidified tribal legal institutions to protect their own class interests and tribal autonomy and viability, seemingly contradictory aims. The next chapter explores the dialectics of Choctaw confrontation, resistance, and accommodation to a new social order to reveal how the Choctaws struggled in the post–Civil War era to retain tribal viability in the face of increasing external threats to tribal economy, polity, and community.

FIVE

The Making of a Choctaw "Internal Colony"

Choctaw Nation, 1871. The rise of the commercial coal industry immediately following the Civil War typified entrepreneurial development throughout the Choctaw Nation and shows the significant role intermarried whites played in the changing course of Choctaw life. J. J. McAlester, an enterprising white man with obvious foresight living in Fort Smith, Arkansas, learned from a geologist conducting land surveys in the region that the best coal deposits could be found at a place called the "Cross Roads," where two famous trails crossed: the Texas Trail, running south to Dallas, and the California Trail, extending from Fort Smith to Albuquerque. He moved to what is today McAlester, Oklahoma, and established a trading business, taking advantage of tribal laws permitting such ventures by whites. He later married a Chickasaw woman, further legitimizing citizenship rights (Debo 1934:128).

The Missouri, Kansas, and Texas Railroad (MKT) won the right to construct the north-south route through Indian territory around the time McAlester established his trading post in 1871:

> McAlester saw a chance to get a railroad by his store and to start a mining industry in the area.
>
> The key to accomplishing both these objectives was coal. ·
>
> Taking the best coal samples he could find, McAlester showed them to the M.K. and T. officials [who] praised it as the best seam coal west of the Mississippi. Convinced of McAlester's plan, the railroad was built through Indian Territory with the first section going directly to McAlester's store. (*Talihina American* 4/28/83:2a)

McAlester soon thereafter convinced the railroad to build a spur to his coalfields, illegal at the time under tribal law. When the spur line was illegally constructed without prior tribal approval, Chief Coleman Cole put out a warrant for McAlester's arrest. Although convicted and sentenced to shooting, he managed to escape until an agree-

58

ment was reached. This pattern became not the exception but the rule during the post–Civil War era (*Talihina American* 4/28/83, p.2a, 16-b; Masterson 1952:162).

The outside world knew little of the Indian Territory Choctaw Nation prior to the Civil War. Sparsely populated, with abundant natural resources, the region became increasingly attractive to westward-expanding settlers and entrepreneurs. As in the previous century, the world economy would soon encroach upon the Choctaw nation to build an "empire to the sea" (see Hall 1987:5) by tapping the West, that "vast warehouse of raw materials for the industrial world" (Robbins 1994:63). Reservation-based Native Americans, as independent "nations," were shielded from colonization, at least on paper. However, indigenous political and economic sovereignty, ambiguously defined in Euro-American jurisprudence and congressional acts, would be no match for U.S. hegemonic interests.

Three factions struggled over Indian Territory during the period between 1860 and 1908. First, the tribe, headed by second- and third-generation mixed-bloods, continued to develop and consolidate its laws, codes, and court procedures to protect its land and people from increasing white encroachment. The tribe also attempted to reconcile its traditional culture with the growing industrial society around it by asserting tribal control over its nascent timber and mining industries in the face of an ever-expanding white entrepreneurial class entering its nation. Choctaw leadership after the Civil War returned for a short period to a traditionalist faction, which mounted a formidable challenge against increased white encroachment on Choctaw territory, assets, and tribal autonomy.

Second, federal, state, and local governments were charged with supervising Choctaws through the Department of the Interior, the Bureau of Indian Affairs, and later county and state bureaucracies. Throughout the era Choctaws confronted the political reality of U.S. hegemony, where national and regional political agendas were shaped by private railroad and timber interests, which controlled virtually every government agency, from the Congress to local courts. Against the unstoppable will of agents of entrepreneurial interests, tribal efforts, including law making and government lobbying, were largely ineffective (see Robbins 1994:63–67).

The third faction comprised America's private and corporate sectors, including the highly powerful railroads and later timber interests, whose major preoccupation was to open up Indian Territory to fuel the expanding late nineteenth-century U.S. industrial economy (see Hoxie 1984; Miner 1976; Littlefield 1993:47; Robbins 1994). "Railroads," according to the historian William A. Williams (1966:261; see also Robbins 1994:64, 71–73), "acted as an accelerator of other industries." They provided transportation for land-hungry western settlers; made accessible natural resources and agricultural products abundant in western lands, including coal, oil, and timber; and facilitated the transport of goods to eastern markets. Railroads were an essential infrastructural component necessary to extract vast Choctaw Nation resources, particularly coal and timber, in an environment that was largely without roads or communications at the close of the Civil War.

With extensive timber, substantial coal and natural gas deposits, quarryable stone, and productive cattle-grazing and agricultural land, the Choctaw Nation was highly attractive to outsiders. Civil War–era events gave the United States the political leverage needed to terminate existing treaties and allow access to Indian Territory, including the Choctaw Nation. Using a variety of weapons, agents of U.S. hegemonic interests rendered tribal political authority powerless, gradually took over tribal resources, and soon simply overran the nation, tearing down the tribal infrastructure, undermining Choctaw cultural integrity, and finally implementing their will to dismantle the tribal estate in the early twentieth century.

CIVIL WAR ERA DIALECTICS OF CHANGE

At the Civil War's eve, tribal leadership was firmly in the hands of the entrepreneurial elite. Brazil LeFlore served as Choctaw chief from 1859 to 1860 and George Hudson from 1860 to 1862. They were succeeded by brothers-in-law, Sam Garland (1862–64) and Peter Pitchlynn (1864–66), all mixed-bloods. Pitchlynn was related by marriage to both the Garlands and Folsoms: Sam Garland was his brother-in-law, and Pitchlynn's wife, Rhoda, was a Folsom. The political inner circle, as Debo noted (1934:154), was tightly and persistently controlled by these individuals, who, when their terms expired, frequently served as Tribal Council members or sought reelection, often successfully.

This period saw the strengthening of the two-class Choctaw society. On the one hand, enterprising Choctaws and intermarried whites controlled substantial tracts as well as coal and other mineral deposits during the era of railroad construction (Debo 1940:17). On the other, the second class continued to inhabit the rural, remote, timbered hill country, subsisting on their ten to twenty acres and largely isolated from more productive agricultural and mining settlements oriented to the wider cash economy. The rural hill country felt the effects of the expanding trade and development sphere once railroad construction increased demand for another local resource, timber, after 1871.

The entrepreneurial class benefited both from tribal land allocation policies and from laws they themselves introduced to protect their formidable landholdings against encroachment. As Morrison (1987:17–18) notes,

It was indeed a planter's paradise in which these Choctaw aristocrats found themselves: good free land in any amount they cared to use; control of the society in which they lived; the help of the United States in preventing an influx of white settlers who might have brought stiffer economic competition; an adequate labor supply; no taxes; and fairly good river transportation via the Arkansas and Red rivers to New Orleans, the cotton capital of the day.

Although tribal leaders often spoke forcefully for preserving traditional tribal ways, they understood and frequently advocated for U.S. political-economic agendas, since they too stood to benefit materially and politically. They were willing to entertain railroad entry, individual tribal land tenure, and outside access to the tribe's wealth, particularly coal, stone, and timber (see Baird 1972; Kingsbury Papers, folder 5, items 2, 50).

Full-bloods, however, continued to be a powerful force in tribal affairs. In the numerical majority for several decades, they held the balance of power into the 1880s (Baird 1972:23, 183; see also Jeltz 1945; McKee and Schlenker 1980:93). Their views were often instrumental in shaping leaders' positions and efforts to protect tribal rights throughout the tribal era (Benson 1860:102). Full-bloods strongly opposed territorial government proposals or division of the tribal estate, issues that surfaced persistently after the Civil War. A vote taken in 1870 showed the strength of the full-blood lobby, when every county voted against a proposed tribal land survey (Indian Archives, Choctaw-Federal Relations, box 17653, "Report of Peter Pitchlynne," 1870).

The tribe until termination in 1903 continued its usufruct land tenure practices. Valuable natural resources, such as coal, stone, and timber, were tribally owned. Timber, stone, and coal were used in small quantities by Choctaw citizens for their own use before the Civil War. Timber, abundant and readily available in the central Choctaw region, was used to construct homes, fences, and other structures and was also used as fuel for home heating and cooking (Debo 1934:134). Coal, discovered before the Civil War, was used mainly as a fuel in blacksmith shops and for other small-scale local enterprises (Debo 1934:128).

As pre–Civil War debates over slavery intensified, Choctaw leaders faced a complex dilemma. As slave owners, many prominent Choctaws sided with the South. Missionaries, especially members of the Boston-based Board of Commissioners of Indian Missions, and some intermarried whites with whom the progressive elite had long worked to promote missionizing and secular education, sided with the emancipationist movement. Although Chiefs Hudson and Pitchlynn urged Choctaw neutrality, secessionists headed by Robert M. Jones successfully lobbied the Choctaw Tribal Council to proclaim Confederate allegiance, and on June 14, 1861, Chief Hudson officially committed the Choctaws to the Confederate cause (see Kingsbury Papers, folder 3, item 40 [1847], folder 5, item 141B [1860], folder 8, items 141B, 148; see also Jeltz 1945:46, 56; McLoughlin 1985: 407–8; Gunning, n.d.:24; Meserve 1942:9–11).

The Confederate defeat dealt a profound blow to the Choctaws, who were penalized heavily for siding with the secessionists. Earlier Choctaw treaties were nullified, and the treaty of 1866 contained several important provisions, including that the Choctaws were henceforth to abolish slavery as well as surrender up to one-third of their territory, called the Leased District, for northern tribes then being displaced in Kansas and Missouri by westward-moving white settlers.

Three additional provisions would have even more far reaching consequences: (1) rights-of-way were granted for two additional railroad lines to be constructed through Indian Territory, one to run north and south, and another east and west; (2) a provision allowed for the surveying and division of Choctaw lands if and when the Indians consented to allotment in severalty (i.e., separate and individual ownership); and (3) U.S. courts were established in Indian Territory for the first time (Debo 1934:89; Miner 1976:11–16; Robbins 1994:63–64, 71–72).

WHITE ENTRY, TRIBAL RESPONSE

With an ever-increasing Euro-American presence, Choctaws faced new challenges to their viability and autonomy. White intruders were an ongoing potential problem because whites were not legally tribal members and were not subject to tribal laws. The 1829 removal treaty, however, allowed for federal government services, such as those of blacksmiths, traders, and

Indian agents, all provided by whites (Graebner 1934:239). Three additional factors also encouraged entry: intermarriage, the hiring of white laborers, and Choctaw entrepreneurial ties with white businessmen.

By 1860 approximately 800 whites, about 5 percent of the population, as well as 2,300 black slaves, 14 percent of the population, shared the region with 13,666 Indians, 81 percent of the population. Throughout the 1860s the white population fluctuated around 700, most working in various Indian agencies, as traders and merchants, or in quasi-legal or illegal capacities. An 1867 tribal census counted only slightly more than 100 intermarried whites, although as previous discussions have shown, this faction constituted a formidable force in tribal affairs (see Graebner 1943; McKee and Schlenker 1980:90–91). The Choctaws, seeking to regulate white entry more rigorously after the Civil War, revised the 1836 law in 1867 to regulate licensing of noncitizen traders. Traders were required to obtain permits directly from the principal chief, pay ad valorem tax (i.e., taxes paid in proportion to estimated value) on goods brought into the nation for sale, as well as post a one-thousand-dollar bond (Choctaw Nation 1973c [1894]: 477; Knight 1953:79).

With passage of the 1866 treaty and transcontinental rail construction, more and more white businessmen, laborers, and entrepreneurs entered the Choctaw Nation to provide tribal services and access tribal resources. Railroad construction also attracted more undesirable whites, including so-called vagabonds, squatters, and even outright criminals. Indian commissioner and Indian Agency reports warned yearly of growing problems of white intruders, "desperadoes," and railroad interests who illegally depredated tribal timber and stone. Trade and intercourse laws, both tribal and federal, were inadequate to keep intruders out. It was necessary during that year to call in federal troops to remove illegal trespassers, since tribal police were unable to deal with the problem adequately (U.S. Board of Indian Commissioners [hereinafter cited as U.S. Board] 1869:33; Commissioner of Indian Affairs to Secretary of the Interior, U.S. Board 1871:6; U.S. Commissioner 1872:77, 91).

Illegal white immigration was abetted by two pervasive problems. First, the tribe lacked jurisdiction over intruders, since it could not try noncitizens in tribal courts. Second, a white tenant labor system emerged after the Civil War, apparently to replace labor lost when close to twenty-five hundred slaves became freedmen in 1865 (McKee and Schlenker 1980:90).

Although federal courts gained jurisdiction over Indian Territory in 1866, the courts were nearly impossible to access, and adjudication was slow and generally inadequate. Trials were frequently postponed for a year owing to the large number of criminal cases being heard. Under these conditions only the most serious crimes were brought to trial, and even those only if the evidence was uncontestable. Most Choctaws "preferred to suffer almost any crime without complaint rather than be subjected to the penalty of bearing testimony," which often meant weeks of travel on horseback (Debo 1934:185). Crime flourished as a result in the absence of readily accessible systems of trial and sentencing (see Graebner 1943:303).

The civil court system was equally as dismal during this period, since it was not until 1889 that the first civil court in Indian Territory was established, at Muskogee (Debo 1972 [1940]: 18). Until then civil transactions involving non-Choctaws, such as debt defaults, contracts, or other business transactions, were outside the jurisdiction of any court system. Many whites took refuge in Indian Territory to transact illegal business and avoid debts in the States (Debo 1934:184). Indian Territory, including the Choctaw Nation, became a haven for individuals willing and eager to engage in illegal activities of all types, including theft of cattle, business fraud, and even murder (see Graebner 1943).

Choctaw entrepreneurs further facilitated white entry by entering into numerous coal mining, ranching, and agricultural business partnerships with whites. Prominent Choctaw leaders, including Wilson N. Jones and the Presbyterian missionary Alfred (Allen) Wright, principal chief from 1866 to 1870, joined in such joint business ventures, not always successfully. A cattle venture between Wright and a white rancher in 1868 ended when the white man absconded with the herd (Wright 1959:295). Jones was more successful, gaining the title of "cattle king" of Indian Territory, leasing land to Texas cattle herders and maintaining a herd estimated at five hundred head (Benson 1860:34; Graebner 1943:311; Jeltz 1945:33; Baum 1940:9–10).

Choctaw farmers seeking to replace slave labor frequently hired whites and sometimes other Choctaws to work their farms in return for wages, improvements, or crops. Even full-bloods occupying smaller farms hired whites, paying one-third of the harvest in exchange for labor (U.S. Congress, S. Rep. 1278, 49th Cong., 1st sess., 2363 [1886]: 228, 246–47; Graebner 1945:241; Baum 1940:37–38, 80). Under a variant of this system, which was not actually legal but which tribal authorities generally overlooked, Choctaws contracted or "leased" land to whites for an extended period, often from five to ten years. Whites were permitted to build homesteads, clear land, and farm unoccupied parcels for stipulated periods of time, in exchange for produce. At the lease's termination the entire land parcel including all improvements reverted to the lessor, that is, the Choctaw landlord. The Indian commissioner in 1886 estimated that one-quarter of Choctaw farms hired white tenant laborers (U.S. Commissioner 1886:vii, 1887:112, 1893:150). Whites under these tenancy arrangements could remain in the nation so long as they were employed by a Choctaw citizen, although they could not obtain actual land titles. Whites accepted these tenancy arrangements because they could earn more than in the States.

As their numbers increased, whites became a force with which the Choctaw tribe had to reckon. It was estimated that by 1876 there were approximately 3,000 whites living in the Choctaw Nation "lawfully" and as many as 4,800 living "unlawfully," that is, without valid permits or legitimate occupations. In that same year there were an estimated 16,000 Choctaw citizens by blood and marriage (U.S. Commissioner 1876:216). By 1890, census figures showed Choctaws to be far outnumbered (Debo 1934:222):

Choctaw	10,017
Blacks	4,406*
Whites	28,345*

*Includes citizens and claimants to citizenship.

The Choctaws, lacking physical or legal means to control whites who were overrunning their tribal domain, faced a serious quandary in reconciling tribal authority with white numerical majority. In 1875 intermarriage laws were strengthened. White males had to procure licenses and pay marriage fees to become official tribal citizens by marriage (Debo 1934:179–80). An 1877 tribal ordinance called for the immediate removal of illegal residents and the sale of their property (Knight 1953:89). Only after review of existing treaties did the Interior Department agree to expedite removal of illegal intruders beginning in 1881, fully ten years after railroad construction (Indian Archives, Choctaw-Federal Relations, box 17675, correspondence, Department of the Interior, June–July, 1881).

ENCLAVE POLITICS: FIGHTING BACK

Following the Civil War, Choctaws faced difficult challenges to their economic, political, and cultural integrity, with ongoing federal government efforts to pass territorial legislation and tribal termination measures. Choctaws were divided over postwar treaty negotiations and the status of freedmen, they faced a nearly collapsed educational system, and tribal debt and lawlessness plagued their nation. Alfred (Allen) Wright, an elected chief, Presbyterian minister, and full-blood, embodied the often irreconcilable poles of Choctaw life, wavering between indigenous and Euro-American worlds in a post–Civil War environment of profound tribal malaise.[1] Wright, as earlier noted, maintained substantial ranching operations and was national treasurer for three terms. Like so many members of the elite, he was trained at an eastern college, Union College in Schnectady, New York, and graduated from Union Theological Seminary in 1855 (Meserve 1941:315).

Following Wright's two-term tenure, a more conservative faction gained tribal leadership until the mid-1880s. William Bryant, chief from 1870 to 1874 and a mixed-blood, represented the newly emerging National Party, also known as the Full Blood or Shaki (Buzzards) party (Debo 1934:164), which represented traditionalist interests of a mainly full-blood faction. Coleman Cole, elected chief in 1874 and descended from the last Choctaw hereditary chief, Robert Cole (1824–26), was also a spokesperson for the traditionalists. Inhabiting a simple one-room log cabin in the Kiamichi Mountains, he worked diligently to protect Choctaw natural resources, institute tribal taxation measures, and resist white encroachment, with only marginal success (Baum 1940:38–39; see Choctaw Nation 1875; Locke 1926; Meserve 1936:16–17, 20–21; Debo 1934:140–41).

COUNTERING WHITE ENCROACHMENT

During the era of increased white encroachment, tribal leaders attempted to stand firm by passing tribal laws to protect against external assaults from all sectors: individual, corporate, and governmental. As already noted, the tribe passed legislation to regulate more closely white entry and intermarriage. Realizing that railroad entry would bring increased demand for timber, stone, and coal, the tribe devised laws for their extraction and use by both citizens and noncitizens, in three major pieces of legislation: the Permit Law of 1867, the Timber Law of 1871, and the Coal Law of 1873. The tribe created the position of national agent, who regulated timber sales, collected royalties, and made contracts (Debo 1934:45; Knight 1953:93).

---

1. John Bartlett Meserve (1941:314) claims that Wright was "a Choctaw of seven-eights blood," although Debo (1934:164) and others claim he was full-blood.

Choctaws were prohibited from selling timber directly to railroads or to private individuals, nor could railroads use timber for purposes other than railroad construction or ship timber out for sale elsewhere. In 1873 coal and other mining enterprises were similarly regulated with passage of the Coal Laws (Debo 1934:134–35). Chief Coleman Cole (1874–78) unequivocally declared in 1875 that "all the mines of coal, lead and other materials, and all the timber belongs to the Choctaw and Chickasaw Nations and not to individual Indians who may occupy the soil," reaffirming long-held principles that the land and natural resources were collective and not individual property (Choctaw Nation 1875; see also U.S. Commissioner 1875:56).

Although the tribe appeared politically in control, white railroad owners circumvented tribal laws to access local timber, not only for their own construction activities but also to supply regional demand, even though exporting Choctaw timber was illegal until the final days of tribal existence. The Missouri, Kansas, and Texas Railroad used an estimated twenty-five hundred ties per mile in constructing its line through Indian Territory, a distance of 250 miles, which it hoped to obtain locally, thereby greatly reducing rail construction costs (Masterson 1952:94). By 1873 four sawmills operated in the Choctaw Nation, which that year cut three million board feet of lumber (U.S. Commissioner 1874:124). The tribe received $54,611 in royalties in 1885 on its various resources, including timber and coal. Timber royalties alone in 1902 amounted to over $43,000, and in 1903 royalties on timber and stone were reported to be about $74,500 (Debo 1934: 145; U.S. Inspector for Indian Territory [hereinafter cited as U.S. Inspector] 1902:42; 1903:48).

From the 1870s until tribal termination after the turn of the century, the Choctaws increasingly faced white abuses of their legal and economic authority, particularly by railroads. Individuals and corporations resorted to any means necessary, legal or illegal, to obtain tribally owned commodities for construction purposes and even for outside export, in flagrant violation of tribal mandates. Whites, refusing to accept tribal jurisdiction, antagonized tribal officials and undermined tribal authority. In 1873 the Indian agent, Albert Parsons, reported:

Much dissatisfaction has been expressed by the Choctaw Nation because the contractors with the Missouri, Kansas and Texas Railway Company have been cutting ties and timber and shipping them out of the Territory without any authority or license from the Nation. Individuals of the Nation would claim to own a certain tract of timber land and sell the timber to these contractors which really belonged to the Nation. A few individuals would thus receive the pay that should have gone into the treasury of the Nation. (U.S. Commissioner 1873:208–9)

Railroad owners, claiming to be unfamiliar with tribal laws and policies, denied wrongdoing and generally refused to operate within the tribe's legal guidelines (Debo 1934:135; Talbot 1981:109; Thompson 1986:31–32).

Even after railroad construction was completed in 1873, railroad owners exported timber and operated sawmills illegally, and even paid individuals not to divulge these activities (Debo 1934:136). "It was commonplace," writes Steve Talbot (1981:109), "for railroads to contract with an individual Indian for timber and coal, disregarding the fact that these resources were tribal property, and therefore communally owned." The railroad companies and individuals in collusion with them could realize far greater cash benefits by ignoring timber and coal royalty laws and purchasing these commodities directly, and railroad owners could easily find individuals willing to ignore tribal laws for their own self-aggrandizement.

Throughout the 1870s and 1880s commissioners and local Indian agents complained about illegal timber depredations, which the tribe was powerless to stop. The major problem was that, although tribal laws were on record, tribal police were inadequate to remove all intruders, estimated in 1880 to number six thousand. Federal laws either did not apply to the Five Tribes or were not sufficiently strong to curb illegal timber cutting. The Choctaw Nation and its agents appealed yearly to the federal government throughout the decade of the 1880s to stop timber depredations by railroad and mining companies as well as private individuals (U.S. Commissioner 1880–89; U.S. Congress, S. Misdoc. 100, 46th Cong., 2d sess., 2261 [1885]; H. Exdoc. 145, 47th Cong., 1st. sess., 2030 [1882]; S. Misdoc. 100, 46th Cong., 2d. sess., 1891 [1883]; S. Exdoc. 17, 48th Cong., 2d. sess. 2261 [1885]; H. Exdoc. 14, 48th Cong., 1st. sess., 2193 [1883]; S. Exdoc. 17, 48th Cong., 2d. sess., 2261 [1886]). Robert Owen, Five Tribes Indian agent in 1886, reported that "*timber and coal thieves* along the border say truly enough that there is no law to punish their trespass, as Section 5388, which protects lands of the United States from depredation, does *not* protect land of Five Nations" (U.S. Commissioner 1886:158; emphasis in original). He urged, like his predecessors, that legislation be enacted to protect this valuable commodity.

TRIBAL TAXATION BATTLE

The Choctaws were engaged in a second battle during this era of increased white encroachment: the right to tax noncitizens doing business in the nation. The dispute over tribal taxation of noncitizens began in 1873 when the MKT manager challenged the tribe's right to tax employees of the Osage Coal and Mining Company, an MKT subsidiary. When the tribe in 1875 raised its tax on licensed traders, the Indian agent, S. W. Marston, declared that the Choctaws did not have the right to levy taxes of any kind on U.S. citizens. Choctaw chief Coleman Cole was outraged by Marston's claims and appealed to Interior Secretary Carl Schurz to have Marston removed from office. When this failed, Cole wrote directly to the president of the United States, Rutherford B. Hayes, to remind him that provisions of the Treaty of 1866 guaranteed Choctaw rights to tax U.S. citizens and govern their own internal economic affairs (Meserve 1936:19–20; Debo 1934:140–41).

The Choctaws enacted several laws to protect their rights to tax white business activities, particularly illegal sawmills. An 1877 law prohibited Choctaw citizens from leasing any part of the public domain to noncitizens. Another law stipulated that failure of illegal intruders to obtain required permits or leave the nation would be punished by sale of their improvements, which was finally enforced by the tribe in 1879, against the opposition of many angry whites (Debo 1934:141).

The federal government used the powerful and effective strategy of withholding tribal annuity payments in 1879 to discourage the tribe from evicting illegal intruders and taxing delinquents. Appearing far more conciliatory than their chief, the Tribal Council agreed to temporarily halt white evictions until the issue could be settled in U.S. courts. In 1881 the Choctaws won an important, although short-lived, victory when the acting U.S. attorney general, S. F. Phillips, ruled for the Choctaws. According to Angie Debo,

Phillips . . .sustained the Choctaws on every point . . . upheld the validity of the permit laws, saying that aside from the temporary sojourners and the internal improvements and federal employees excepted by the treaties of 1855 and 1866 all other noncitizens were subject to the conditions of admission and residence prescribed by the tribal authorities; and he ruled that all who did not conform to those conditions were intruders, and that it was the express duty of the United States to remove them. (Debo 1934:142)

This court victory revealed just how tenuous Choctaw legal rights were against U.S. imperialism. Throughout the era the Choctaws struggled as a weakening nation against a society committed to an ideology of global expansion and Manifest Destiny.

TRIBAL RESOURCE EXPLOITATION: TIMBER AND COAL

Throughout the nineteenth century tribal leaders, seeing the benefits of resource exploitation in much-needed tribal revenues, provided a legal framework to allow outside access to tribal wealth through permit laws and other legislation, even at times allowing whites to evade these laws when they were unenforceable (Debo 1934:134). The transformation to white domination, however, occurred insidiously, without the clear perception by many tribal members that whites were indeed overrunning their nation.

The tribe's own entrepreneurial ventures in coal, stone, and timber industries were at best only marginally successful during the period 1831–1906. Chief Coleman Cole (1874–78) lobbied to increase taxes on tribal assets and to nationalize various industries, including coal, timber, and railroads, although his efforts also proved unsuccessful. Instead, these commodities were exploited by white capital and in many instances white laborers, many of whom by the 1880s were recent southern European immigrants (Debo 1934:116–17, 130, 140–42; Meserve 1936:19–20). The tribe did attempt to build a railroad infrastructure immediately after the Treaty of 1866 was drafted permitting one east-west and one north-south route through the nation. In 1870 the Tribal Council granted charters to two private railroad companies to construct these rail lines, and at that time the tribe voted to purchase stock in the companies with revenues from the sale of its right-of-way land.

For a brief period in the 1880s the tribe also attempted, under the tribal permit system, to regain control of its coal and natural gas resources, which at the time were dominated by white entrepreneurs such as J. J. McAlester, an intermarried white trader called "founder of the Oklahoma coal kingdom." Again the tribe was unable to nationalize their coalfields successfully, since the resource had already been fully dominated by whites and enterprising Choctaws who were unwilling to relinquish their profitable enterprises at the whim of tribal officials (*Talihina American* 4/28/83:2a; Debo 1934:129).

Choctaw Nation, 1982. Although few Choctaws work directly for Weyerhaeuser, many work part-time in timber-related industries, cutting timber, planting trees, and maintaining forests. Locals work for independent contractors who hire their own crews to harvest and maintain Weyerhaeuser's extensive forest reserves. Although Choctaws like the independence and kin camaraderie that contract work affords, jobs are scarce, intermittent, and dangerous. Workers for the independent contractors earn less than Weyerhaeuser's unionized work force; layoffs and short paychecks are frequent.

Few Choctaws seemed to work as loggers or mill hands or in other capacities in the nascent timber industry of the nineteenth century. One former logger who worked in the sawmills around Antlers, in Pushmataha County, just before the turn of the century said that there were over two hundred loggers and timber workers in the Kiamichi Valley, although few were Native Americans. He claimed that "the Indians didn't take to sawmill work. . . . They took to this more as a sport than a job" (see Debo 1934:141; Heerwagen 1963:13; U.S. Congress, S. Rep. 1278, 49th Cong., 1st sess., 2363 [1886]: 246). Timber region Choctaws, mainly full-bloods, were largely subsistence farmers at the time, using timber for cooking, heating, and construction needs (see *Bishinik* 4/88:9). Timber was not a marketable commodity for them, since they participated only minimally in the wider cash economy.

The northern Choctaw Nation, inhabited by widely disbursed, traditionally oriented Choctaw subsistence farmers, became a prime area for infiltration by those interested in harvesting Choctaw timber, as well as those willing to evade permit laws and cut timber illegally. Since the region was sparsely populated and poorly policed, with only a rudimentary system of roads, illegal activities could continue for months unnoticed by tribal authorities. Rural full-bloods became easy targets for exploitation and permit law abuses, since they were not well informed concerning entrepreneurial "wheelings and dealings," and they participated only marginally in the cash economy.

Four crucial factors constrained the tribe from taking control over its resource base and the railroad infrastructure. First, it lacked expertise in timber management, harvesting practices, and other extractive enterprises, such as coal mining. The tribe also lacked sufficient development capital of its own to undertake large-scale extractive development and therefore permitted outsiders to commence operations.

Second, the tribe was constrained by the structure of dependence within which it was embedded as a colonized tribe and ward of the federal government, which oversaw all tribal activities – economic, political, and social. The federal government, as previously shown, paid lip service to Choctaw rights as an independent nation but was more strongly influenced by industrial developers and white land grabbers in forming and, even more importantly, in enforcing Indian policy. Federal officials never took the aggressive steps necessary to protect Choctaw rights to autonomous self-rule or self-determination in tribal resource development, since government officials were not committed to such a policy in the first place (see U.S. Commissioner 1886:vii+, 1887:xii, 1894:141; Debo 1934:116–17). Federal officials continually failed to curb white entry and illegal resource extraction, abuses the tribe was unable to stop.

A third constraint was that railroad penetration, so crucial to other development enterprises, particularly coal and timber, was controlled by white-owned corporations. Control of the railroads gave these entrepreneurs access to tribal wealth even before the tribe was able to articulate sufficiently stringent legal mechanisms to protect its wealth or otherwise direct access away from outside intruders (see Robbins 1994:63–72).

The fourth obstacle was the tribal composition itself and the class divisions alluded to previously, both of which undermined the tribe's ability to present a united opposition to white development interests. Increasingly after 1871 whites entering both legally and illegally had access to tribal land and resources, either through intermarriage or through the tribal permit system. Tribal leadership, drawn from all tribal segments but concentrated among more progressive members, had to reconcile diverse traditional and progressive interests. Leaders generally allowed whites access to tribal wealth so long as they met tribal permit and taxation guidelines.

In the 1880s the two Choctaw political factions were split along racial/class lines. The Progressive party, called "Eagles," composed mainly of mixed-bloods, openly favored tribal termination, land allotment, and U.S. citizenship; while the Nationalists, called the "Buzzards," mostly full-bloods, retained traditionally conservative views toward change. The Progressive candidate for chief in the 1888 election was Wilson N. Jones, long a representative of the elite Choctaw aristocracy. Among his allies included then-Chief Edmund McCurtain and his brother, Green. The opposition candidate, Benjamin Smallwood, was elected that year, although the era was characterized by ongoing factional strife and acrimony (*Daily Oklahoman* 5/12/35: sec. D; Gunning n.d.:50–52; typescript copy, *Daily Oklahoman,* Jones Collection).

Tribal sovereignty and self-determination became so weakened by congressional mandates and white penetration in the late nineteenth century that the Choctaws could no longer stop what had become an inevitable march toward tribal termination. The U.S. government possessed real power to implement congressional policy, irrespective of tribal interests. Choctaw land alienation was finally realized with passage of the Dawes Severalty Act in 1887. By this act and the Curtis Act of 1898 lands were to be allotted in severalty to each Choctaw citizen, the tribal government was to be dismantled, and the Choctaws were to become citizens of the new state of Oklahoma. The Choctaws strongly opposed the Dawes Act, and their tribal legislature refused to cooperate with the Dawes Commission. It was not until passage of the Curtis Act in 1898 that the Choctaws reluctantly consented to allotment (U.S. Department of the Interior [hereinafter cited as U.S. DOI] 1898:75). Between 1893, when the Commission to the Five Tribes was created to terminate tribal affairs, and 1898, the Choctaws and other Five Civilized Tribes stood firmly against the dissolution of communal land-ownership and tribal sovereignty. The federal government, however, used the standard tactic of hammering away at resistance through conciliatory channels, while ever holding the trump card that it could at any time enact legislation to enlarge its powers over the Five Tribes and thereby force allotment. The Curtis Act was just such a piece of legislation, which, when passed by the House of Representatives in 1896, indicated unequivocally to the Choctaws that they were the weaker party and must eventually consent to negotiations for termination (Brown 1931:88, 92; Debo 1934:246–53; 1972 [1940]: 23–30).

Even before the Curtis Act's final passage, the tribe signed the Atoka Agreement in April 1897, subject to ratification by their members. Full-bloods in particular strongly opposed this agreement, which embodied all provisions necessary for full tribal termination. With this act, the Choctaws relinquished their right to self-government; lost the power of revenue collection, which was to be taken over by agents of the federal government; were obliged to accept enlarged jurisdiction of the U.S. courts and police powers; and agreed to the enrollment of all Choctaw citizens, the allotment of tribal lands, and the sale of surplus unallotted land.

When a ratification vote was taken in August 1898, many full-bloods refused to cast votes, thereby silently voicing their disapproval of such an agreement. The Atoka Agreement was ratified anyway, even though only an estimated 2,164 voted for ratification, while 1,366 voted against, out of an estimated population of 16,000 (Debo 1934:262; Phillips 1982:34). The ratification vote was really again a moot point, since the Curtis Act, which had already been passed by Congress, superseded whatever action the tribe might have taken (Brown 1931:100–105).

Between the Atoka Agreement in 1897 and about 1912, provisions of various acts of Congress transferred the governing privileges from tribal to federal control and permanently undermined the tribe's ability to operate as a governing body. Federal officials took over disbursement of tribal funds, and the tribe was no longer able to operate independently in fiscal matters (U.S. DOI 1899:113). The Curtis Act also stipulated that the tribal government would be dismantled after March 4, 1906, since it was assumed that by that date allotment would have been completed. Gilbert W. Dukes, Choctaw chief in 1900, perceived the full implication of tribal termination:

It means the end of our political existence; it means a disruption of all government tribal; it means the breaking of concert and political unity in our actions. . . . Having no political existence, no official organization, our efforts at protection of our interests would be necessarily desultory and ineffective. Without political status and standing, we could not expect recognition from Congress or the Departments of Governments; except perhaps, by reason of our political disarmament become charges of the government. (Indian Archives, box 19452, Choctaw–Principal Chiefs, "Message to Members of the Senate and House of Representatives, G. W. Dukes," 1900)

Choctaw tribal demise meant that Choctaws were transformed from an autonomous, independent tribal entity, however imperfect that had been, into a marginal enclave of U.S. political-economic interests.

The period 1865–1908 marked the demise of autonomous Choctaw nationhood, as private and U.S. government sectors chipped away at tribal sovereignty and opened a wedge for non-Indian land taking. The Treaty of 1866 was the tool needed to allow railroad access, thereby increasing white entry from a manageable trickle to an unstoppable deluge. The Indian Territory Choctaw Nation, although legally protected from encroachment by treaty, became highly desirable to U.S. private- and public-sector interests in the Civil War era, for its extensive coal, timber, and stone, and for its vast virgin forests. The Choctaws were transforming from tribe to rural hinterland enclave, an internal colony valuable as a source of land and labor for the U.S. metropolitan-based export-oriented industrial economy.

Throughout the contact era, Choctaws had confronted the full thrust of U.S. colonizing efforts, as public and private interests worked to dismantle the Choctaw Nation. Choctaw land was being converted from collective to individual property. Choctaw land, timber, and stone were particularly valuable to the core economy's infrastructural development, crucial to the nineteenth-century U.S. mercantile-industrial economy. Politically, the Choctaws were rendered powerless, as tribal political decision making was expropriated by the majority culture's political apparatus. Tribal government was virtually dismantled when the U.S. government took over chiefly appointments after 1906.

The contact dialectic fostered a spectrum of Choctaw responses, ranging from accommodation to resistance by a fractionated tribe. Choctaw progressives responded to changing definitions of landownership by maximizing opportunities for their own economic success. Traditionalists tried to retain remnants of indigenous production and consumption strategies, which became increasingly difficult with land allotment. Choctaw political, economic, and cultural transformation moved dangerously toward tribal annihilation, a process that would not reverse until tribal political resurrection with the election of Hollis Roberts in 1971.

SIX

Local and National Dialectics of Change

Choctaw Nation, 1982. The 1920s and 1930s were a desperate time for timber region Choctaw allottees. Most had lost their land to timber and land thieves. Choctaws subsisted on odd jobs, scratched a subsistence on inferior land, worked as migrant farm laborers, and took public handouts. "I don't know how we made it," said one informant who yearly brought his family, including six children, to work in migrant farm labor camps in Texas. "Every one of them worked in the fields. They didn't go to school. We couldn't afford to send them."

Angie Debo (1972 [1940]: 91) characterized the postallotment era as "an orgy of plunder and exploitation probably unparalleled in American history." The era was marked by two processes: first, the tribe's separation from its land and resources, and second, incorporation into the U.S. welfare state and global political economy (see Cornell 1988:88; Robbins 1994). Choctaw tribal government was dismantled and replaced by an externally controlled bureaucracy that took over all aspects of Indian administration, rendering it powerless to act as a sovereign entity. The Choctaw Nation's 6.8 million acres were allotted in severalty to its approximately twenty thousand eligible citizens and quickly alienated by unscrupulous private land grabbers and public officials.

Hinterland incorporation into the global economy, as the Choctaw instance reveals, is not a benign or passive process. Human agents and actors located in core centers of power wielding and decision making execute development strategies that affect peripheral hinterlands directly. In the global development arena, governments act; multinational corporations influence; and sectoral strategies are implemented to serve larger capitalist entrepreneurial agendas.

Private corporate interests dominated the U.S. political arena in the nineteenth century, working to penetrate Indian Territory and break down the tribal structure to access tribal resources. This was part of a larger entrepreneurial strategy that saw the vast untapped resources of the West as fuel for the emerging U.S. global economy. This chapter in Choctaw history recounts how U.S. political-economic hegemony was achieved: through individual and collective machinations emanating from the very core of American political and economic power and decision making. Among the major culprits in the land-grabbing conspiracy were the Interior Department, the agency directly charged with managing tribal affairs; the Commission to the Five Civilized Tribes, responsible for tribal land allotment and termination; and powerful corporate lobbies, including railroads. Legislative acts and policies, such as railroad land grant legislation, tribal land allotment, and the demise of tribal government, abetted the Choctaw Nation's transformation from a self-sustaining autonomous people into a dependent, largely landless class.

GOVERNMENT "WHEELING AND DEALING"

William Robbins argues that the U.S. government's policies and bureaucratic structure in the decades following the Civil War served virtually every private capitalist development interest "through its unrestricted, indeed sympathetic, support for the activities of most business enterprises, through subsidies to scientific and transportation infrastructures necessary to industrial expansion, through a politics that gave primacy to economic matters (especially the handling of natural resources), and through an outright hostility to labor." Federal land and infrastructure development policies – particularly railroad land grant legislation and speculative land sales – allowed for private land taking and rail construction to open up the vast resources of the West. The United States in those years, with enormous untapped hinterland resources, transformed itself from merely a player to a global economic leader by buttressing its private entrepreneurial sector and converting rural regions into colonies of capitalist enterprise (Robbins 1994:62, 64–65).

Indian Territory was one region shrewdly targeted for exploitation. Federal policies disregarded prior treaty agreements altogether, allowing the dominant white society between 1871 and 1908 to expropriate tribal wealth and resources at an ever-increasing rate. Not only did Native Americans face a highly politicized policy-making process closely tied to private corporate interests, but Indian resource administration was subject to abuse and even outright fraud, facilitated by close ties between various Interior Department branches, with their seemingly conflicting and often partisan interests and aims.

The Interior Department, responsible for Indian affairs since 1849, also oversaw several other government branches, including the General Land Office, railroads, land surveys, territorial lands, and national parks (Waltman 1962:44). Interior Department policy decisions were generally made between the secretary of the interior and the commissioner of Indian affairs, both presidential appointees. As political appointees, officeholders routinely endorsed the ruling party's Indian policies, ignoring tribal interests and legal mandates. In its dual role as manager of public lands and supervisor of the land grant system, the General Land Office consistently protected railroad interests, even at the expense of homesteaders and indigenous tribes (Julian 1883a:206, 1883b:238). The Land Office ignored court rulings protecting Indian land takings by railroad companies and gave railroad companies title to lands illegally (see *Leavenworth, Lawrence, and Galveston Railroad Company* v. *United States,* 2 Otto, 733, 1875; Julian 1883b:240–43; Gates 1936; see also Robbins 1994:64–67).

Railroads, seeking to extinguish Indian land title by one means or another, organized what became known as the Territorial Ring, a powerful lobbying group that infiltrated several branches of government. Included in its ranks were J. P. C. Shanks of Indiana, who served as head of the House Committee on Indian Affairs. Other members of the ring included a vice president of the Atlantic and Pacific Railroad and a member of the Board of Indian Commissioners, the so-called philanthropic organization created in 1869 to monitor potential abuses and conflicts of interest in Indian policy making and implementation (Miner 1976:77, 83, 90; Debo 1940:21). These obvious conflicts of interest among top-level government officials seriously inhibited objective policy making within the highest federal government agencies during the period, although undoubtedly private corporate interests were well served. The ability of these men to perform their assignments in Congress and on various committees without bias was doubtful, a circumstance that boded poorly for the tribes under their charge.

THE DIALECTICS OF RESOURCE EXPROPRIATION
The Commission to the Five Civilized Tribes, created in 1899 to undertake land allotment as stipulated in the Atoka Agreement, was charged with both the land survey and the entire tribal termination process, including estab-

Table 6.1. Classification of acreage in the Choctaw Nation, estimated
number of acres, and appraised value in 1903

Class	Description	Acres*	Appraised value/acre**
1	Natural open bottomland	1,066	$6.50
2a	Cleared bottomland	3,400	6.50
2b	Best black prairie land	35,236	6.50
3	Bottomland with timber and thickets	86,190	6.50
4a	Best prairie, other than black	89,765	6.00
4b	Bottom land subject to overflow	281,234	5.50
5a	Prairie land, smooth and tillable	526,188	5.00
5b	Swampland, easily drainable	21,281	4.50
6a	Rough prairie land	129,021	4.00
6b	Upland with hard timber***	2,134,427	3.25
7a	Rocky prairie land	145,314	3.00
7b	Swampland, not easily drainable	37,588	2.50
8a	Alkalai prairie land	19,125	2.00
8b	Hilly and rocky land	1,390,481	1.50
8c	Swampland, not profitably drainable	14,666	1.00
8d	Mountain pasture land	289,277	1.00
9a	Sandy land with pine timber***	265,594	.75
9b	Mountain land with pine timber***	765,896	.50
10	Rough mountain land	514,296	.25

*Source: Commission to the Five Civilized Tribes, *Annual Report* 8 (1901): 35–36.
**Rounded to nearest acre. *Source*: Commission to the Five Civilized Tribes, *Annual Report* 10 (1903): 31–32.
***If land so classified contained timber of commercial value, timber was appraised separately.

lishing citizenship rolls and surplus tribal land sales. Choctaw and Chickasaw lands would be allotted in severalty, with each allottee receiving approximately 320 acres of "average allottable land," valued at about fourteen
hundred dollars. All tracts were to be surveyed and graded according to location, character, value of standing timber, proximity to market, and suit-
ability for agriculture. Surplus unallotted lands would then be sold at public
auction after all allotments were made. The commission devised a schedule
of ten classes and subclasses according to which surveyors were to grade
each land parcel (see table 6.1). Land was appraised at from $6.50 per acre for
choice farmland down to $.50 per acre for rocky mountain terrain. Standing
timber, appraised separately, was added to the parcel's value, thus reducing
the amount of acreage that each individual would receive. The survey com-
menced in 1899 and was not completed until 1903 (Mills 1919:70; U.S. DOI
1898:159; U.S. Commission to the Five Civilized Tribes [hereinafter cited as
Five Tribes Commission] 1900:27, 1903:31–32).

Soon after the land survey was completed in 1903, allotment began. In all, 20,799 Choctaws were enrolled, and offices were established at various locations throughout the nation where allottees went to file claims on their occupied lands and choose additional acreage if necessary to receive the stipulated total land allotment. In January 1902 the Commission to the Five Tribes fixed the value of pine timber in the nation at $.50 per thousand feet of timber, regardless of its location, well below market value (Five Tribes Commission 1903:33; Brown 1944:191; U.S. Inspector 1901:41).

Choctaw Nation, 1982. Choctaw informants told how their parents had lost their allotments. Some had been swindled out of their land, forced as children to sign phony "leases" that turned out to be deeds of sale. Others had failed to pay taxes they were unaware of, having been falsely told that Indian allotments were not subject to tax liabilities. Others were forced to sell when their allotments became entangled in family heirship disputes and relatives forced land sales. White neighbors sometimes obtained Choctaw land by enforcing easements, which Choctaw owners little understood. "If families today own two or three acres they're lucky." said one informant. "Many have no land at all to pass on to their children or build an Indian home."

TIMBER COUNTRY LAND-GRABBING

Certain provisions of the Atoka Agreement and subsequent congressional acts made it especially easy for individuals to defraud unsuspecting Choctaws of their allotments, particularly what was called their "surplus" land. The Atoka Agreement gave approximately 320 acres of "average allottable land" to each allottee, frequently chosen in widely scattered parcels. Individuals typically chose a 160-acre tract as one's "homestead," which was generally the land where they lived when allotment took place. The remaining "surplus" land would be assigned elsewhere, often in the western Chickasaw Nation prairie region, which most allottees had never seen. (Owing to the relationship of joint landownership between the Choctaws and Chickasaws, allottees were permitted to choose allotments in either tribal region.)

The Supplemental Agreement of 1902 between the Choctaws and the federal government permitted allottees to sell their "surplus" holdings, that is, any land not designated as homestead, at a specified rate: 25 percent one year from the date a patent was issued by the tribe, another 25 percent after three years, and the remainder after five years. It also stipulated that prior to expiration of the tribal government, land could not be sold for less than its appraised value (32 Stat:641, 7/1/1902, in *Laws* 1915:392; Mills 1919:81–82). Congress in 1904 revised this plan and enacted that all surplus lands of intermarried whites and freedmen allottees could be sold as soon as a patent had been issued. Mixed-blood and full-blood adults were also permitted to sell their surplus lands, but only with the consent of the secretary of the interior. This decision placed on the market over 1.5 million acres among the Five Tribes shortly after its passage (Debo 1972 [1940]: 89–90).

The result of these congressional acts was that timber speculators and so-called grafters became especially interested in all Choctaw "surplus" and timberlands and used several tactics to obtain it. Timber speculators would induce full-blood allottees to take possession of widely scattered tracts of ten or more acres, all but the homestead being of little value to the allottee. Allottees would then be induced to sell their surplus lands for a fraction of its worth. Many full-bloods were induced to turn over deeds to surplus land merely in return for assistance in choosing sites and transportation to the land office (Five Tribes Commission 1904:42; Hargett Collection, box A-58, file 9, correspondence, Attorney E. L. Matlock to E. B. Pierce, Esq., Van Buren AR. July 25, 1901, box B-58, file 18, Attorney Chester Howe to Azel F. Hatch, Esq., Chicago IL, August 18, 25, 1902; see also Debo 1940:95). Lumber dealers similarly assisted Choctaw allottees in making selections of choice timberlands, and then offered allottees a mere pittance for the timber, leaving them with a tract of denuded and nearly worthless land in the mountainous timber region to cultivate. Fraudulent agreements were also written by which allottees were induced to cede land once restrictions were removed. They were not told by the "grafters" that the agreement was actually a deed of sale, but that the so-called lease would enhance their property's value (Debo 1972 [1940]: 96, 101–2; Thompson 1986:101).

Lands allotted to children of allottees and the valuable timber on it also became the target of graft and exploitation. Indian Territory courts routinely declared natural parents, particularly full-bloods, incompetent, and whites were assigned as substitute guardians for minor children, with little or no scrutiny as to their motives. Timber dealers, acting as "guardians" for Choctaw minors, would select allotments for them in the choice timber region, then sell the timber, often to themselves at bargain rates, taking most of the money as payment for their services (Indian Archives, Choctaw Estates, box 17632, "Letter of McCurtain and Hill, Attorneys for the Choctaw Nation," ca. 1904; Debo 1940:106–13; Thompson 1986:101).

Attorneys for the Choctaws reported one case where an individual who was actually a citizen of Kansas City, Missouri, was petitioner in 171 guardianship cases involving about 250 minors. This individual purchased timber from the estates of his wards and entered into leases of their lands while serving as their guardian. Through these transactions he defrauded them of their land and timber by undervaluing these resources (Indian Archives, Choctaw estates, box 17632).

The Commission to the Five Tribes proposed in 1903 that the practice of allowing speculators or agents to accompany full-blood allottees to "assist" them in choosing allotments be declared illegal. They further resolved that full-bloods not be allowed to choose widely scattered tracts if such tracts were not obviously to benefit the allottee in some way. The U.S. attorney general ruled against these resolutions, declaring that such resolutions deprived the allottees of their legitimate rights. That they were in fact being severely deprived of their land and resources without these restrictions apparently had no bearing in this case (Five Tribes Commission 1904:42–44).

During 1903 the Indian Rights Association uncovered irregularities in practices of the Commission to the Five Tribes itself, the very agency charged with implementing the allotment process and terminating tribal business. An investigator charged that members of the commission were dealing in Indian lands as members of various trust and investment companies that leased and managed the estates of Indian allottees. Every member of the commission, including its chairman, Tams Bixby, was found to be a high official of these trust companies, some of which had offices in the same building as the office of the Commission to the Five Tribes. It was reported that Indians would select their allotments at the commission office, then immediately be taken to the office of one of these companies, often the Canadian Valley Trust Company, located in the same building as the commission office, whose president was Tams Bixby (*New York Times* 8/27/1903:1).

Canadian Valley and other trust companies were accused of paying Indians very low rates for leases and defrauding them of their lands by entering into agreements to sell their property as soon as restrictions were removed after the stipulated period of time. Indians were lured into these agreements because of the promise of ready cash when such agreements were signed (*New York Times* 8/27/1903:1). Also implicated in these land scandals were officials of the Justice Department, the Internal Revenue Bureau, the inspector for Indian Territory, town site commissioners, and even the U.S. marshal for Indian Territory. The federal government subsequently made it illegal for commissioners or anyone associated with the allotment process to deal in any manner in Indian lands, which activities were finally recognized as a serious conflict of interest (*New York Times* 8/27/1903:1; *Independent* 55 [8/20/1903]: 1951; U.S. Commissioner 1907:105–7).

Between 1906 and about 1912 Congress undertook to gradually reimpose greater restrictions on allotted land, largely because land was so quickly being alienated under the various allotment provisions. The government sought to protect full-blood allottees, while allowing mixed-bloods greater freedom to govern their own business affairs, it being assumed that they were competent and ready to take on that responsibility. The congressional act of April 26, 1906 (34 Stat. L., 137) reimposed restrictions on all full-blood landholdings for twenty-five years, until April 1931. Full-bloods could not sell or alienate any of their lands, either homesteads or surplus, until that date without the consent of the secretary of the interior. Allottees of less than full Indian blood were still permitted to sell surplus land, although homesteads remained inalienable for a maximum of twenty-one years (Mills 1919:97–99, 166; *Laws* 1915:505; U.S. Commissioner 1908:100).

Congress on May 27, 1908, enacted new legislation with respect to allotted lands, reaffirming the long-standing philosophy that individuals with less than full Indian blood should be

intrusted with the untrammeled management of their lands [and] should be authorized to sell their surplus lands because as they too had opportunities for education, very few would have any excuse for making a foolish use of the privilege, and if they did sell their land for less than it was worth or make improvident use of the proceeds, they would still have their homesteads to fall back upon and would have learned a needed lesson. (U.S. Commissioner 1908:100)

This so-called Restrictions Act permitted all lands – homesteads and surplus – belonging to intermarried whites, freedmen, and Indians of less than one-half Indian blood to be sold. Restrictions on surplus land alienation by individuals of one-half to three-quarters Indian blood were also removed. The restrictions on alienation of all lands of individuals of three-fourths or more Indian blood were retained, except with the consent of the secretary of the interior. This act, again, freed for sale more and more allotted land and permitted tribal members of all categories to be deprived of their most valuable

permanent resource: their land. Rather than protecting tribal land alienation, these congressional acts actually had the opposite effect. The act of
May 27, 1908, alone removed the restrictions on the alienation of 3,629,238
acres of allotted Choctaw land, more than half of the original Choctaw Nation's 6,688,000 acres (U.S. DOI 1920:2:22).

Such vast land alienation was a direct result of the tribal ethnic composition at the time. When Choctaw citizenship rolls were closed on March 4,
1907, the Choctaw Nation included full- and mixed-bloods, intermarried
whites, and freedmen, each entitled to allotments of various sizes. As the
data below show, full-bloods were already in a numerical minority in 1907.
Allotments were made to more than fifteen thousand mixed-bloods, whites,
and blacks in addition to the approximately eight thousand restricted full-
blood allottees. This meant that much Choctaw land went directly to individuals quickly permitted to alienate their land, regardless of the nature of
the land sale or the allottees' ability to manage their personal economic affairs successfully.

Choctaw full-bloods	8,319
Choctaw mixed-bloods	10,717
Intermarried whites	1,585
Freedman	5,994
Total	26,615

Source: U.S. Commissioner of Indian Affairs, *Annual Report* (1907), 112.

Table 6.2 shows the tribal composition in 1917 by degree of Indian blood
and status of allotments, either restricted or unrestricted. This table reveals
that nearly sixteen thousand Choctaw allottees owned unrestricted land in
1917, while close to eleven thousand still retained restricted land. It was estimated that the 1908 Restrictions Act had removed restrictions on two-thirds
of the Five Civilized Tribes' land. Only 36,000 of the 101,228 Five Tribes allottees still retained restricted land after 1908. By 1920 only 5,409 of the more
than 26,000 original enrolled Choctaw Nation citizens still possessed restricted land (U.S. Commissioner 1908:101; U.S. DOI 1920:2:7).

FROM INHERITANCE TO ALIENATION

Federal legislation enacted during the allotment era also contained guidelines for allotted inherited land. According to the Supplemental Agreement

Table 6.2. Tribal composition and status of allotments, 1917

	Blood quantum	Number	Total
Restricted	Full-blood	8,444	
	≥¾	799	
	½ to ¾	1,674	
			10,917
Unrestricted	< ½*	9,882	
	Freedmen	6,029	
			15,911

Source: U.S Department of the Interior, *Annual Report*, 1917:2:50.
*Includes intermarried whites.

of 1902, inherited land could be sold by any heir, whether full-blood or not, so long as it was not sold for less than its appraised value. Inherited land, then, wholly free of federal supervision, became subject to easy exploitation by white land grabbers. Each year brought more and more land into the "inherited" status, as original allottees died and passed on their allotments to their heirs.

After 1906, when land allotments ceased, newborn children regardless of their degree of Indian blood were no longer entitled to allotments, even though more than two million acres remained unallotted. This new generation depended solely on their status as heirs to obtain land, which by law was fully alienable when inherited. One historian commented that "coupled with the loss of surplus lands, the sale of inherited estates meant that the third generation – the heirs of the allottees' heirs – would virtually be landless" (Holford 1975:14). As later pages will show, land alienation became aggravated with each generation, such that today access to land remains an unsolved problem of ever-increasing proportions.

GRABBING UNALLOTTED TRIBAL LAND

Not only were Choctaw allotted lands subject to expropriation by non-Indians during the first decade of the twentieth century, but also devastating to the Choctaws was the loss of over two million acres of unallotted Choctaw timberland, located mainly in McCurtain, Pushmataha, and adjacent counties, the heart of the Kiamichi Mountain region. This region, long the home to Choctaw full-bloods, became the last target of the white land-grabbing frenzy. When surveying parties arrived in the Kiamichis in 1899, much timber had already been taken by railroaders and timber thieves. Surveyors in 1901 found that cedar, used principally for railroad ties, had nearly disappeared (Five Tribes Commission 1901:37).

Choctaw timber reserves, estimated to contain about one billion board feet of timber, became especially valuable after the turn of the twentieth century, when timber resources in the northern and eastern states were growing scarce and depleted as a result of decades of harvesting. In 1900 Choctaw principal chief Gilbert Dukes, recognizing the value of this tribal resource and the potential for its depredation, requested the Dawes Commission to postpone surveying until actual allotments were assigned to reduce the potential for illegal timber removal once surveying parties revealed the location and extent of valuable timber stands. The region was particularly vulnerable to exploitation owing to several factors, including the impossibility of policing the region, the fact that railroads were permitted by Congress to cut timber for their own use, and that it might be years before actual allotments were made. The Dawes Commission denied his request, claiming that timber appraisal could not be delayed, nor could anything of value be gained by such a delay (U.S. Inspector 1900:28, 1901:38; Indian Archives, sec. X, Gilbert Dukes Papers, 12/10 and 12/17/1900).

Tribal concerns were well founded, particularly when Congress in January 1903 authorized that railroads operating a continuous line "extending into Indian Territory" could use timber and stone obtained from that region outside the territory, a decision that violated tribal laws enacted since the Timber Act of 1871 and reaffirmed by tribal legislation in 1899. A member of the House Committee on Indian Affairs, defending U.S. entrepreneurial interests over indigenous rights, stated, "Active railroad construction in, through, and from that Territory is now in progress, and the use of stone and timber from the Indian Territory for railroads . . . is found to be absolutely necessary" (Indian Archives, box 23548; Choctaw Nation 1973a [1897–99], 3/25/1899, p.64; U.S. Congress, H. Rep. 2881, 57th Cong., 2d. sess., 4413 [12/16/1902]; U.S. Inspector 1903:28). The 1903 act also permitted Indians to dispose of their timber once they had received allotment certificates. Both congressional decrees laid open the Choctaw timberlands for vast exploitation, which is exactly what began almost as soon as Choctaw allottees were handed their certificates, and even in some cases before (see Hargett Collection, box A-58, file 9, box B-58, file 18).

The Commission to the Five Civilized Tribes, the agency overseeing Choctaw land allotment, realized in 1903 that a substantial timberland tract, estimated at over 2.3 million acres, would remain unallotted after all allotments had been made. The commission took two actions, ostensibly to curb ongoing flagrant losses to timber thieves and speculators (Morrison 1954:90). First, in April 1903 it withheld from allotment all land in the nation containing pine timber of commercial value (1,247,473.63 acres), so as to protect the resource from further depredation and allow for its disposal in a manner more profitable to the tribe. Simultaneously the commission chairman, Tams Bixby, informed various federal officials, including the Departments of Agriculture and the Interior, that the time was ripe for the government to obtain these timberlands for a proposed forest reserve (Five Tribes Commission 1904:42, 43; Morrison 1954:90; U.S. Congress, "Forest Reserve in Indian Territory," H.Doc. 509, 59th Cong., 2d sess. [1907]: 2-11).

Setting aside Choctaw lands for a forest reserve had been proposed both publicly and privately. A private developer at the time offered to purchase one hundred thousand acres of forestland for a private forest reserve. The federal government was also extremely interested in the forest reserve proposal, as the acting director of the Geological Survey alluded in November 1906:

These forests deserve special consideration, since the United States Bureau of Forestry is, and has been for some time, engaged in devising means of extending the native forests in the regions of Oklahoma and Indian Territory. The Kiamichi Mountains are but a small part of the stony, mountainous forest lands in the southeastern Choctaw Nation, the most of which are public Indian domain. . . . The income to be derived from these forests, properly conducted, would, without doubt, more than pay the appraised value of the lands, and at the same time the forest may be kept intact for continuous enjoyment and profitable use of the inhabitants in the future. (U.S. Congress, "Forest Reserve in Indian Territory," H.Doc. 509, 59th Cong., 2d sess. [1907]: 4, 13; see also Ise 1920)

This proposal would have permitted the government to purchase tribal land from profits accrued from tribal timber sales. Not only would the U.S. government obtain a desired forest reserve in Indian Territory, but they would obtain it at almost no out-of-pocket cost.

The Choctaws almost unanimously opposed the commission's decision to withhold the prime timberland from allotment, since many allottees, particularly full-bloods, would be deprived of homesteads on which they had already built improvements and constructed homes. Following an October

1903 request by the tribal council, the secretary of the interior declared in May 1904 that lands could not be withheld from allotment by arbitrary decision of the Commission to the Five Tribes (Debo 1940:78; Phillips 1982:42; Choctaw Nation 1973b [1903], bill 28 [October 1903]). Allotments in the timber district increased significantly, with over 1,400 made the month the order was rescinded (May 1904), amounting to over two hundred thousand acres, compared to only 938 allotments the previous month. The commissioners charged that Indians "in nearly every case have been influenced by speculators . . . who have used every means to induce full-blood Indians to select timber land in allotments, hoping to obtain the timber at its appraised value, or even a lower price" (Act of 4/26/1906, sec. 7 [HR 5976], in *Laws* 1915:498; Five Tribes Commission 1904:42–43; U.S. Commissioner 1910:51; U.S. Congress, "Letter from Secretary of Interior, January 15, 1907," H.Doc. 509, 59th Cong., 2d sess. [1907]: 1–5, 10–18; Phillips 1982:42). Once the timber was cut, the Commission believed, the land would be of little value to allottees or anyone else. Subsequent developments in the course of tribal land alienation, however, made the logged-off homesteads of the early Choctaw allottees seem very valuable indeed alongside the prospect of landlessness faced by their descendants.

The disposition of this choice timberland was still uncertain in 1906 when Congress again officially sanctioned the segregation and removal from allotment of certain lands in McCurtain and Pushmataha Counties at the request of Commission chairman Tams Bixby, Secretary of the Interior Ethan A. Hitchcock, chief forester Gifford Pinchot, and Secretary of Agriculture James Wilson, again with a view to creating a forest reserve (Act of 4/26/1906, sec. 7, in *Laws* 1915). It was estimated that about 840,000 acres of timberland set aside by this act had already been allotted by 1907, leaving 1,373,304 acres of choice timberland estimated to have been worth nearly $1.6 million (Act of 4/26/1906, sec. 7:498. U.S. Commissioner 1910:51).

Suspending allotment assignments in this prime timberland tract profoundly affected the future course of private landownership in the region. Rather than protect Choctaws from unscrupulous developers, the suspension in fact led to the eventual sale in large undivided parcels to the very class of speculators whose abuses this policy was ostensibly designed to curb, including the Dierks family, who later became the region's largest private landowner. Furthermore, the temporary (and at the time illegal) withdrawal of timberland from allotment left unresolved the tribe's legal interest in the timberland, which amounted to nearly 20 percent of the Choctaw Nation's land base prior to allotment and comprised the heart of the local timber wealth (Phillips, 1982:53, 65–67; U.S. Congress, "Letter of December 28, 1906," H.Doc 509, 59th Cong., 2d sess. [1907]: 8–9). According to Richard Phillips (1982:54),

The Secretary of the Interior, in withdrawing the Choctaw timber lands from allotment, accomplished by unilateral administrative fiat what could not be done by Congressional legislation. . . . The initial orders withdrawing the timber lands from allotment were issued before anyone in the executive branch had looked for statutory authority. The final order of 12 January 1907 was issued after extensive Senate hearings on the subject, during which the executive officers responsible were made painfully aware that no statute could be found which authorized their actions. The Secretary of the Interior was able to thwart the will of Congress, however, by simply ordering the Dawes Commission not to comply with the law, and not to allot the Choctaw timber lands.

The proposal to create a forest reserve, ostensibly why the land was withdrawn from allotment in the first place, was never sent to Congress for ratification, and therefore the reserve never became a reality (see Phillips 1982:62; U.S. Congress, "Report of Select Committee to Investigate Matters Connected with Affairs in the Indian Territory" [11/11/1906–1/9/1907] S. Rep. 5013, 59th Cong., 2d sess. [1907]: 1689–94).

The tribe still possessed more than two million unallotted acres in 1908, when Interior Department officials and members of Congress began to propose selling the land under procedures for disposing of surplus tribal land in the act of April 26, 1906 (Phillips 1982:62). The tribal leaders, facing a glutted land market, agreed to sell their surplus land for cash so allottees could construct urgently needed improvements on their own allotments. Principal Chief Green McCurtain, in his annual message in 1909, explained the tribe's dilemma:

If the unallotted lands, consisting of several millions of acres, should be offered for immediate sale, its effect upon the market price of land would be in the very nature of things depressing, and we would realize a very small average price per acre for said lands. However, to defer the sale of said unallotted lands awaiting the opportune time or better market would delay the final disposition of the said property indefinitely, and that is not desired. (Indian Archives, Choctaw principal chiefs, box 19457,

"Annual Message of Green McCurtain, Principal Chief, to the Choctaw Council,"
10/4/1909)

The tribe's worst fears were realized when Congress offered to purchase approximately 1.2 million acres of unallotted land at a flat rate of $1.50 per acre for the standing timber, far below market value. Said one individual:

There is not an acre of this land that the timber on it is not worth three times the amount which is proposed the Government should pay – not an acre within the timber belt. It is proposed to take the land in which these people have vested rights under the Act of Congress at an arbitrary price for less than the actual market value today. (U.S. Commissioner 1910:19; see also Phillips 1982:62–65)

COUNTY COURT LAND FRAUDS

The Restrictions Act of May 27, 1908 (32 Stat. 312), dealt another blow to Choctaw allottees by transferring jurisdiction over Indian estate and inheritance administration from the Interior Department to local county courts, ostensibly to expedite landownership transactions (see Mills 1919:541–42). Strategies used earlier by grafters and land speculators to fraudulently obtain Choctaw allotments continued to plague allottees well into succeeding decades as local courts became responsible for administered Indian estates and as more and more land became subject to alienation through acts of Congress and inheritance. Local white citizens and officials, familiar with local land values and property laws, and under little direct federal scrutiny, proved even more adept than federal officials had been at acquiring Choctaw land through means both on the edge of the law and outside it.

Charges began to mount that local court officials were colluding with Choctaw guardians and attorneys to defraud allottees. Court investigations of transactions during 1909 and 1910 resulted in federal indictments of more than one hundred persons for unlawful timber cutting on tribal land. Numerous sawmill and cutting operations were closed during this period for operating illegally in the Choctaw Nation (U.S. Commissioner 1909:55, 1910:19).

In 1911 the McCurtain County probate court judge and other court officials were implicated in land fraud involving the sale of more than forty-one hundred acres. Investigations resulted in the resignation of the county judge and reimbursement of over sixty-five thousand dollars to minor allottees. Three large landowners in the county were directed to submit to arbitration all land acquisitions they had obtained. Other charges against the courts themselves included the following: exorbitant fees to administer the estates of allottees, as much as ten times what whites paid for the same services and in some instances nearly what the entire estate was worth; children allowed to die by guardians seeking to obtain their estates; and phony wills "signed" by already deceased individuals but fully notarized and accepted as evidence in probate court (U.S. Commissioner 1911:45; Holford 1975:17; U.S. Congress, "Investigate Indian Affairs in Oklahoma," H.Doc. 678, 68th Cong., 1st sess. [1924]: 2).

An Indian Rights Association report in 1924 further documented local court abuses and implicated county judges, guardians, attorneys, bankers, and merchants in schemes to defraud allottees of fair prices for their estates (U.S. Congress, H. Rep. 678, 68th Cong., 1st sess., 8228 [1924]). One individual, James Eggleston, a land agent for a Texas oil company, testified in hearings before a congressional committee in 1924 that "twenty men, with the cooperation or toleration of the courts, controlled all Indian lands in southeast Oklahoma," charges that he substantiated by name (Holford 1975:17).

Contradictions in the evolving land policy enabled outsiders to amass great wealth in timberland, against the expressed will of tribal, state, and federal officials. By 1913 more than 1.7 million acres of unallotted land had been sold in the Choctaw and Chickasaw Nations in successive rounds of bidding. The average price per acre received by the tribe was $5.82, $1.30 above the appraised value set by the government. By 1916 the average price per acre had fallen to $3.36. Yet a comparable tract of private timberland in Arkansas had increased in value from $1.00 per acre in 1900 to $13.50 per acre in 1904. By 1917 about 419,000 acres of timberland remained unsold in Pushmataha, McCurtain, LeFlore and Latimer Counties, of which 248,000 acres was in the McCurtain and Pushmataha County timber region (U.S. DOI 1914:2:418, 1917:52; U.S. Department of Commerce and Labor 1913:197).

By 1920 restrictions on more than four million acres – nearly two-thirds of the former tribal estate – had been removed. The federal law of May 27, 1908, had freed over 16,000 of the estimated 27,000 Choctaw allottees to sell their land. By 1920 all but 36,502 acres had been allotted, sold, or otherwise alienated, not counting 145,063 acres reserved for town sites, railroad rights-of-way, and other specified uses (U.S. DOI V. II, 1913:50, 1917:50, 1920:7).

Legislation enacted in January 1933 again attempted to slow Choctaw land alienation by providing that lands inherited by heirs of one-half or more Indian blood be "restricted" from sale through the heir's lifetime until 1956, except with the consent of the Bureau of Indian Affairs. The state of Oklahoma strongly opposed this legislation, and it was repealed in 1947. New legislation permitted heirs to sell undivided inherited land if an heir demanded a distribution of shares. Since few tribal members could buy out all the joint heirs of an undivided parcel, much jointly held land was typically sold to outsiders, a process that has continued to the late twentieth century (Debo 1951:5–6).

The Choctaw Nation, although granted "in perpetuity," survived for only seventy years, overrun by global capitalist hegemonic forces. The rhetoric of tribal sovereignty, sacred treaties, and self-determination was meaningless, as the Choctaws were alienated from their land and stripped of tribal political authority. Choctaws were politically and economically marginalized and peripheralized with land allotment and the ensuing land-grabbing frenzy.

Several crucial factors contributed to making Choctaw land particularly vulnerable to exploitation and alienation the early twentieth century. First, the allotment process itself and subsequent legislation put a vast amount of tribally owned land on the market early in the century, flooding the market and depressing land prices. Second, the inability of the tribe and its members to develop and manage a viable timber enterprise created an economic vacuum that helped outsiders penetrate the timber region. Tribal members without capital resources were easy prey for outside entrepreneurs, just as they had been during the tribal period. Third, many Choctaws, particularly full-bloods, were new to the concept of private landownership and were chronically short of cash, particularly in the timber region. After allotment, when both federal and tribal subsidies were severely cut, the region's mainly full-blood Choctaw subsistence farmers, trying to make a living on their inadequate land, saw their surplus land as a source of desperately needed cash.

No longer able to sustain a self-sufficient subsistence mode of production, Choctaws turned increasingly to mixed subsistence and wage labor, serving as an unskilled labor force for the land thieves who now occupied their homeland. Choctaws in the twentieth century became a captive rural labor force, wedded to their tribal homeland culturally and historically, and easily exploitable.

In the twentieth century private timber companies, first family-owned

Dierks, and later the multinational timber giant Weyerhaeuser Corporation, would become the driving force in the local timber extraction industry, a multimillion-dollar enterprise from which the Choctaw people would only minimally benefit. Abetted by U.S. government complicity, private entre-preneurial activity soon fully subsumed the Choctaws within the emerging twentieth-century Euro-American political economy.

SEVEN

Dierks Locally, Weyerhaeuser Nationally: The Rise of a Contemporary Political-Economic Structure

Choctaw Nation, 1982. A Choctaw woman living in McCurtain County explained how her father had lost part of his allotment to the so-called Choctaw Loan Company in the 1920s. The loan company – not tribally connected – offered her father about $150 to $200 for 160 acres, which he agreed to sell because of his desperate need for cash. When she investigated the matter a decade later assisted by an attorney, the loan company offered her $300 to silence and appease her. The timber on her father's land was lost by another common practice. A lumberman approached her father wanting to purchase standing timber; although her father never consented, a "signed" agreement was simply registered at the local courthouse verifying an alleged timber sale. She confided that "a lot of Indians have been tricked out of their land" and timber in similar incidents.

During the half century from 1850 to 1900, competing internal and external social forces worked to bring the Choctaw Nation into the sphere of U.S. political, economic, and cultural dominance. As Hall argues (1987:4–5), Native American incorporation was neither abrupt nor unidimensional; it occurred as a "continuum . . . from initial contact through complete absorption." By 1900 Choctaws could no longer hope to retain tribal sovereignty, and the tribal government was officially terminated in 1906. Green McCurtain was the last elected tribal chief until 1971, when a new tribal constitution was adopted.

With the demise of tribal government, land allotment, and eventually, Choctaw citizenship, the Choctaws became simply an impoverished rural enclave. What was formerly an independent "nation" was now a weakened "tribe" and would become just another ethnicity entering the U.S. melting pot, like other ethnicities before and since: at the bottom of the social hierarchy (see Hall 1987; Nagel and Snipp 1993). In the context of tribal demise, the timber region was ripe for full takeover by externally based entrepreneurs, bringing two family-owned timber giants to southeastern Oklahoma.

TRANSFORMING TRIBAL TIMBERLAND OWNERSHIP

Around the turn of the twentieth century two families, Dierks and Weyerhaeuser, established themselves in the timber business, the Dierks primarily in the southcentral region of Nebraska and in Indian Territory, and the Weyerhaeusers in the Far West. These two family business would play an important part in the political economy of southeastern Oklahoma, intersecting with many Choctaw families whose impoverishment contrasted sharply with the wealth of these industrial giants. The history of these two companies during the early part of the century reflects timber development regionally and nationally, and in each instance family-owned businesses blossomed into impressive regional timber enterprises.

The Dierks family began its lumbering operations in the 1880s in Iowa, and by 1900 Dierks family members owned twenty-four lumberyards, mainly in central Nebraska. In a pattern typical of the era, the Dierks opened yards along a railroad supply route, tapping a regional market. It was possible to operate lumberyards profitably as close as seven miles apart, since transporting lumber was difficult and relied heavily on access to rail lines (U.S. Department of Commerce and Labor 1913:3–4).

During the era when Choctaw tribal land, both allotted and unallotted, was being sold to private developers through the highly questionable practices described in chapter 6, the Dierks family began to penetrate southeastern Oklahoma in earnest, taking advantage of extremely favorable timberland prices and lax legal structures to add to its already impressive regional timber asset base. The Dierks family began in 1898 to obtain lumber from a small mill in Indian Territory, located in Petros, near Heavener (Smith 1986:19). Tribal records show a permit granted in that year to Dierks Lumber and Coal Company for "manufacturing and shipping of lumber on the Kansas City Southern Railroad" (Tucker Collection, box 40). Lumber purchased by Dierks was cut on tribal land and conveyed to the Dierks yard for cutting and retail sales (Dierks 1972:15). The Dierks family later purchased the Petros mill, gaining access to extensive southeastern Oklahoma and western Arkansas forests for their Nebraska operations. This mill later closed, and the Dierks operation was concentrated mainly in Arkansas by the turn of the twentieth century.

By 1900 the Dierks family operated fifty miles of railroads, including a controlling interest in the DeQueen and Eastern Railroad, which connected with the Kansas City Southern (Moody's *Railroads* 1908:288). Arkansas purchases prior to 1900 had brought under Dierks ownership a complete mill operation, including a sawmill, dry kilns, and air drying yard, plus a five-mile logging railroad (Dierks 1972:15).

Choctaw Nation, 1982. One Choctaw informant told how his family's land was lost between 1929 and 1933 to Dierks, which paid approximately four dollars per acre for a 110-acre tract, well below market rates. He was a boy of thirteen at the time, but his signature appeared on a deed, although he cannot recall how it got there. County records showed that the court had fully approved the land sale and determined that the price paid was fair. (LeFlore County, Oklahoma, miscellaneous deeds, book 174:514–16, 170:152–53, 178:8–9, 200:621–22, 1929–38. Author's interview, 6/17/81, Ludlow OK)

The Dierks family reentered the Oklahoma timber region in 1909 when they took over the Choctaw Lumber Company, based in McCurtain County. This brought to Dierks an additional 112,000 acres in McCurtain and several Arkansas counties (Poor's *Industrials* 1915:3769). By 1910 the family-run partnership controlled 97,000 acres of land in Arkansas, of which 82,000 was owned in fee (Poor's *Industrials* 1910:2288). Over the following three decades the Dierks family "exercised a singleminded passion for acquiring timber" (K. Smith 1986:76), building their southeastern regional timber company into an impressive enterprise. Dierks-owned Choctaw Lumber, renamed Dierks Lumber and Coal Company in 1936 and owned principally by Hans and Herman Dierks, purchased timberland throughout the region using practices similar to speculators investigated previously. Page after page of land conveyances are documented in Pushmataha, McCurtain, LeFlore and Latimer County court records, showing Choctaw allottees turning over land titles for a mere pittance to Dierks purchasers. Land conveyances were even made to Dierks by minor heirs as young as nine years of age.

Lawyers for the Dierks-owned Choctaw Lumber Company used the unscrupulous practice described earlier of serving as guardians for Choctaw minors whose land was later acquired by Choctaw Lumber Company. Richard Phillips (1982:126), citing 1911 U.S. Interior Department correspondence, found "121 guardianship sales to the Choctaw Lumber Company, involving the rights of about 242 full-blood Indian minors, . . . approximately one-hundred of [which sales] were conducted and managed by the salaried attorneys of the Lumber Company, who were also the attorneys of record for

Table 7.1. Representative Choctaw Lumber Company land purchases
from Choctaw allottees, 1911–1914

Approximate date, court transaction	# of sales	Acres obtained	Purchase price	Price/ acre
1911	1	995	$640	$0.64
1911	1	34,200˙	n/a	n/a
ca. 1911–14	121	31,780	$39,430	$1.25
ca. 1911–14	115	32,432	$41,292	$1.27
ca. 1911–14	n/a	33,815	$45,855	$1.36
1914	1	11,415˙	n/a	n/a
Total		142,642		$1.28˙˙

˙*Source*: Phillips 1982:123, 126.
˙Allotted land acquired from other lumber companies in quit claim transactions.
˙˙Average price/acre computed on prices/acre previously listed.

the guardians." Choctaw Lumber obtained in these transactions 31,780 acres of land for $39,438, paying allottee a mere $1.24 per acre. The Dierks brothers in 1906 and 1907 – a period of depressed lumber prices according to Kenneth Smith (1986:38–39) – paid for and sold land and stumpage rights at prices ranging from $6.75 to $7.00 per acre, in marked contrast to the $1.24 paid to Choctaw allottees. Choctaw Lumber acquired land, including some which by law was inalienable because it was owned by full-blood allottees, although county courts had fully approved these illegal sales (Phillips 1982:126). Table 7.1 shows a representative sample of transactions through which Choctaw Lumber Company acquired more than 142,000 acres at an average $1.28 per acre.

The Dierks family also acquired substantial amounts of unallotted tribal land during this same period, including land that had originally been set aside for the proposed forest reserve discussed earlier (Phillips 1982:120). Table 7.2 shows the original allotted and unallotted status of the once-Choctaw land acquired by Dierks (but owned by Weyerhaeuser when data were collected by Phillips). This table shows that both allotted and unallotted land provided substantial timberland for the emerging Dierks empire during this early period.

Choctaw Lumber Company eventually was charged and pled no contest for violating the Oklahoma State Constitution, which prohibited purchase of Oklahoma real estate for the sole purpose of resale at a profit (Phillips

Table 7.2. Weyerhaeuser landownership by original status prior
to purchase, allotted or unallotted

County	Acres owned	Acres subject to allotment	Unallotted (proposed forest reserve)
Pushmataha	246,515	80,400	116,115
McCurtain	553,605	298,090	255,515
Total	886,530	388,590	497,940

Source: Phillips 1982:117, 118, 120.

1982:127–35; Smith 1986:76–77). Although the law called for the penalty of "escheat to the State of Oklahoma," that is, land forfeiture, the state instead permitted Choctaw Lumber to plead no contest to fraud charges, pay a ten-thousand-dollar fine plus attorney's fees, and promise to refrain from further land dealings in the state (Phillips 1982:131). To comply with the latter, Choctaw Lumber simply "sold" its timberland back to the company's owners, Hans and Herman Dierks (Phillips 1982:132). The Dierks brothers were penalized a mere sixteen thousand dollars for what should have cost them all of their fraudulently acquired timberland (Phillips 1982:133–34).

The Dierks family by 1910 was permanently established in southeastern Oklahoma. The following year Choctaw Lumber opened a lumber manufacturing mill in Bismarck, today called Wright City, Oklahoma, on the Dierks-owned Texas, Oklahoma, and Eastern Railroad, which connected with the Saint Louis and San Francisco Railroad (Poor's *Industrials* 1913:1122; K. Smith 1986:75). A second Dierks-owned lumber mill began operations in Broken Bow, Oklahoma, in 1912. The Dierks family owned about 1.5 million acres in the southeastern Oklahoma/southwestern Arkansas region by 1930, about 80 percent wholly company-owned. In 1929 the Oklahoma affiliate, Choctaw Lumber, had fifteen hundred employees. Dierks timberland alone was estimated to have been worth almost nine million dollars in 1929 (Moody's *Investments* 1930:1237).

The Wright City, Oklahoma, Dierks plant was an impressive enterprise. It was a typical "company town" in its early years of operation, similar to mill towns of the Northeast. Company housing was built for employees, who used scrip to make purchases at company stores. Today Wright City, with a population of one thousand, is still dominated by the lumber mill. Nearly 90 percent of the town's work force is employed at the Wright City plant, most of them third- or fourth-generation industry lumber employees (Hankins 1982). Wright City, today the center of Weyerhaeuser's southeastern Oklahoma operations, houses not only the mill operation but also a modern office complex.

Forced into bankruptcy during the Great Depression, Dierks Lumber and Coal Company merged its two subsidiary companies, the Choctaw and Pine Valley Lumber Companies in 1936 and was renamed Dierks Forests, Inc. (Phillips 1982:136). At that time, in addition to the approximately 1.5 million acres already mentioned, Dierks owned controlling interests in five manufacturing mills, with an annual capacity of two hundred million board feet of timber, and approximately seventy-five miles of railroad (Moody's *Investments* 1936:2625). Dierks enterprises had about two thousand employees in 1934. By 1938 their lumber operations appeared to have weathered the depression in relatively good financial health (Dierks 1972:94).

Hans and Herman Dierks had attempted to introduce sustained-yield forestry management and timber conservation measures in the 1920s under the guidance of William L. Hall, earlier responsible for surveying the Ouachita Forest region in 1906 for Gifford Pinchot, then chief forester of the Department of Agriculture. The Dierks' efforts, however, did not prevent the depletion of their eroding forest base, and in 1941 the Dierks plant at Pine Valley, Oklahoma, closed. The post–World War II era brought a boom in timber demand, but Dierks still faced several challenges, particularly competition from other, smaller operators, problems of depleting timber resources in the Ouachita National Forest region, and pressure from the Congress of Industrial Organizations (CIO) to unionize the Forester, Oklahoma, plant. In 1952 the Dierks sawmill at Forester shut down permanently (K. Smith 1986:114, 116, 181–82, 197–201). By 1962 Dierks Forests, Inc., had nearly three thousand employees in its Oklahoma and Arkansas operations.

WEYERHAEUSER ENTERS THE PACIFIC NORTHWEST
TIMBER REGION

While the Dierks family was consolidating its southeastern Oklahoma and Arkansas operations in the first half of the century, the Weyerhaeuser family, headed by Frederick Weyerhaeuser, was expanding into the yet-untapped region of Oregon and Washington. A series of transactions in 1900 enabled Weyerhaeuser and his associates to become America's second-largest private timber owners by 1913 (U.S. Department of Commerce and Labor 1913:16), and today Weyerhaeuser Corporation is the largest owner of private timber resources in the United States.

The Far West had been unavailable to private developers before 1897, when Congress enacted a piece of legislation called the "forest lieu selection clause," which allowed landowners, mainly railroads with vast tracts of land, to exchange worthless land located within public forest reserves for tracts in another region. The Northern Pacific Railroad exchanged approximately one million acres located on forest reserve land in the Northwest for other timber-rich property under this "forest lieu" legislation, which it then turned around and sold to Weyerhaeuser. In one transaction in 1900, Northern Pacific sold to Weyerhaeuser approximately 900,000 acres at a flat rate of six dollars per acre, far below the prime timberland's actual value. This single land purchase increased Weyerhaeuser's landholdings by 80 percent. A few years later Weyerhaeuser sold a one-quarter section – 160 acres – for seventy-six thousand dollars. Weyerhaeuser's estimated profit in this single 900,000-acre land purchase was an estimated twenty million dollars. The forest lieu selection law was repealed in 1904 once it became obvious that private developers were siphoning off vast tracts of timberland. By that time, however, Weyerhaeuser had purchased from railroad owners a fortune in timberland (U.S. Department of Commerce and Labor 1913:xxi, 18–19; Norcross 1907:255, 257–58).

Weyerhaeuser by 1905 had enlarged its landholdings to 1.5 million acres, valued at $9.5 million. By 1913 Weyerhaeuser, the nation's second-largest private timber owner, controlled almost two million acres of timberland, mainly in the Pacific Northwest (Weyerhaeuser ca. 1975:10; U.S. Department of Commerce and Labor 1913:xxii).

Timber and timberland concentration by private timber owners, including Weyerhaeuser, became increasingly evident during the first decade of the twentieth century. According to a 1913 U.S. Department of Commerce and Labor report (1913:xx), three companies, Weyerhaeuser Timber Company, the Southern Pacific Company, and the Northern Pacific Railway, together controlled about 11 percent of privately owned timber in the nation. These companies monopolized both timberland and the railroad infrastructure so essential to the timber industry. They also dominated many allied industries, including lumber mills, logging activities, processing plants, and even retail establishments (U.S. Department of Commerce and Labor 1913:xxii, 3–4).

Standing timber was the key to the lumberman's wealth, since there was no cost to maintain it, its value appreciated with each succeeding year of timber growth, and the nature of the timber market in the early twentieth century was such that withholding timber from the market accrued even greater wealth to the timber owner. A profitable strategy was to curtail timber cutting, thereby artificially inflating the value of their marketed timber as well as their timber holdings (U.S. Department of Commerce and Labor 1913:38–42).

Land monopoly in the southern pine region, then being penetrated by the Dierks family, was not so startling as in the Pacific Northwest. Monopoly was more prevalent in the ownership of the more valuable species of timber, including shortleaf and loblolly pine and cypress, however (U.S. Department of Commerce and Labor 1913:21). Land values were also escalating during the first decade of the twentieth century in the southern timber region, but, as previously shown, Dierks benefited by a declining price for Choctaw timberland due to the timberland market glut when their purchases were made.

Weyerhaeuser by 1951 owned about 2.75 million acres of land, mostly in the Pacific Northwest, and by 1959 southern acquisitions had increased the total to almost 3.5 million acres. In 1969 the Dierks family, the second largest timber producer in the South, sold its entire operations to the Weyerhaeuser Corporation in a sale reported to be one of the largest in the history of the American forest products industry. This transaction added approximately 1.79 million acres of land (in two states) to Weyerhaeuser's already sizable worldwide holdings, estimated prior to the Dierks purchase at 3.8 million acres (Hidy, Hill, and Nevins 1963:212, 224, 556; *Business Week* 5/17/69:120; *New York Times* 5/10/69: p.37, col. 5).

Since the mid-nineteenth century, the Choctaws were alienated from their vast tribal resources as a result of government and private-sector intrigue, handicapping the tribe's effort to maintain control over their own tribal assets. Outsiders stepped into a vacuum created by federal complicity, unenforced laws, a lack of indigenous economic development initiatives, and overwhelming white pressures for access to the tribal domain.

Dierks and later Weyerhaeuser, archetypes of capitalist entrepreneurial strategists, controlled the resource base and infrastructure essential to timber business success. Weyerhaeuser's entry into southeastern Oklahoma brought timber region Choctaws into a classic contemporary political-economic relationship between a centrally based multinational corporation and rural hinterland inhabitants, where an outside elite controls a valuable local asset: timberland.

Today Choctaws are embedded in a situation of dependent development similar to dependent satellite or peripheral economies throughout the Third World. Southeastern Oklahoma is what Jorgensen (1978:3; see also Coppedge and Davis 1977:ix) calls a "domestic dependent niche," serving private-sector interests as a source of cheap, readily available labor. Weyerhaeuser Corporation was attracted to southeastern Oklahoma not only for its vast timber resources but also for its reputation for paying low wages and hostility to union organizing (see K. Smith 1986:197–98, 208; Students of the Multinational Corporation Group Contract [hereinafter cited as Students] 1975:48). Since Choctaw social and cultural ties are deeply rooted in the region, many Choctaws remain in (and continue to return to) their homeland, working to preserve their identity as a tribal people in their ancestral homeland. The next chapter explores the contemporary Choctaw nation, its people, and its socioeconomic conditions.

EIGHT

Timber Region Communities:
Persistence and Change

Choctaw Nation, 1982. The McCurtain and Pushmataha County timber region still retains the flavor of its nineteenth-century past. Long home to traditionally oriented Choctaws, it still is home to the largest number of full-blood Choctaws of any Choctaw Nation county. As in the past, it contains dense forests, clear mountain streams, dirt roads, and sparsely populated villages. Small homes nestled in the woods, some dilapidated and without electricity or running water, display a wood pile, an occasional wringer washer, toys, automobiles, and various farm animals.

Interspersed throughout are the dramatically visible Weyerhaeuser clear-cuts, often as large as 350 acres, the maximum allowable, transforming the dense forest into a wasteland of denuded, treeless stubble, removed of every visible sign of life, including most undergrowth.[1] Choctaws don't have to fight back the forest; Weyerhaeuser sometimes clear-cuts right to their front door.

In early spring, work crews – men, women, sometimes children, young and old – plant tiny loblolly pine seedlings amid the stubble of a Weyerhaeuser clear-cut. The work is hard, poorly paid, and intermittent, but for many locals it's all the work there is at this time of year, or ever. It's piecework. "The more you plant, the more you earn. If the stand dies, you pay to replant," said one worker.

An estimated twenty thousand Choctaws still occupy their former tribal homeland in Oklahoma, although they are only a remnant of their earlier status as owners of the Choctaw Nation. Choctaw nationhood was extinguished long ago, receding into ever more distant cultural memory. A century ago Choctaws made up 80 percent of the region's population, while today they constitute less than 15 percent. Between 1906 and 1971, when the Choctaw tribal government was reinstated, the Choctaws retreated into a

---

1. Weyerhaeuser in 1993 curtailed its clear-cutting practices and now relies more extensively on modified sustained yield.

mixed subsistence/wage labor existence, eking a living in an externally controlled regional economy dominated by Dierks and later Weyerhaeuser. Tribal identity was submerged – impoverished both economically and culturally – as Choctaws adjusted to their new reality as rural poor "citizens." Their status was now as a disempowered ethnic minority subsumed under state political and legal jurisdiction (see Hall 1987:9, 11–13, 1988; see also Castile 1993:273).

As uneducated, unskilled rural proletarians lacking both structures and opportunity for effective self-determination, Choctaws, like rural blacks and whites, were exploited as cheap labor for the increasingly hegemonic U.S. economy before and after World War II. The Choctaw internal colony was being transformed into a peripheral economic sector of the United States: a reservoir of raw materials and cheap labor.

The Choctaws today share the ten and one-half counties of their rural homeland with two prominent ethnic groups: whites, about 80 percent of region's inhabitants, and blacks, about 5 percent (Geography Extension Division 1975; Oklahoma IMPACT 1981:31–32; U.S. Census Bureau 1990). Although these three population segments share many similarities, Choctaws in certain important respects are a unique class of rural poor who, after a period of near-extinction, have devised their own strategies to maintain their ethnic autonomy and satisfy their basic subsistence needs (see Jacobsen 1984; Nagel and Snipp 1993).

SOUTHEASTERN OKLAHOMA: DEMOGRAPHY AND COMMUNITY
Southeastern Oklahoma has become a year-round recreation area with its many man-made lakes and reservoirs, attracting tourists from other parts of Oklahoma and neighboring states to view the colorful late fall foliage, a display unique to that part of the country, nearly equal to New England in beauty and seeming to surpass it in duration owing to the temperate climate. Large tracts of the naturally reforested wilderness have been set aside as public forests, including the Kiamichi Forest, Broken Bow Reservoir, and Sardis Lake wilderness area (see map 8.1).

Numerous villages, many from five to fifteen miles apart, dot the rural landscape, including Bethel, Smithville, Honobia, and Ludlow. These smaller incorporated villages with populations of one hundred or less contain only a gas station, post office, and perhaps a small general store. Descen-

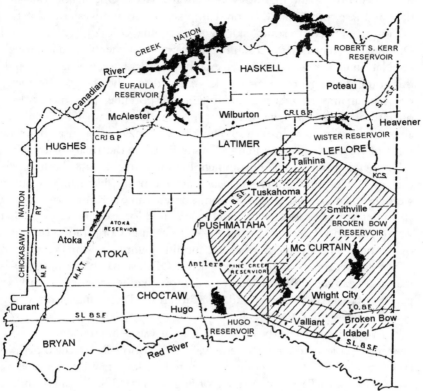

Map 8.1. Choctaw Nation, showing current county boundaries, regional towns, and major forest concentration. *Source*: Adapted from Choctaw Nation of Oklahoma, *Comprehensive Plan of the Choctaw Nation* (Durant OK: Choctaw Nation Planning Department, 1980).

dants of the first Choctaw inhabitants still live in these settlements, many bearing names familiar from Choctaw history. The somewhat larger towns, with populations of five hundred to twenty-five hundred, such as Broken Bow and Antlers, house several stores and infrequently a movie theater. Larger cities, such as McAlester, Idabel, and Durant, range in population from five thousand to fifteen thousand and serve as regional centers of commerce. Villages and towns of all sizes are linked by rural, sparsely traveled networks of two-lane highways, not always paved. One major four-lane thoroughfare, the Indian Nation Turnpike, bisects the western Choctaw Nation from north to south, skirting the regional cities of McAlester and Durant. The Saint Louis and San Francisco Railroad, the third built through the Nation in 1882, was abandoned exactly a century later, in 1982. Although this route, linking Fort Smith, Arkansas, with northeast Texas, formerly provided an important human and freight transport line, it was too costly to operate profitably and the track was torn up, leaving a narrow swath of abandoned railroad right-of-way. The tribe was finally compensated for the right-of-way, but only after filing a lawsuit based on the Treaty of 1866.

Timber continues to be a prominent local resource. In 1958 about 75 percent of McCurtain County and nearly 85 percent of Pushmataha County were classified as forest-woodland, while only about 9 percent of McCurtain and 3 percent of Pushmataha County were used for growing crops in that year (Peach and Poole, n.d.: chart 18). Weyerhaeuser Corporation currently owns approximately one-third of McCurtain County, an estimated 556,000 of the county's estimated 1,678,000 acres. Of Pushmataha County's estimated 910,720 acres, Weyerhaeuser owns more than 262,700 acres, nearly 30 percent of that county's total land (McCurtain and Pushmataha County Assessor's Offices, 1993).

Between 1925 and 1970 the region's economy was being transformed from an internal colony to a racially, ethnically, and regionally stratified peripheral sector of the U.S. corporate-dominated welfare state (see Flora et al. 1991:82–83; Cornell 1988:60–62). According to a 1973 U.S. Bureau of Indian Affairs (BIA) report (1973:4), "until the 1940s the major source of [Choctaw household] income was from cotton and corn on small subsistence farms." In a trend typical of rural America generally, between 1929 and 1959 the number of farms in McCurtain County declined by more than 50 percent, and in Pushmataha County by nearly 60 percent. Farm size and acreage under cultivation actually increased during that period, however, reflecting patterns of farm consolidation and ownership concentration prevalent nationally since the 1920s (Peach and Poole, n.d.: chart 17; Jorgensen 1978:19).

Also like the rest of rural America, the region experienced a noticeable population decline between 1930 and 1960, felt by all sectors, especially the Choctaws, whose population fell by nearly 40 percent (Dillman and Hobbs 1982:62–63; U.S. BIA 1973:13). Depopulation was prompted by a combination of push and pull factors, including declining agricultural employment

Table 8.1. Pushmataha and McCurtain County population trends, 1960–90

		1960		1970		1980		1990	
McCurtain	Overall	25,851		28,642		36,151		33,433	
		#	%	#	%	#	%	#	%
	Indians	2,010	7.8	2,493	8.7	3,638	10.1	4,873	14.6
	Blacks	4,524	17.5	n/a	n/a	3,849	10.6	3,452	10.3
Pushmataha	Overall	9,088		9,385		11,773		10,997	
		#	%	#	%	#	%	#	%
	Indians	573	6.3	n/a	n/a	1,222	10.4	1,669	15.2
	Blacks	180	2.0	n/a	n/a	101	0.9	112	1.0

Sources: U.S. Bureau of the Census, 1960, 1970, 1980, 1990; Oklahoma Department of Commerce, State Data Center; Oklahoma IMPACT, 1981.

opportunities, coupled with federally sponsored Indian relocation programs during the 1950s. Since 1960 the trend has begun to reverse, as many Choctaws returned to take advantage of the "mutual help housing" program instituted in 1969 by the Department of Housing and Urban Development (HUD). In Pushmataha County alone, as shown in table 8.1, the Native American population doubled between 1960 and 1980. Southeastern Oklahoma was home to about sixteen thousand Choctaws in 1980, about 10 percent of the region's population.

The Choctaws, although still a socially recognized and legally viable tribal entity, became even more racially diluted than they were at the time of Oklahoma statehood. In 1988, of 41,000 Choctaws holding tribal certificates based on degree of Indian blood (CDIBs), only about 8 percent were full-bloods, and 72 percent were less than one-quarter Indian by blood quantum (*Bishinik,* 1/88, 2/88). Currently the Choctaw tribe – which imposes no restriction on tribal membership other than traceable descent from an enrolled tribal member – numbers more than 98,000 nationwide.[2]

Table 8.2 summarizes the findings of a 1975 census, showing the distribution of full-bloods, mixed-bloods, and non-Indian household members in Indian households, both in the ten and one-half counties of the Choctaw region and more specifically in Pushmataha and McCurtain Counties, which are the central focus for this study. McCurtain County remains the center of the largest concentration of Choctaw full-bloods and was the only Choctaw

2. The Choctaw tribe does not require a specific minimum blood quantum to qualify for tribal membership.

Table 8.2. Choctaw Nation population by blood quantum, 1975

	Ten-county region		McCurtain County		Pushmataha County	
	#	%	#	%	#	%
Full-blood	2,613	15.4	1,415	45.7	183	15.2
¼ to < full	5,112	30.1	786	25.4	404	33.5
< ⅛ to ¼	6,092	35.8	515	16.6	416	34.5
Non-Indians in household	3,169	18.7	380	12.3	203	16.8
Total	16,985	100.0	3,096	100.0	1,206	100.0

Source: Geography Extension Division 1975:2–16; table 6.

Nation county where full-bloods outnumbered non-Indian household members in the 1975 survey.

During the Great Depression and World War II the Choctaw Nation's "socio-economic structure . . . underwent a fundamental change. . . . Land was converted into a commodity and labour into a factor of production," as Barnett (1975:206) showed among the Gaziera. And like the Walpole Island Ottawa reserve described by Hedley (1993:196–200), the era marked the demise of Choctaw household self-sufficiency with further land alienation, wage labor dependence, and state welfare subsidies. The Choctaws increasingly entered the wider cash economy, in Works Projects Administration (WPA) jobs both before and after the war, and in military service. WPA jobs programs continued after World War II and served as common sources of intermittent employment into the 1950s (author's interviews 1980–82; see also Quinton 1967). Although many Choctaws became fully embedded in the wage labor economy, most timber region Choctaws relied on multiple livelihood-maintaining strategies, combining wage labor, petty commodity production, household subsistence, and transfer payments.

Choctaw Nation, 1982. Older Choctaws told how they survived the 1930s and 1940s. Men, and sometimes women, cut and stripped posts and hauled timber from the woods using farm animals before modern mechanized timber-cutting operations made these jobs obsolete. Men worked as casual farm laborers for local white families, while women did washing, ironing, and sewing, paid in groceries or a combination of commodity and cash payments. Some were migrant laborers picking cotton in Texas and other southern states. Other older workers were employed in depression-era WPA projects constructing bridges and roads.

Rural Choctaw farm families supplemented their meager earnings with home-based subsistence activities, a strategy not unique to Choctaws during the era (see Hedley 1993:200–203; Jacobsen 1984; also Meyer 1994). Several were raised on or ran farms that produced nearly all of the household's food supply. Hogs and chickens were slaughtered for home consumption. Fruit trees grew in many yards, and large gardens were maintained. A small number of Choctaw farm families were able to provide for their own subsistence needs on farms averaging about twenty acres in size around 1950 (author's interviews 1980–82; Debo 1951:4–5).

Farming was not an option for the many Choctaw households with access to little or no land. Approximately 20 percent of households surveyed between 1980 and 1982 grew up on church grounds, since their families owned no land. Families undertook subsistence farming when they could, raising chickens and planting small gardens, which they supplemented with casual wage or bartered labor.

Rural farm families weathered periods of extreme need by selling tracts of inherited or allotted land. Land, since allotment's inception in 1902, was bargained in exchange for subsistence commodities when necessary, a practice that saw nearly complete Choctaw land alienation by 1950. Nearly every household surveyed told of kinfolk who had sold land to obtain much-needed cash. During the 1950s and 1960s land was sold for as little as thirty dollars per acre, generally to whites.

The Oklahoma Indian Welfare Act was passed in 1936 to revitalize dying rural Native American economies by providing loans to tribal members to purchase farm equipment and modernize farm operations. These attempts largely failed in the timber region, where money was used instead for day-to-day living expenses. Greater success was achieved among Choctaws living in the valley rangeland, mainly mixed-bloods who invested in improvements for cattle-raising operations (Debo 1951:14–15).

By about 1960 Choctaws controlled only about 144,000 acres of allotted and less than 10,000 acres of collectively held land, holdings so reduced that they could no longer be relied on for traditional subsistence activities. Land alienation had reached a near-desperate state for some Choctaw families. As Angie Debo (1951:4–5) noted, many "live[d] in appalling poverty." Many landless Choctaw families resorted to living in substandard church dwellings used formerly for church gatherings. "Always a religious people, they have collected on their church grounds, using the camp houses that were

Table 8.3. Average landholdings by household type, Choctaw sample

	Younger nuclear	Older nuclear	Extended
# Households surveyed	20	16	14
Average acres/household	5.65	21.55	36.07
Average acres/individual*	1.15	8.21	5.61

*Computations include only permanent residents living in household.

erected in happier days for their weekend or week-long meetings. They live in a close-knit fellowship essentially tribal; and their support also comes from Public Assistance and veteran's benefits" (Debo 1951:8). A Choctaw household survey conducted by the author between 1980 and 1982 found that nearly every Choctaw Nation Indian church ground, some without electricity or running water, was occupied by at least one landless Choctaw family unable to afford to purchase even the single acre needed to qualify for a federally subsidized "mutual-help" Indian home. Of fifty households surveyed, 65 percent owned five acres or less, while only 8 percent owned forty acres or more. Table 8.3 summarizes the results of this land survey, showing landholdings according to household type: younger nuclear, older nuclear, or extended (these terms are defined below).

Southeastern Oklahoma's rural economy since the Depression has been typical of hinterland economic sectors globally and rural America generally: mixed subsistence economies; part-time, intermittent employment opportunities; a preponderance of unskilled, low-paid jobs; and ever-increasing state subsidies through both public-sector employment and various transfer payment programs. Southeastern Oklahoma has experienced a dramatic decline in agricultural and forestry employment, accompanied by notable increases in service and government jobs. Overall employment in both McCurtain and Pushmataha Counties declined by nearly 50 percent from 1940 to 1960, despite a 50 percent increase during the same period in government jobs, a sector that employed far fewer workers than did agriculture (Peach and Poole n.d.). Table 8.4 summarizes employment in selected industries in the two-county timber region from 1940 to 1990.

Southeastern Oklahoma's poverty and unemployment woes persisted throughout the 1960s and 1970s. In 1970 Choctaw unemployment in the ten-county region was more than twice the state average (Choctaw Nation of

Table 8.4. Employment in selected industries, 1940–90[*]

County	Industry	1940	1950	1960	1980	1990
McCurtain	Agriculture, fishing, forestry	5,485	3,337	1,020	430[**]	605
	Services	1,307	1,207	1,077	n/a[***]	1,404
	Government	169	221	257	1,830	n/a
Pushmataha	Agriculture, fishing, forestry	2,383	1,621	469	130[**]	403
	Services	557	518	498	n/a	778
	Government	82	127	130	720	n/a

Sources: Peach and Poole n.d.; Oklahoma Employment Security Commission, 1980, 1989; U.S. Census Bureau, 1990.
[*]Excluding 1970.
[**]Data include only agricultural workers.
[***]Not available.

Oklahoma 1980:50). By the early 1980s this region boasted the state's highest unemployment rate, about 10 percent, while the state's overall jobless rate was 4.8 percent. In Pushmataha County only about 35 percent of Indian males worked full-time (from fifty to fifty-two weeks) in 1969, an unemployment situation the BIA report termed "critical" (U.S. BIA 1973:30). Local minority unemployment in 1981 was the highest statewide, 18.6 percent (Oklahoma IMPACT 1981:31). In 1987 Choctaw sources estimated timber-region Choctaw unemployment at 37 percent (*Bishinik* 5/87:2). A statistical summary of unemployment data between 1970 and 1990 is shown in table 8.5.

In 1990 Native Americans in both McCurtain and Pushmataha Counties continued to show high unemployment rates, with unemployment in Mc-Curtain County at 13.3 percent and in Pushmataha County at 14 percent. White unemployment was at 10.5 and 11 percent respectively in those counties (U.S. Census Bureau 1990).

The extreme Choctaw unemployment problem is not fully apparent in general statistical data, however. As the 1973 BIA report indicated, Choctaws must contend with not only unemployment but also underemployment. In 1969, this report said, less than half of Indian males held full-time jobs, and about 24 percent worked twenty-six weeks or less during the year. Although whites experienced a similar difficulty finding full-time work, their ten-county underemployment rate was less severe, 17.2 percent (U.S. BIA 1973:28–29).

Native Americans in the ten-county area were further disadvantaged since they were overrepresented in laboring and nonskilled service jobs and

Table 8.5. Unemployment data, McCurtain and Pushmataha
Counties, 1970–90

County	Group	1970 rate	1980 rate	1990 rate
McCurtain	Native American	n/a	13.3%	15.6%
	White	n/a	6.9%	8.9%
	Minority	n/a	15.0%	16.6%
	Overall	8.5%	9.0%	10.5%
Pushmataha	Native American	n/a	11.8%	14.0%
	White	n/a	6.3%	6.0%
	Minority	n/a	20.0%	13.0%
	Overall	11.0%	10.9%	6.6%

Sources: Oklahoma Employment Security Commission; U.S. Census Bureau, 1970, 1980, 1990.

underrepresented in managerial jobs (U.S. BIA 1973:33). These employment patterns, as discussed in the following chapters, reflect current employment quandaries experienced by Choctaws throughout the region today.

This tenuous employment situation has fostered welfare dependence in both McCurtain and Pushmataha Counties, since wages often fall below federally established poverty levels. Between 1950 and 1963 public assistance payments in McCurtain County rose by 60 percent and in Pushmataha County by one-third (Peach and Poole n.d.: chart 16). In 1980 nearly half of Pushmataha County's population, 45.4 percent, lived below the poverty level. McCurtain County fared somewhat better, with 37.1 percent below poverty, while the overall state average for the same year was 18.8 percent (Oklahoma IMPACT 1981). Southeastern Oklahoma also claimed the lowest average per capita personal income of any Oklahoma region in 1981, $8,394 (Oklahoma IMPACT 1981:29–39); by comparison, the official poverty level for a family of four in the same year was $9,287 (U.S. Census Bureau 1982).

Contrary to the glaring need, Oklahoma's public assistance programs consistently have neglected the substantial needy populations in Pushmataha and McCurtain Counties. For example, although nearly half of Pushmataha County's residents lived below the official poverty level in 1981, only 10.2 percent received food stamps. Throughout the state similar findings were reported, indicating that only about one-quarter to one-third of those eligible actually received public assistance benefits (Oklahoma IMPACT 1981:29–39). In 1989 slightly more than 20 percent of McCurtain County's population and about 16 percent of Pushmataha County's residents received food stamps, while 7 and 4 percent respectively received Aid to Families with Dependent Children (AFDC) benefits. The state as a whole had a 3.1 percent AFDC caseload that year (Oklahoma Department of Human Services 1989).

CHOCTAW NATION FIELDWORK, 1980–82

Participant observation fieldwork was conducted in the Choctaw Nation's Pushmataha and McCurtain Counties between 1980 and 1982, the "ethnographic present" in the following narratives. Additional visits were made in 1983 and 1993, and telephone contacts have been ongoing with a number of informants. The author lived with her family for two years in Talihina in adjacent Latimer County, on the grounds of the Talihina Indian Hospital, renamed the Choctaw Nation Indian Hospital, where she gave birth to her third son, Benjamin, in 1981. She traveled to various timber region communities several days per week throughout the duration of fieldwork, meeting with Choctaw families and individuals, conducting formal interviews, making impromptu visits, and observing and participating in various activities, including socials, family crises, shopping trips, and gardening. Research also took her to county courthouses, the tribal council complex at Durant, Weyerhaeuser corporate headquarters at Wright City, offices of the Woodworkers Union Local Lodge W15 (formerly IWA) in DeQueen, Arkansas, and research data bases in Oklahoma City, Tulsa, and Norman, Oklahoma.

Initial contacts with Choctaw families were facilitated by a hospital staff member whose extended family has lived in southeastern Oklahoma since the Trail of Tears. Several trips to remote rural Choctaw communities, located fifty to seventy-five miles from Talihina, permitted me to meet more than enough families who agreed to participate in in-depth interview sessions, from whom were chosen the fifty households for the comprehensive study.

Early in the fieldwork phase it was found that many Choctaw families inhabit small residence enclaves shared by closely related kin, many on remnants of former family allotments. These residence enclaves became a basic unit of the current study. Through subsequent visits a sample was selected of households belonging to several residence enclaves located in three distinct named communities dispersed throughout Pushmataha and McCurtain Counties. Interviews were conducted mainly over a period of one year, January through December 1981.

Lengthy interview sessions were scheduled in advance. Impromptu visits were also made to several families whose members became key subjects for this study. Relations were further broadened through hospital channels of communication, not only by informal contacts but also through work as a volunteer counselor for diabetic patients, which I performed for approximately a year. Since many Choctaws are diabetic, including quite a few in the study sample, this provided additional access to subjects as well as direct knowledge of family crises. Several household members became key informants, with whom the author participated in family crises, and through whom was gleaned a sense rural Choctaw life in the 1980s and 1990s.

Semistructured in-depth interviews conducted with fifty rural Choctaw families, using an interview instrument shown in appendix 2, provide the data base for discussions to follow. Open-ended discussions were incorporated into interview sessions to ascertain informants' attitudes toward tribal membership and participation, Weyerhaeuser's local presence, self-identification as Choctaws, participation with other Choctaws in church and tribal institutions, and other areas of interest and concern. Interviews were nearly all conducted in English with English-speaking household members; learning Choctaw would have been extremely time-consuming, and only a small number of Choctaws were monolingual in that language. Three interviews were conducted with the assistance of a bilingual interpreter or English-speaking family members. Each household was paid a small sum through National Science Foundation research grant funds. Payment was a vital component in allowing access to confidential household economic data, a way of reimbursing informants for their time, and a means of compensating families often short of cash and food.

Southeastern Oklahoma and its Choctaw minority are not marginal to global economic forces that swirl around them, and perhaps never were. This rural "frontier," like the Cherokee region discussed by Dunaway (1996), occupies a focal position as a resource enclave in the relationship between core and peripheral global economic sectors. Since allotment the region, although rich in natural resources, has not sustained the local population economically, as outsiders extracted surplus wealth to benefit core sector industries.

Hall (1995:7) argues that "through careful attention to local histories . . . we can . . . develop an understanding of how incorporation into the European world-system reshapes Native American cultures, and conversely how Native American cultures adapt in order to cope with incorporation and maintain their own cultural identities." Choctaws responded to the core/periphery contact relationship both as a rural enclave and an indigenous ethnicity, adapting preindustrial traditions, modifying means and relations of production, and creating new strategies for economic and cultural maintenance. Using Nagel and Snipp's (1993) terminology, the Choctaw cultural survival strategy in the post–World War II era has been for some segments to accommodate and amalgamate into the majority culture while they redefine Choctaw cultural traditions and the role of the Choctaw Nation in their lives. For others, "ethnic reorganization" has meant resistance and retreat into subsistence, petty commodity production, and intermittent wage labor, topics to be discussed more fully in later chapters.

NINE

Rural Choctaw Community Life

Choctaw Nation, 1995. Little more than a decade ago the Choctaw timber region seemed more remote. Many Choctaws were without automobiles and telephones. Roads were generally unpaved, sometimes nearly impassable. Today, rural Choctaw Nation towns such as Bethel, Smithville, and Honobia appear more spiffy: dirt roads have been paved, bridges widened and rebuilt; modern Choctaw community centers stand proudly in every Choctaw county; post offices and gas stations have been modernized.

Let us hear the Choctaws tell their own stories, about land, work, church, kin, subsistence, Choctaw identity, Weyerhaeuser, chicken plants, housing; "making do" in an environment of scarce resources, incipient racism, rural hardships; defining and negotiating the meaning of being Choctaw in late twentieth-century America.

Choctaw Nation communities may be framed as a series of smaller and larger, sometimes overlapping, circles of spatially and ethnically shared space, constituting "different levels of inclusion" (see Blu 1993:281–85), as diagramed in figure 9.1. Kin-based Choctaw residential enclaves, frequently named, are set within larger circles of named villages, towns, and cities inhabited by whites and blacks who share community resources such as schools, government agencies, and retail shops. Choctaw families are focal aspects of Choctaw communities, just as among North Carolina's Lumbees/ Cherokees described by Blu (1993).

Approximately twenty-five named villages, variously referred to as "towns" or "communities," incorporated and unincorporated, dot the Pushmataha and McCurtain County countryside.[1] The town centers are

---

1. Incorporated towns are units recognized by the state of Oklahoma that contain a town structure of government and usually a post office. The unincorporated settlements are often named but are not official towns.

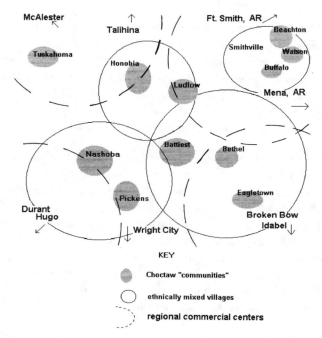

KEY

⬤ Choctaw "communities"

◯ ethnically mixed villages

⌒ regional commercial centers

Figure 9.1. Choctaw residence enclaves, towns, and cities in spatial perspective.

meeting places and centers of activity for all rural citizens. Choctaw children attend district schools with white and black children from their and neighboring villages. The town post office, if one exists, a local grocery store, if available, and gas station are located there and serve as the lifeblood for the rural folk, particularly those without means of transportation to larger regional centers of commerce.

Meetings among townsfolk are permeated with personal familiarity, acknowledging long-standing acquaintances that transcend ethnic boundaries. Longtime residents go daily to town to pick up mail and need no introductions to identify themselves to the postmaster or storekeeper, who knows them by face alone. Choctaws, like rural whites, depend on the external world for subsistence needs, information, and access to the services of the wider society. The town centers long ago ceased to be strictly Choctaw settlements managed by white government officials. They have become the domain of the secular Western society. One must travel to the more hidden Choctaw settlements to find where rural Choctaws live.

Choctaw Nation, 1982. One need not know the exact whereabouts of a particular Choctaw family, regardless of how deeply in the woods they reside. "Just ask at the store; they'll know how to find us," was how Choctaws often gave directions. A shopkeeper, gas station attendant, or neighbor invariably provided adequate directions. The difficult task was traveling over twisting dirt roads, which became more impassable as they wove deeper into the woods, especially during spring rains, when streams overflowed the roadways, making them impassable.

Rural Choctaw settlements, called "communities" both on official maps and unofficially by Choctaws themselves, are occasionally but not always named. An unincorporated settlement, such as Buffalo, Beach, or Spring Hill, may not possess even a post office or store, but its population, often nearly exclusively Choctaw, maintains its own unique cultural flavor. These Choctaw communities are frequently situated close to one of the many Choctaw church grounds located throughout the region and reflect strategies Choctaws have long used to maximize economic opportunities and preserve ethnic and social identities in an environment that contains formidable obstacles to preserving Native American cultural autonomy.

CHOCTAW HOUSEHOLD AND FAMILY: SOME DEFINITIONS

As among other economically marginal population segments, households and extended families are crucial to rural Choctaw economic survival and to capitalist production within which Choctaws are embedded. Randall McGuire and Cynthia Woodsong (1990:168) argue that households must be viewed not simply as units of analysis but as sets of social relations between core and periphery, where power wielding and exploitation take place over ownership and control of productive resources and labor power. Households and families are embedded in specific historical situations and relations of production, and they interact dialectically within an asymmetrical relationship between core and periphery (see Glazer 1990; Collins 1990).

Households and families use a variety of strategies to achieve basic levels of subsistence, successful rearing of children, and access to strategic resources (see Stack 1974). Choctaw production and reproduction strategies are opportunistic and varied, combining traditional subsistence, petty commodity production, and wage labor. Households are mobilized in day-to-day social and economic livelihood-maintaining strategies, while extended family networks operate more intermittently (although at times, daily), de-

1. Choctaw church ground with camp
houses circling main church building,
Bethel, 1981

2. Wheelock Academy, near Wright City,
1993. Wheelock Academy is a Choctaw girls'
boarding school named after the founder of
Dartmouth College, Eleazar Wheelock; it
was founded in 1832 on the grounds of the
Wheelock Church and Seminary.

3. Willie H. Dyer (in black dress) with his
brothers and sisters, photographed in
Eagletown, ca. 1900. Dyer, the father of Etta
Mae James, of Talihina, died in 1976 at age
eighty-five; he, along with his siblings, was
an original Choctaw enrollee. (Photo
courtesy of Etta Mae James)

4. Choctaws congregate beneath brush arbor for noontime meal, reminiscent of traditional tribal gatherings, Tuskahoma, 1981

5. Unimproved church ground home, used for camp meetings and frequently as permanent residences, Honobia, 1981

6. Unimproved residence located adjacent to recent Weyerhaeuser clear-cut (in background) near Honobia, 1981

7. Contemporary mutual-help Indian home in clustered neighborhood, Bethel, 1981

8. Choctaw tribal member Frances Willis works at quilting board, Choctaw Community Center, Bethel, 1993

9. Choctaw dancers perform at Tuskahoma
wearing traditional ribbon shirts and
dresses, 1981

10. Tree planters work in rugged terrain near
Smithville, 1981

11. Weyerhaeuser clear-cut showing logging
roads and uncut acreage in background,
Bethel, 1981

12. David Noah, a member of the last remaining Oklahoma Weyerhaeuser timber-cutting crew, near Wright City, 1993

13. Tribal council member Billy Paul Baker, an employee of Weyerhaeuser Corporation for more than twenty-eight years, Wood-workers Union shop steward, and member of the last remaining Weyerhaeuser timber-cutting crew, with the author, near Wright City, 1993

14. Chief Hollis E. Roberts, at tribal headquarters, Durant, 1993

15. Choctaw Nation Bingo Palace, opened in 1985, Durant, 1993

16. Wilma J. Robinson, director of tribal development, at tribal headquarters, Durant, 1993

pending on a particular family's class membership and adherence to traditional cultural practices.

The term *extended families* refers to the entire network of consanguineal, affinal, and fictive kin (Keesing 1966:271–72), including those members who are geographically dispersed. Following McGuire and Woodsong (1990:170–71), *households* are resource-sharing networks of individuals, frequently related and generally coresident, who labor to meet householders' livelihood maintenance and reproduction needs. Householders perform a variety of productive activities, both waged and unwaged – what McGuire and Woodsong call "householding" – to meet livelihood maintenance needs. Households are constrained in their livelihood-sustaining efforts by larger global market forces, which define the value of waged and unwaged labor and limit household livelihood-deriving opportunities (see Collins 1990; Collins and Gimenez, eds., 1990).

Fifty Choctaw households were surveyed in depth over an eighteen-month period between 1980 and 1982 as part of the current study, using participant observation fieldwork methods along with an oral questionnaire and open-ended interviews. Household selection was developed through personal contact networks, through which initial contacts were made with prospective households. The families interviewed, many related consanguineally or affinally, inhabited several residence enclaves in three Pushmataha and McCurtain County timber region districts, each nearly thirty miles apart. This allowed comparison and contrast of widely separated Choctaw settlements, all located within the two-county timber region dominated today by Weyerhaeuser's presence.

Weyerhaeuser has become a visible part of the local landscape throughout the area of investigation. Families knew of Weyerhaeuser, and most had opinions about its effect on the area. Clear-cuts were often visible along roadsides – some abutting Choctaw homesteads – and Weyerhaeuser trucks were prominent on roadways. Many householders were personally tied to Weyerhaeuser, mainly as seasonal laborers doing tree planting, spraying, or timber cutting. Other householders worked in Weyerhaeuser's full-time paid labor force, both in the field and at mill sites.

Although full-bloods are prominent among timber region families, Choctaws today are fully embedded in white-dominated society after two centuries of contact. Of fifty households surveyed, thirty-six were headed by couples where both spouses were three-quarters or more Indian by blood.

Table 9.1. Ethnic composition of household heads by household
type, Choctaw sample

Family type	¾ to Full blood	<¾ Full blood	White spouse
Older nuclear	11	4	2
Younger nuclear	14	7	2
Extended	11	3	1
Total	36	14	5

Five male household heads were married to white women, and one household included a non-Indian, nonwhite spouse. Table 9.1 summarizes the ethnic composition of the Choctaw sample. Ethnically and culturally, the
households sampled showed features earlier noted as "typically Choctaw,"
including residence and village settlement patterns, church activities, diet,
and a mixed subsistence economy. This region, then, represents the heartland of the traditionally oriented Choctaw community in the late twentieth
century.

Households varied widely in composition, access to resources, and subsistence patterns. Three distinct household types were found, each containing specific constellations of inhabitants and reflecting unique responses to
limited resources, a problem shared by nearly every household. Households
were classified as *nuclear* if they consisted of one independent conjugal unit
that shared income and other resources among all members. Nuclear households were of two types: younger and older. Households where spouses averaged forty-five years of age or younger were classified as *younger nuclear,*
while those above forty-five years were placed in the *older nuclear* category.
This distinction was not arbitrary but reflected two quite different household constellations with different relations to economic resources. Younger
nuclear households were in their prime years of productive life, while older
nuclear households represented the generation of adult retirees. Each population segment was found to operate differently in subsistence strategies.
Divorced, widowed, and separated households were classified as nuclear,
since these households operated economically as nuclear household units
and shared resources similarly. There were three such households in our
sample, two in the younger nuclear and one in the older nuclear category.

Table 9.2. Distribution of household types and family size,
Choctaw sample

Family type	Number	Average household size	Average number of children
Older nuclear	16	2.63 permanent 0.00 temporary	0.69
Younger nuclear	20	4.9 permanent 0.02 temporary	2.95
Extended	14	6.43 permanent 1.7 temporary	3.93

Table 9.2 shows the distribution of the three household types found in the sample investigated, their relative sizes, and the number of children residing in each household. Of the thirty-six households categorized as nuclear households, twenty were younger nuclear, while sixteen were classified as older nuclear. The fourteen remaining households were *extended households,* consisting of two or more conjugal units and several income sources and typically including three generations. A common extended household constellation was one where adult children shared a home with elderly parents, along with spouses and grandchildren.

Younger nuclear households were not especially large, apparently a departure from the previous generation's norm of six or more children. Younger nuclear households contained an average of slightly fewer than three children per household, although there was great variation of household size among households surveyed. Signs of a permanent commitment to the region were noted among younger families. Many were in the process of purchasing a home, participated actively in local church activities, and otherwise nurtured roots in the local community. Fourteen of twenty younger nuclear families occupied mutual-help homes, while four lived in substandard dwellings, with cold running water (if at all) and no indoor plumbing facilities. Younger nuclear household heads were on average older than might have been expected, approximately thirty-five years. Their age reflects the common pattern of returning to their homeland after attempting to establish a life elsewhere.

Older nuclear households, consisting mainly of adult retirees, averaged the smallest of all three household categories and contained the fewest number of children. They frequently included minor children or unmarried adults, especially grandchildren or other kin temporarily left with grandparents while their own parents sought employment elsewhere.

Extended households were larger than either nuclear type, as table 9.2 shows, particularly when temporary residents are included in household totals. Temporary residents often remained for extended stays, particularly young married adults who returned for seasonal work or had exhausted employment opportunities elsewhere. Extended households averaged 8.13 individuals, when both permanent and temporary residents were included.

CHOCTAW SPACE

Choctaw homesteads dot the countryside in two typical residence patterns. Isolated homesteads located on the remnants of former Choctaw allotments continue to be occupied by a small number of original allottees or, more often, their descendants, who inhabit an old home or a more recently constructed mutual-help home. These homesteads may be adjacent to other Choctaw homesteads or to white-owned farms interspersed throughout the region. Often, whites occupy land that was sold twenty or thirty years earlier by a Choctaw neighbor. Choctaw homesteads frequently also border Weyerhaeuser or other privately owned timberland, another reminder of the history of land sales to whites Choctaws unwittingly undertook to meet subsistence needs.

A second residence pattern is more recent. This is the clustering of recently built homes located on adjoining one- or two-acre parcels. Home clustering has become common since 1969, when a federally subsidized home construction program was introduced through the Department of Housing and Urban Development (HUD). So-called mutual-help homes or "Indian homes" are available to Native American families who qualify under strict eligibility requirements, including that the family must own at least one acre of suitable land, meet income guidelines, and show proof of Indian descent. Families must also assist in home construction, for example, by unloading construction materials, landscaping, or cleaning up after construction crews. Currently more than twenty-five hundred mutual-help homes have been built in the Choctaw Nation (*Bishinik* 3/88:1).

Residence clustering is a by-product of land division (or in many cases, subdivision). Small parcels are typically deeded to each child around the time of marriage to provide the young adult generation with homesteads.

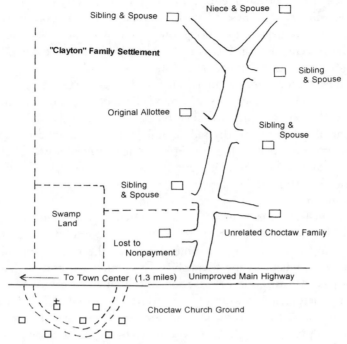

Figure 9.2. Residence subdivision, Evergreen Community: Typical mutual-help home subdivision of a twenty-acre parcel*. Note proximity to Choctaw church ground and town center.

A twenty-acre parcel, which in many households is all that remains of the parents' family inheritance, is typically subdivided among six or eight offspring. Figure 9.2 diagrams a typical residence subdivision, called Evergreen Community.[2]

Mutual-help homes constructed in clustered neighborhoods are generally occupied by genealogically related kin, often siblings, with an occasional unrelated family inhabiting one house. Houses are built in close proximity, linked by a network of dirt roadways. Homes in a particular settlement are typically built the same year in a similar style. A mutual-help home's age can often be detected by materials used or the style or color of

2. The names of particular settlements and families have been changed to protect their anonymity. Events described are representative of the timber region.

the brick facing, although efforts are being made to vary external facades. Occasionally an old homestead will remain standing next door, or the dilapidated structure may be torn down once the new home is occupied. If an older home remains intact, it is quickly occupied by family members, since young families face a serious housing shortage.

Clustered and more isolated homesteads are situated near Choctaw church grounds, to which most nearby residents belong. Choctaw churches represent the physical and social focal points of rural Choctaw life. Churches are generally the only nearby public buildings, since town centers shared with whites are usually at least a couple of miles away. Many families maintain close and continuous daily contact through church, tribal, and secular activities, and through kin networks.

Evergreen Community is a typical Choctaw settlement. This community's main feature is a rural Choctaw church ground that serves ten to twelve Choctaw families living within a mile or so of the church, as well as a small number of additional families linked to the nucleus of members through kin affiliations and friendship. This church community has had a stormy past. The tiny one- or two-room outbuildings surrounding the main church structure served as homes to several Choctaw families during the 1930s and 1940s. In the early 1980s the buildings were in extremely dilapidated condition, although one was occupied by a young nuclear family desperate for a place to live.

The church community was temporarily abandoned during the 1950s and 1960s as children of member families left the area to find employment or housing elsewhere and the few remaining elderly members lost interest. In about 1980 interest in the church rekindled, when several younger families built mutual-help homes near the church ground and formed the nucleus of a revitalized church community. The church's current permanent membership numbers ten or more families, most residing in newly constructed homes nearby. The resurgence of this church community and the nearby Choctaw neighborhood was a direct result of local mutual-help home construction, which brought younger Choctaw families back to Evergreen Community to reestablish an enlarged Choctaw settlement.

Several mutual-help homes in the Evergreen settlement were built on a single parcel adjacent to the church owned by the Clayton family, in a pattern typical of local land-use practices. On this family's twenty-acre parcel, part of the father's original allotment, was the homestead where the eight

Clayton children were raised. The senior Clayton served as an Evergreen Church elder for many years during its earlier existence. Before his death in the late 1970s, he subdivided his land, giving each child a tract of one or two acres, anticipating their subsequent housing needs.

Several children left the community during the 1960s to find work or attend college after completing high school locally. Slowly family members returned to Evergreen from Dallas, Tulsa, or elsewhere in the Southwest. Some brought young families with them, hoping to reestablish roots in their native community. A couple of the children had successful careers as skilled laborers, although others told of hardships they endured: difficulty finding employment, job-related illnesses, and discrimination in jobs and housing.

As the children returned, they claimed their small land parcels, and those who qualified built mutual-help homes. Land parcels were also sold by the elder Clayton to two landless Choctaw families. This practice of selling land to an unrelated needy family at a nominal fee, usually fifty dollars for an acre, is not uncommon and represents both the giver's personal generosity and the core tradition of mutual reciprocity.

The Clayton family settlement is today a permanent residential community containing eight mutual-help homes situated in a wooded setting linked by a short unpaved roadway. Four homes are occupied by siblings, who were among the original land inheritance beneficiaries. A fifth home is occupied by their elderly widowed mother, and a sixth is occupied by an unrelated family who purchased an acre under the arrangement alluded to above. Another mutual-help home was lost to foreclosure by another sibling, who could not pay the mortgage. The home was temporarily rented to a white family. The tribe ostensibly purchased the property after foreclosure, although the house stands empty and family members were unclear as to its ownership status or what would become of it. The original owner moved to Broken Bow, about thirty miles away, and paid in rent about three times what he would have paid had he been able to meet his mortgage payments. Another house constructed on the property was later sold by its original owner (another sibling) to a niece, when he, too, could not maintain payments and left the area to find work.

A couple of heirs never build on their parcels. One parcel located on marshlands was unsuitable for home construction, a potential liability when subdividing the hilly and irregular local terrain. Unless the subdivision is carefully planned, individuals may end up with property unsuited for home construction. In fact, the housing authority that supervises the mutual-help housing project routinely rejects potential homesites, thereby leaving the family with a piece of worthless land.

Another obstacle to satisfactory permanent residence is the pervasive employment problem. As noted previously, two siblings were forced to leave the area, and one even lost his home to foreclosure, owing to a lack of sustainable family income. This region, where tree planting and harvesting or work in local chicken-processing plants are principal employment sources, offers few permanent job opportunities, a quandary discussed in detail in a later chapter.

Today families occupying the Clayton settlement include at least twenty-five grandchildren and several great-grandchildren, who will soon face the predicament of searching for a place to live and raise a family. Obviously, the original family tract has reached its carrying capacity and will not sustain all who may wish to settle there. This problem of an ever-diminishing land base is common, although little is said among a folk who have continually devised new strategies to cope with conditions of adversity.

CHOCTAW HOUSING

Living conditions among the fifty households varied widely, from a small run-down shack with a wood stove, cold water, and outhouse to a modern three-bedroom centrally heated mutual-help home with contemporary furnishings. By far, most families tended toward modest furnishings, although the majority did occupy mutual-help homes constructed within the past fifteen years. Homes were typically furnished with the bare necessities. Furniture was old and often in disrepair, made more presentable with a throw cover. Living rooms doubled as sleeping quarters where two large couches (often the only pieces of furniture) served as beds. Decorations typically included family photographs prominently displayed on a living room wall and sports trophies won by teenagers and young adults in various tribal and school athletic leagues. Much pride was shown in sports accomplishments, which represent a popular tribal social activity and a common mechanism for Choctaw children and young adults to participate in regional competitive sports.

Characteristics of the fifty housing units are summarized in table 9.3. Thirty were mutual-help homes, one was a home constructed through Fed-

Table 9.3. Characteristics of housing, Choctaw sample

Characteristics	# Homes	%
House and furnishings modern, in good repair	18	36
House and furnishings modest, in disrepair	32	64
Overcrowded living conditions	12	24
House and furnishings dilapidated	19	38
House lacks indoor plumbing, bathroom (absent or in disrepair)	13	26
House lacks electricity	3	6

eral Housing Authority (FHA) financing, two were trailers, and the remaining seventeen were substandard older homes lacking at least some modern conveniences, with many in disrepair. Five families lived on church or other public grounds in severely dilapidated housing. At least a couple of the mutual-help homes constructed within the past fifteen years had fallen into disrepair and were without indoor plumbing, running water, or both.

Of houses surveyed, eighteen were furnished with new furnishings in a modern style. Approximately two-thirds had living room rugs and three homes had upright pianos. Many "lavishly furnished" homes, however, were heated with wood to reduce fuel costs. Nearly all families cut at least some of their own wood and most cut their entire supply. Thirty-seven families heated their homes predominantly with wood because they could not afford to pay for butane. Three homes were entirely without electricity, one having been shut off for several months for nonpayment, while two had never been electrically wired.

The more than twenty-five hundred mutual-help homes built locally since 1969 have brought much needed housing to Choctaw families, particularly younger nuclear families. Thirty households lived in homes constructed through the mutual-help program. Three more families moved into mutual-help homes by 1985. Without this source of housing assistance, which was seriously curtailed by the Reagan administration, many Choctaw families have little prospect of affording their own homes.

Table 9.4 summarizes household appliances found in the fifty households surveyed. The most common durable items, aside from refrigerators, were washing machines and deep freezers. Freezers were not luxury items, but essential to take advantage of seasonally available foodstuffs, particularly wild foods gathered, products of hunting or fishing, and commodities purchased

Table 9.4. Distribution of household appliances, Choctaw sample

Appliance	# Dwellings	% Households
Washer–Wringer	10	20
Washer–Electric	27	54
Dryer	12	24
Freezer	19	38
Telephone	21	42
Refrigerator	47	94
Television	46	92

in quantity or on sale. Telephones, found in only twenty-one households, were a luxury many households simply could not afford. Television sets, however, were seen as indispensable, although reception in the rural hill country is poor and limited to two or three stations. Like rural folk throughout peripheral regions nationally and even globally, television is both a link with the outside world and an important source of cheap entertainment.

A SCARCE COMMODITY: CHOCTAW LAND
An adequate livelihood in the timber region continues to be elusive for many Choctaws because the essential elements – jobs and land – remain in short supply. Land is an essential resource for rural Choctaws, not only as a housing site, but also as a source of foodstuffs and fuel and as a focus of family and tribal continuity. Choctaws today continue to be beset with a severe land shortage and an inability to productively use the land they do own, both tribally and individually. Tribal members currently hold only about 160,000 acres individually, with about 40,000 acres held in trust (*Bishinik* 1/88:1).

   Land is inherited bilaterally and usually apportioned equally to all offspring. The older generation typically inherited land from both mother and father, although some land remains undivided. One's inheritance, then, may be merely a share of an undivided estate, which often means that its disposition is uncertain and the land cannot be used by one's descendants. Land is occasionally given to offspring as needed in small one- or two-acre parcels, rather than undertaking a complete subdivision. This permits the family to qualify for a mutual-help home while preserving the rest of the estate intact.

   Certain population segments, particularly younger nuclear families, are

Table 9.5. Acreage size by household type, Choctaw sample

# Acres	Younger nuclear	Older nuclear	Extended	Total
0–5	18	7	7	32
6–20	1	4	3	8
21–40	0	4	2	6
41–100	1	0	0	1
101–200	0	1	2	3

experiencing an acute land shortage, and their children will be truly landless in the next generation as a result of land subdivision. Whereas the last generation was a beneficiary to as many as twenty acres, the current generation, as noted, typically receives only one acre of land for home construction. Land was a scarce commodity among all households surveyed, as tables 8.3 and 9.5 and figure 9.3 show. Among the fifty households, six owned no land at all, while twenty-two owned only one acre. Sixty-five percent of younger nuclear, 25 percent of older nuclear, and 35.7 percent of the extended households surveyed owned only one acre or less.

Younger nuclear households today are recipients of extremely small parcels, often simply 1 or 2 acres. The twenty younger nuclear households sampled together owned only 113 acres. One household owned 79 acres, while the remaining nineteen households together owned only 34 acres. Extended households were found to be little better off than were nuclear households, as table 9.4 shows.

A small number of households in our survey have held onto between 120 and 200 acres, some purchased by retirees returning from Texas or other states. One family acquired through purchase and inheritance about 80 acres. They have, however, had to collect disability payments owing to serious health problems that make the husband unable to work, while the wife works seasonally as a tree planter to supplement their meager unearned income.

The greatest reservoir of land remains with older nuclear and extended households who have managed to retain undivided land. Older nuclear households averaged about 21.5 acres per household, while extended households owned an average of 36 acres. Two or three households retained surplus allotted land located in western counties of the Choctaw or Chickasaw Nations, which they lease to ranchers, cattlemen, or oil exploration companies. None received more than five hundred dollars per year in revenues,

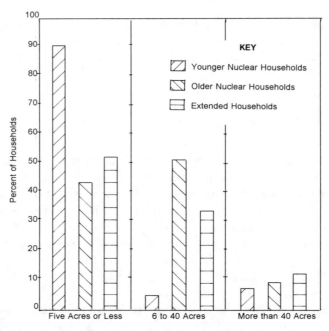

Figure 9.3. Distribution of land by household type, Choctaw sample.

and the land is frequently more a liability than an asset, since the asset may make the household ineligible for full public assistance benefits, a problem not unique to Choctaws (see Moore 1993a:265).

One elderly widow received only about $120 per month from public assistance because she owned about 160 acres, including a large tract in a western county leased for a negligible amount. The family retains the land more as a symbolic gesture than for profit. None of the household members desires to relocate there, and many have not even seen it. As one individual explained, showing receipts for money received from an oil lease on his mother's land, including monthly checks for $1.67 and $3.65: "We don't benefit from owning this land. Exxon and Standard Oil, they benefit, but not us. This land just keeps her from receiving her welfare payments 'cause she owns this land. They think she's rich, and we don't even know where this land is out there in Garvin County somewhere" (author's interview 5/12/1981).

To obtain land for home construction, landless families must either purchase land directly from a local landowner, usually white, or obtain it from a benevolent Choctaw neighbor or kinsman. To purchase land privately is far more costly and represents one way Choctaws are exploited by the white community. Local white landowners may sell one or two acres to a desperate Choctaw family for as much as one thousand dollars per acre. The seller, often a prominent local citizen, may also serve as a casual moneylender to Choctaw families. Choctaws desperate to improve their housing situations are driven to these land transactions.

THE TANGLED WEB OF LAND INHERITANCE

Many larger tracts remain entangled in multiple ownership status, where several or even dozens of heirs may jointly own a tract ranging in size from as little as 20 acres to an entire undivided homestead of 160 acres. Typically an elderly Choctaw owns the tract jointly with several siblings, one of whom may reside on the property in the old homestead or in a newly constructed mutual-help home. Heirs frequently want to subdivide an estate to provide land for their children so they can meet mutual-help home eligibility requirements. Heirs for and against subdivision frequently disagree on a course of action. The argument against subdivision is that once land is subdivided it will be broken into tracts too small to be useful to anyone. As in earlier days, few heirs can afford to buy out fellow shareholders, and the only recourse is to sell the entire estate to outsiders, usually whites.

The BIA rules governing Indian land further complicate land inheritance and promote land alienation. Since all heirs must be consulted in a land division, tracts often remain in limbo if not all claimants can be located. In one instance an old homestead stood empty for several years because four stepchildren of one heir could not be located to endorse a course for disposing of the property. The house cannot be sold, occupied by any of the claimants, or even leased to another family, although the area's housing shortage is acute.

Current land laws, rooted in allotment-era mixed-blood/full-blood designations, also allow that a mixed-blood shareholder less than one-half Indian may force the sale of the entire estate, even if some of the owners are full-bloods. This may occur when joint heirs cannot agree on a fair and equal land distribution. The mixed-blood heir may simply force a land sale to obtain his or her share. County court judges, when faced with the problem of dividing an estate among multiple heirs, often choose simply to sell the entire estate and subdivide the proceeds rather than trouble themselves with dividing the land into equal parcels.

Land litigation and subdivision, as in earlier decades, has continued to promote exploitation and expropriation by whites familiar with legal aspects of landownership. Many Choctaws are unfamiliar with the legal intricacies of landownership and unable to afford costly legal advice or assistance in litigation when it becomes necessary. Whites, including corporate landowners, have taken advantage of legal ambiguities and Choctaw inexperience to obtain privately owned Choctaw land. Chapter 7 examined unscrupulous practices used by Dierks in the early twentieth century to amass its substantial local land base, including buying up entire Choctaw estates once they became alienable under congressional enactments. Dierks also bought up countless partial interests in Choctaw estates between about 1906 and 1969 to enable it to purchase remaining interests under court-approved land sales.

Whites, including Dierks and more recently Weyerhaeuser, have also undertaken the common practice of paying delinquent taxes on Choctaw-owned property over several years, intending to purchase the tract at delinquent-tax land sales, a practice Dierks used to amass land between 1920 and 1969 (see bills of sale copies, Nelson Collection, box 1, no. 8, file 5; Phillips 1982; deeds and land records, McCurtain and Pushmataha County Courthouses). Often the landowner is unaware that taxes are even owed on the property. Numerous instances were recorded where Choctaw landowners learned only much later that their land had been sold, when statutes of limitation had expired, and had no recourse to recover the property. Corporate landowners have in this way used the landownership system to benefit themselves and to amass the vast land estates they currently hold.

One McCurtain County Choctaw family's plight reveals how Choctaws, when faced with formidable corporate interests, fail to be protected by either landownership laws or the BIA, which is charged with protecting full-blood interests. The Deacon family occupied a 120-acre tract in 1981 in the heart of McCurtain County Weyerhaeuser timberland, inherited by five now-elderly full-blood siblings from their father, an original allottee who died in the 1920s. A dispute originated many years ago when one heir ostensibly sold his share to Dierks, a transaction actually illegal under Five Tribes law and later nullified in a county court transaction.

The homestead was temporarily abandoned when several siblings joined the armed forces during World War II. Dierks then began to pay taxes on the property, unbeknownst to the rightful owners, who in fact as full-blood heirs were exempt from tax liability. Dierks eventually applied to the county court to purchase the land, calling the land tax-delinquent property.

The family later appealed to the BIA and tribal officials for assistance in regaining their land, once they learned of the title dispute. Several years had passed since the Dierks land sale, and the statute of limitations on their claim had run out. The family was told by the BIA in the late 1970s that what was now Weyerhaeuser's claim (Dierks sold out to Weyerhaeuser in 1969) was valid and that nothing could be done to reverse it. Chief Hollis Roberts advised that the tribe could not afford costly litigation to defend them, which might take years to resolve.

The Choctaw claimant was further discouraged when Weyerhaeuser corporate representatives informed him that they intended to fight the case diligently, reminding him that he could lose everything if they were to win the suit in court. The family, on the advice of the chief, agreed in the early 1980s to settle out of court, giving up all but a 40-acre tract and allowing Weyerhaeuser clear-cutting rights on the entire 120 acres. As Mr. Deacon said, "Timber will grow back. I'd rather have the land to live on" (author's interview 6/17/81).

Land disputes have not occurred solely with large corporate landowners. Informants also reported cases of outright fraud in land transactions with whites. Several members of one large family described how they had been defrauded of nearly twenty acres when an elderly parent prior to his death in the early 1970s deeded one acre to an intermarried white man for a nominal sum so the landless family could have a piece of land. A bill of sale was signed and notarized by a local attorney. At some point during the transaction, the deed was altered to twenty acres instead of the single acre actually sold. The family was unable to regain title to the disputed land because the individual to whom the land was sold refused to cooperate. The family could not afford to pay for an attorney to assist them and were unable resolve the problem (author's interview 4/30, 5/14/81). To add to the insult, the families continue to live as neighbors, a permanent reminder of the humiliations and corruptions Choctaws historically faced.

White families have also expropriated Choctaw land or made Choctaw estates inaccessible by altering fences or constructing roadways over Choctaw homesteads, then claiming to own the property. The rightful Choctaw owners, unable to afford costly litigation to challenge the claim, may be forced to sell or subdivide the land. One family said that they had sold their 160-acre homestead just three years earlier when pressured by a white neighbor over disputed tax payments and road easements. The white neighbor had in fact fenced across the only access road to an uninhabited Choctaw homestead. None of the family members could afford to buy out fellow heirs and thus were forced to sell the entire estate and subdivide the proceeds (author's interview 6/4/81). Whites, aware that Choctaws may be unfamiliar with land-ownership laws and unable to afford attorney's fees, freely exploit them when they think they can get away with it.

Tribal representatives, BIA employees, and individual tribal members complained that BIA officials at the area office in Muskogee were "not doing the job that they're supposed to do" to protect individual Choctaw or tribal interests, a charge common in tribal-BIA relations nationwide (see Champagne 1983). Individuals, such as in the Weyerhaeuser land claim discussed above, have sought BIA legal assistance, only to be rebuffed. BIA attorneys were widely viewed as unwilling to assist tribal members with landowner-ship problems and inclined to discourage tribal landowners from pressing lawsuits.

Weyerhaeuser was working to clear ownership on approximately fifteen Choctaw-owned parcels in McCurtain, Pushmataha, and LeFlore Counties in the early 1980s. Several were jointly held by twenty or more heirs, all of whom would face a reduced inheritance or become entirely landless if Weyerhaeuser's claims prevailed. This rigid adherence to land acquisition policies regardless of human cost brought to Weyerhaeuser and its predecessor Dierks its massive Choctaw Nation land estate. Weyerhaeuser's land acquisition practices, although not always illegal, are blatantly unethical when the results are calculated in terms of human suffering. Weyerhaeuser's and Dierks' land acquisition practices are typical of multinational corporate single-minded profit-making strategies. The local population is unable in most instances to provide monetary resources and expertise to protect itself from land or resource taking.

Rural Choctaws in the twentieth century became marginalized and periph-eralized as a rural ethnic minority, depleted of tribal and individual land re-sources, and subject to exploitation as a cheap, unskilled labor force. Timber region Choctaw families accommodated to the legacy of early twentieth-century land grabbing by adapting families and households to maximize livelihood-maintaining opportunities in a resource-scarce environment.

Choctaws, particularly younger families, continue to face a severe land shortage, which has been alleviated in part by generations of land subdivision and the mutual-help housing program. Choctaw families reduce costs to maintain and reproduce themselves by reducing housing costs however possible, including heating with firewood, contending with substandard accommodations, and tapping public-sector subsidy programs such as federal and tribally sponsored mutual-help housing. Cheap and inferior housing is one way that workers under capitalism subsidize their own maintenance and reproduction while reducing corporate-sector labor costs. Corporations can pay lower wages to workers who accept inferior or substandard housing or depend on public-sector inputs to subsidize housing costs.

As the Choctaw subsistence economy was incorporated as a peripheral segment of the U.S. economy since the turn of the twentieth century, Choctaws have adapted preindustrial subsistence strategies rooted in kin-based reciprocity networks, petty commodity production, and wage labor. Choctaw subsistence strategies are explored in the following chapter to reveal how the community has adapted its prior mode of production to new capitalist relations of production, thereby increasing household labor value. That chapter examines conditions that have made it difficult for Choctaw households to make ends meet in an environment of apparent abundance.

TEN

Maintaining and Reproducing
Choctaw Households, 1:
"Just Making Do"

Timber region Choctaws face formidable obstacles to earning a decent living, since the region offers few full-time job opportunities. Choctaws are further limited economically by their diminished land base, which provided a means of subsistence in earlier generations. Choctaws have devised various household, family, and community-level strategies to meet their livelihood needs. They maximize economic opportunities by taking advantage of available wage labor, efficiently distributing land resources, and tapping non-wage sources of cash and commodity income when available. Choctaw women and men both play focal, and sometimes complementary, roles in devising strategies to broaden household resources, relying on both wage labor and informal household economic activities. Choctaw household economies reveal that despite incorporation into the wider wage labor economy, Choctaws have retained preindustrial production, distribution, and consumption strategies to maximize livelihood-sustaining options. Women are crucial economic contributors to household maintenance, both as wage workers and in informal economic activity, thereby contributing to Choctaw household reproduction within the world system (see Ward, ed., 1990:5–7; Ward 1993; Collins and Gimenez, eds., 1990; Collins 1990; Gimenez 1990; McGuire and Woodsong 1990; Glazer 1990).

Within larger and smaller circles of interaction, modeled in figure 9.1, Choctaws have learned to negotiate opportunities and minimize costs in their livelihood-gaining strategies. Choctaw interaction webs are subsumed within kin, town, and urban interaction spheres, each providing Choctaws with essential resources.

THE CHOCTAW SUBSISTENCE CYCLE
Choctaw households – nuclear or extended – constitute basic economic units of production, distribution, and consumption. Households vary in

composition, as noted in chapter 9, with members largely related biologically or through marriage. Resources are generally pooled within households and redistributed as needed, although where two or more conjugal units share a household, incomes may be managed separately.

Choctaw wage labor and domestic subsistence activities take on a cyclical rhythm in many households. Various activities are undertaken to maximize seasonal job opportunities, seasonally available produce, and winter months of indoor activity. Mid-January through May is the season of tree planting, when many households contribute young workers to plant trees for Weyerhaeuser contractors. Households fill with visiting kin who return to work at temporarily available jobs. Tree-cutting activities are also in full swing, after a wintertime slowdown.

Spring comes early to the Choctaw timber region, and by February the gathering of pokeweed (*Phytolacca americana*) begins. Households also look for wild onions during the spring months. Fishing is a popular activity in the early spring, along with small game hunting, especially squirrel. Gardening also begins at this time, with an early crop of mustard greens and beans. Many households gather wild fruits in large quantities throughout the late spring and into the summer. These include blackberries, muscadine, huckleberries, and strawberries. Peaches are often purchased by the bushel from vendors and canned for later use. Fruits, generally made into jams and jellies, are consumed by the household or shared at church suppers.

Potatoes, peas, beans, cucumbers, tomatoes, turnips, and onions fill large gardens planted by a small number of Choctaw households. Enterprising households plant sufficient quantities to last until Christmas or even until the following spring, although these households are rare, constituting about 20 percent of those surveyed. Throughout the summer, fishing and hunting of small game continue, although catches are light as the heat (often breaking one hundred degrees in July and August and even into early September) takes its toll on enthusiasm.

Summer is also when families cut timber for winter needs. Weyerhaeuser allows limited timber cutting by Choctaws on its land and issues permits to local families, many of whom take advantage of the opportunity. Weyerhaeuser generally tags trees that can be cut, although some complained that pine was unsuitable for their wood stoves. The tribe also permits Choctaw families to cut up to five cords of wood on tribal land, through a similar permit system.

Once autumn comes, and with it a break in the heat, second crops of mustard and turnip greens are planted, which are harvested until the winter frost kills them. Late November is an important season for many Choctaw households. Thanksgiving week is deer hunting season, and schools close for the week while entire families take to the woods to camp, hunt deer, and socialize. A deer kill brings a substantial amount of fresh meat, and all households are eager to take a deer during the short season. Wild turkeys are also hunted during the winter, although the expense of obtaining a hunting license precludes some households. A couple of families admitted that they hunt illegally regardless of the season to supplement their food supply. Some younger Choctaws expressed a strong urge to hunt and fish and pleasure at being able to provide for themselves in this way.

Winter months are taken up with indoor crafts in many households, particularly by women. Quilt making is especially common, and many living rooms are taken over with a large quilt frame. Quilts are made for home use, given to close kin, and sometimes sold. Church and tribal community center quilting parties are common winter pastimes, and women gather weekly to make quilts to be sold by the church. Quilt making is a craft most Choctaws identify as their own, and they take pride in producing an attractive product. Households produce an average of two or three quilts per year. Most who engaged in quilt making undertook it both as a necessity and for the pleasure of producing an attractive quilt top.

Sewing is also done by many women to reduce the cost of store-bought clothing for family members. Clothing is generally made for girls and women of the household, and occasionally for grandchildren. A couple of the older women also continued an earlier practice of sewing dresses, skirts, and blouses for local white women, for which they were paid at piecework rates.

A few native crafts are also produced. Some Choctaws weave reed baskets, and the sewing of Choctaw-style dresses and shirts is becoming more popular. A couple of households engaged in beadwork, a popular Choctaw craft today. One informant told how beadwork was revived in the late 1970s by a group called the Choctaw Nation Homemakers Association when a woman taught several members how to do beadwork. Some of the ladies have their own beadwork patterns by which they have become known. Choctaw native dresses and ribbon shirts have been popularized mainly through contact with Mississippi Choctaws at annual festivals linking the two regions.[1] Choctaw dresses and shirts are elaborately decorated with bold patterns in contrasting colors and are commonly worn at the annual Choctaw tribal festival held over Labor Day weekend at Tuskahoma, the tribal capital, and at other tribal festivals throughout the year. One individual has begun to sew Choctaw dresses and shirts for retail sale, hoping to revive the style for her kinsmen and women.

Basket making, too, is being revived as a traditional Choctaw craft. A couple of local colleges offer courses in traditional basketry and two local Choctaw craft centers actively produced Choctaw basketry in traditional styles. Silver work, although not an indigenous craft, is also locally produced. Silver work became popular as a result of a tribal initiative to train several Choctaws in silversmithing. One silversmith still practices locally, although the high cost of silver has reduced the amount of silver work currently being produced. Choctaws voiced strong enthusiasm for continuing to revive their traditional arts and crafts, and many were eager to learn basketry or beadwork, thereby reviving links to their indigenous past.

GENDER AND COMMODITY PRODUCTION

Choctaw women, like women workers in other peripheral sectors globally, use diverse resource-deriving strategies, combining unwaged household work with formal economic participation to maximize their household's economic opportunities. Women opportunistically enter paid and unwaged labor sectors, using a variety of skills and exploring multiple resource-deriving niches, to supplement their own and other householders' wages. Women's work, both waged and unwaged, is a crucial component of the global marketplace, contributing to the maintenance and reproduction of peripheral households like those in the rural Choctaw Nation. Women's skills, time, and energy are tapped in so-called second- or third-shift unwaged work performed in addition to wage labor and housework. Ward (1993:53) notes that "women's total contributions to the household through their informal and formal sector activities and housework provide *most* of the subsistence for many households" (emphasis in source; see also Ward,

---

1. This segment of the Choctaw tribe is descended from indigenous Choctaws who remained in Mississippi and selected allotments at the time of removal. The two tribal groups acknowledge kinship and cultural links and maintain active, ongoing social ties (see McKee and Schlenker 1980).

ed., 1990:5–7; Ward 1993:52–57; Collins and Gimenez, eds., 1990; Collins 1990; Gimenez 1990; McGuire and Woodsong 1990; Glazer 1990).

Household resource-deriving work is reminiscent of indigenous preindustrial home work; and Choctaw women are purveyors and conservators of indigenous Choctaw traditions, instrumental in reviving indigenous technologies and introducing exogenous traditions, such as basketry, the making of ribbon shirts, beadwork, and quilt making (see Ward 1990:15). A brief look at typical households from each Choctaw segment will show just how Choctaw families tap available resources to meet their members' livelihood needs.

THE RAYMONDS AND JEFFERSONS: YOUNGER NUCLEAR HOUSEHOLDS

The Raymond family inhabits a well-furnished fifteen-year-old three-bedroom mutual-help home. The household includes Jerry and Minnie Raymond and their three children, ranging in age from six to fourteen years. Jerry Raymond works as a log cutter, part of a local contracting crew. He has worked about three days per week with occasional layoffs of two or more weeks since the housing slump reduced Weyerhaeuser's demand for timber in the late 1970s. Before that he averaged about four days per week with annual layoffs of three to six weeks. In 1981 he earned slightly less than six thousand dollars after job-related deductions amounting to more than one thousand dollars, including costs to maintain his equipment and purchase a new chain saw, which for him is an almost yearly expense. Jerry Raymond's wife, Minnie, is not employed outside the home. She cares for their three children and spends much time devising ways to economize on clothing, food, or other household necessities. She sews all her own and her daughter's clothes. Assisted by her husband and children, she also does extensive gardening, canning, and freezing and raises poultry for home consumption. She proudly noted that generally at year's end there is still food remaining in the freezer from the previous year's garden produce. The members of this household also cut their own wood for home heating.

The Jeffersons, another younger nuclear household, also rely on the timber business for their livelihood. Like Jerry Raymond, Virgil Jefferson cuts timber part-time for the same contractor that employs Raymond. This household includes a teenage son and a young nephew who lives permanently with the Jeffersons. Virgil's income of about $125 per week is supplemented by his wife's wages as a teacher's aide at the local elementary school. She earns slightly more than $100 per week. Together the household earned about $12,000 in 1981, considered a moderately comfortable income.

The Jeffersons own a freezer for storing garden produce, although their returns are not so great as the Raymonds. They also cut their own firewood on Weyerhaeuser-owned land, allowing them to heat their home for nothing during the winter months. Neither the Jeffersons nor the Raymonds receive public assistance benefits of any kind, except for the Women, Infants and Children (WIC) program for their preschool children. Each household pays a mutual-help housing payment of approximately twenty-one dollars per month. Each also makes payments of about three hundred dollars per month for automobile loans, household furniture payments, and other miscellaneous loans.

The Jeffersons and Raymonds were all born and raised in the timber region, all but one to large Choctaw families. While the Jeffersons have both graduated from high school, the Raymonds each completed only about seven years of formal schooling. The Raymonds shortly after marrying moved to Texas seeking work, but returned as their children grew older so they could take advantage of the housing program and raise their children among kin. Neither household currently expects to leave the region, although all are somewhat dissatisfied with job opportunities available locally. They do not foresee many opportunities for their children as they complete high school and begin to look for work. Since each household owns only one acre of land, neither knows how their children will meet future housing needs.

LIVING ON CHURCH GROUNDS: AN ANCIENT STRATEGY

Marie and David Cotter, another younger nuclear family, have lived in an unimproved church dwelling for the past five years, since David began collecting disability benefits because of high blood pressure and other ailments. They are both in their early thirties and have two children, one living at home and the other permanently residing with grandparents. The Cotters receive about four hundred dollars per month from disability and food stamp benefits, their only income. Their house lacks running water and electricity, so they cook with a wood stove. They owe about one hundred dollars to the utility company that shut off their electrical service five months previously. They spend much time with relatives living within a mile or two, who often share garden produce and rides to the store. Most of their food shopping is done at the local grocery, where they have credit amounting to at least three hundred dollars per month.

Both David and Marie have tried various jobs, including chicken processing and odd jobs working for white landowners. David likes to work with his father at odd jobs for whites, although his health has kept him from working steadily. The family cannot afford car repairs, so they have no transportation to travel to the chicken plants or elsewhere. They would very much like to own a mutual-help home, although they have no land and cannot obtain any from relatives, since none have any to give. Their only prospect is to buy land from a local landowner who wants one thousand dollars per acre. This is far too expensive, so they expect that they will continue to make do as they are.

The Cotters were both raised in traditional Choctaw homes; both sets of parents still occupy homes lacking indoor plumbing and running water. Both grew up "making do" in the old way, living where they could find a roof over their heads, cooking with a wood stove (as both sets of parents still do), attending school infrequently because their labor was needed at home or transportation was unavailable, and relying on casual labor and work for white families when cash was needed. This young couple relies heavily on extended kin for information, commodities, and daily support. Neither wants to leave their homeland, since kin ties are crucial, even more important than finding satisfactory jobs or a more comfortable place to live. They both feel that they are getting by as best they can and don't think that their lives will change much in the foreseeable future.

AN OLDER NUCLEAR HOUSEHOLD: THE ELDER JEFFERSONS

Virgil Jefferson's parents, Hazel and Montgomery, live in a mutual-help home next door to their son, just a short walk to the church ground where they lived for many years before moving into their own home. Both are full-bloods in their early sixties (she is part Cherokee), and both have lived locally nearly all their lives. Another unmarried son in his midtwenties, currently unemployed, lives with the Jeffersons. Montgomery Jefferson has no formal schooling and speaks little English, although his wife, fluent in English, completed the sixth grade. The Jeffersons qualify for retirement and disability benefits owing to severe diabetes, a common ailment among Choctaws. Their home is modestly furnished, with a couch and table in the living room and an old table and a couple of chairs in the kitchen.

From various public-assistance sources, the household brings in about five hundred dollars per month. When additional cash is needed, Mrs. Jefferson works temporarily on the night shift at a chicken plant located about thirty miles away, although she knows that the work is becoming too strenuous. The Jeffersons have in the past sold tracts of inherited land to provide for their seven children, although they have managed to hold onto thirty-seven acres. They gave one acre to their son, Virgil, as well as two additional acres to a landless family desperate for a home.

Since they are heavily in debt and have difficulty making ends meet each month, they have had to borrow money just to meet current expenses. They pay about two hundred dollars per month on various personal loans and have talked with a banker about obtaining another loan, for which they plan to use their land as collateral. This strategy could jeopardize their only asset if they fail to meet loan payments.

The elder Jeffersons often care for their grandchildren, in return for which Virgil and his siblings cut wood for their parents. The elderly couple also does a small amount of gardening and canning, particularly wild berries, which they share at church dinners and consume.

THE CHIDERS FAMILY: AN EXTENDED HOUSEHOLD SUBSISTENCE STRATEGY

Viola and Max Chiders, like the Jeffersons, were the parents of a large family of eight children and already have more than twenty grandchildren. They live in their own four-bedroom mutual-help home next door to Mr. Chider's elderly parents, who share their fifty-year-old dwelling with a married granddaughter and her husband and children. Several other married children live nearby in mutual-help homes. Mr. Chiders, a twenty-five-year veteran of Weyerhaeuser, works as a casual laborer and maintenance man. The Chiders are both full-bloods in their midfifties, neither with more than six years of formal schooling. Their home is very modestly furnished with two large couches and a console television set in the living room. They own a freezer, which they try to stock, although they don't always have sufficient funds to buy food other than what they need for their immediate use.

The Chiders home includes four unmarried children and two school-age nephews in their permanent custody. One married son and his wife and three children also live in the household. Two other children, also married with young children, return frequently to work at seasonal timber industry contract jobs. Children are left with household members while both spouses work. This household contains approximately twelve permanent and five temporary members at any one time. The younger working adults only infrequently contribute to household expenses, and most of the food is purchased and prepared by the elder Chiders. There is some strain in the household as a result, since the elderly parents find it difficult to meet the needs of all who come and go.

Mr. Chiders takes home about $150 per week, working on average thirty-two hours. The household also receives public-assistance benefits for their nephews amounting to about $175 per month. Sons and daughters living at home work sporadically, earning anywhere from nothing to $100 per week depending on seasonal job availability; most of that money is kept by the wage earners to purchase clothing and other personal necessities. About two months before the interview, the household ran out of butane, which they could not afford to refill, so the house lacked hot water. The Chiders heat their home with wood cut by family members, and make a monthly payment of $47 on their mutual-help home, as well as about $110 per month to a local furniture company where they purchased a freezer and a couple of other items.

The elder Chiders own about three acres, including the one acre where they live. Mrs. Chider owns two acres a couple of miles away, inherited from her mother when the family estate was subdivided several years earlier, although the land is unsuitable for home construction. Since neither parent can provide their children with any land, the next generation faces difficult circumstances in meeting their housing needs, so they continue to live with relatives until they can devise alternative housing strategies.

Mrs. Chiders acknowledged that the family runs low on food nearly every month, and when that happens, "we just eat beans and potatoes," she said. The family occasionally borrows from their in-laws next door — elderly non-English-speaking traditional full-bloods — and takes advantage of credit at local white-owned stores.

CHICKEN PLANT WORKERS: THE WILSONS

The Wilsons, another extended household, consists of seven permanent and five temporary residents. An older child and grandchild share the three-bedroom mutual-help home for extended periods with five younger siblings. Another married son also returns from time to time with his wife and child.

All adult family members work intermittently at nearby Arkansas chicken plants, where the parents have worked on and off for fifteen years. They each earn about four dollars per hour and receive a five-cent raise each year if they don't get fed up and quit. When that happens, they claim, their seniority pay is cut to minimum wage. In 1981 the household earned about $11,500, too much to qualify for food stamps. The elder Wilsons have tried to subsist on just one income but were unable to meet expenses. Most of the time both spouses work on night shift, since it pays more and generally offers more hours each week. Each spouse generally works about four nights per week, from twenty-five to thirty-five hours. They are not paid when the line breaks down, which it frequently does, in which case they simply sit and wait until work resumes or the next shift arrives.

The one acre the Wilsons own was obtained as a gift from a relative. They would like very much to obtain more land for their daughter's housing needs, but are afraid to ask relatives again and cannot afford to purchase land. Their home, although only about fifteen years old, already shows extensive wear, and the plumbing is not in working order. Although the tribe provides maintenance assistance for mutual-help homes, they have been unable to obtain the necessary parts to fix the water pump.

This family, acutely aware of their economic exploitation, view their current situation as precarious and unsatisfactory. Their strategy has been to continue working at the chicken plants until they can no longer stand the routine, then quit for a while. Well aware that this is their only local employment option, they tolerate their predicament, albeit with difficulty. Fighting alcoholism, they face passing onto their children their legacy as poor unskilled labor.

Household members did little in the way of gardening or other home subsistence endeavors. The wife did some sewing occasionally. Their home was heated with butane rather than cutting their own wood, which they claimed was too time consuming and strenuous after a night's work at the chicken plant.

The dirty and demeaning work at chicken-processing plants appeared to be a far more distasteful employment option for local Choctaws than was work in timber-related occupations. Timber work, however, was less available and even more intermittent. Furthermore, older workers simply could not perform difficult outdoor jobs cutting and hauling timber, and most families could not afford high transportation costs to travel seventy or more miles to Weyerhaeuser's Wright City or Valliant mills, where full-time jobs might be available. Older workers often turned to the chicken plants, where they were generally guaranteed at least a distasteful job. This work still entailed traveling twenty or more miles each way, for which most paid $2.50 per night for transportation supplied by plant owners.

SUBSISTENCE AND PETTY COMMODITY PRODUCTION

Choctaw households, inadequately poised to sustain and reproduce themselves solely through wage labor, rely on diverse nonwage activities to supplement substandard household incomes. Petty commodity production, unwaged labor, informal sharing networks, and subsistence production continue to be essential for Choctaw families to meet household maintenance and reproduction costs. As one informant aptly said, "We Choctaws do everything we can on our own to make it here, from gardening to sewing to cutting our own wood. Otherwise, we'd starve!"

Studies by Stack (1974) and Lomnitz (1977) have shown how poor urban families maximize available resources by mobilizing family and household members in complex, predominantly kin-based sharing networks, which allow families to extend their resources during lean times of the month or year. Native Americans have devised similar methods to cope with the lack of available resources, particularly housing, jobs, and cash (see Hedley 1993; Jacobsen 1984). Max Hedley (1993:200–203) has reported diverse household nonwage production and exchange practices among Canada's Walpole Island Indians in the 1920s and 1930s, practices that allowed householders to produce and reproduce their own livelihood needs in an environment of scarce and inadequate resources. Walpole Islanders, like Choctaws since allotment, were increasingly incorporated into the wider wage laboring economy. And like timber region Choctaws today, they retained a culturally distinct "agrarian household economy" rooted in preexisting reciprocal labor and resource exchange networks, bartering, nonagricultural subsistence activities, and other extramarket activities (see Hedley 1993:197–200).

Choctaw production practices represent two aspects of U.S. capitalist penetration into rural Native American communities: First, Choctaw household production is an aspect of capitalist incorporation of rural hinterland regions into a global economy, where local householders subsidize their own reproduction by creating surplus value in a multiplicity of household unpaid laboring activities. Choctaw subsistence strategies directly ben-

efit market-based capitalist production by reducing employer costs to reproduce a local captive labor force.

Second, the Choctaws constitute a particular rural ethnic enclave with adaptation strategies rooted in their indigenous past, modified to accommodate to an environment of scarcity in the late twentieth century. Choctaws as
a tribal ethnic minority, however, are placed somewhere between a status of
sovereign self-determination as a "nation" and a weakly defined "ethnic minority" category. Ethnic minority status signifies the stripping away of prior
sovereign rights and the merging into parity with other U.S. ethnic groups.
As the Choctaws adapt to new constraints on household maintenance and
emerge as a rural ethnic minority proletarian class, their tribal status is challenged and a new identity as rural ethnic minority is defined.

Choctaw adaptations represent what Nagel and Snipp (1993) call "ethnic
reorganization": indigenous ethnic survival strategies implemented in colonized societies such as that of rural southeastern Oklahoma. Ethnic survival
strategies are dynamic and dialectic, involving negotiation and contestation
among core and hinterland segments. Ethnic minority groups create new
cultural features, meanings, and institutions to promote cultural survival,
albeit in an altered form. Since the contact era, Choctaws have undergone
ethnic reorganization economically, politically, and culturally. In the twentieth century, Choctaws have devised several adaptive strategies at household, family, and tribal levels to insure the tribe's economic survival, political integrity, and cultural continuity.

"ECONOMIC REORGANIZATION" STRATEGIES
Economic reorganization, according to Nagel and Snipp (1993:213), has
been a common feature of Native American survival strategies in the postcontact era. Choctaws in their preremoval phase, as discussed previously,
adopted and adapted for their own use many externally introduced components of the nascent U.S. economy, including agricultural implements,
guns, cash crops, and private land tenure. In the twentieth century, Choctaws continue to cope with severe land, labor, and resource shortages by
combining indigenous with contemporary cultural practices.

Choctaws rely on extensive reciprocal and redistributive exchange mechanisms, including informal exchange networks and more formal cycles of religious and secular food sharing at religious "sings" and tribal gatherings.
Various forms of labor, resources, and commodities enter sharing networks.

Firewood may be cut by a son, son-in-law, or grandson for an elderly widow. Grandparents provide child care for grandchildren while parents work. Food, child care, personal services such as transportation, and even land are made available to others when needed. Exchanges are sometimes even formalized in what appear to be "giveaways," as Moore (1993a) reports for central Oklahoma tribes, when Choctaw elders sponsor church feasts. Sharing of resources and services occurs almost exclusively among related households and often among households situated in close proximity to one another, frequently between parents and their grown children, although it also occurs among siblings and distantly related kin as well.

Informal resource sharing occurred in nearly all households surveyed, although this was not the only way Choctaw families broadened their resource base. Other resource-expanding strategies included sharing of housing space and nonwage subsistence-based production, including hunting, gathering, gardening, and fishing, in a lifestyle reminiscent of traditional indigenous subsistence strategies. Choctaw households also participate in a variety of home industries, including quilt making, sewing, canning and freezing foods, and silver and beadwork, as earlier noted.

A common resource distribution strategy was to share housing and, by extension, subsistence resources originating within the household. Shared housing was particularly evident in extended households (28 percent of those sampled), although younger unmarried adults also took advantage of shared housing space. Young newlyweds often resided with parents or in-laws while they attempted to adjust to married life, a new baby, bleak employment prospects, and a lack of suitable housing. The fourteen extended households surveyed contained twenty-eight separate conjugal units (both husband and wife present), an average of two per household. In at least two households surveyed, three married couples with numerous grandchildren (plus other adoptees) lived with parents, who served as caretakers while younger adults worked at seasonal timber industry jobs or on the night shift at chicken plants located over the Arkansas border. Working nights brought a slightly larger paycheck and also permitted more efficient use of severely limited sleeping quarters, which amounted to two bedrooms for four couples plus children in one instance. This postmarital practice is not unique to the present generation. Many older informants said that they, too, had spent many years living with their own parents or in-laws until a home was secured, often waiting for years or moving into a shack on one of the numerous church grounds that dot the local countryside.

Household heads, particularly the elderly, showed a willingness to accommodate to fluctuating residents regardless of constraints on living space or the inevitable drain on household resources. Sleeping quarters were rearranged to accommodate an entire family of five or more in a household with two or even three other conjugal units. Coresidents relied heavily on parents to run the household, as in the example above. The mother often did much of the cooking and child rearing, since young parents worked sporadic hours and were often unavailable to care for their children during the day. Parents also paid most bills, not only for household upkeep and utility and house payments, but also for food; with younger married children contributing only sporadically and irregularly to food and shelter costs. Money appeared to go toward job-related expenses, such as maintaining an automobile, rides to work, or other expenses, including cigarettes and entertainment.

Household resource pooling protects members from being left wholly without essential housing and food, a strategy Rayna Rapp (1978:228) notes is common among working-class families: "The ideal autonomy of an independent nuclear family is constantly being contradicted by the realities of social need, in which resources must be pooled, borrowed, shared. . . . When a married child is out of work, his (or her) nuclear family turns to the mother, and often moves in for a while." Rapp concludes that "ties to family, including fictive family, are the lifelines that simultaneously hold together and sustain individuals" (1978:294).

The extended household atmosphere was frequently highly charged in a small, substandard, and extremely overcrowded living space. Living arrangements often became permanent when no suitable housing options could be found or where a young couple simply could not manage their personal affairs alone.

Younger workers in particular struggle with the region's prevailing problem: an abundance of resources that are out of their reach. A common strategy young couples resort to is seasonal relocation, moving from in-law to in-law to take advantage of work opportunities in different regions. Often the entire family relocates, and children are left with grandparents while parents work as seasonal tree planters, in other timber-related operations, or at chicken-processing plants.

Nuclear households are also used as temporary repositories for minor children while parents leave the timber region altogether to test job opportunities elsewhere. Approximately 20 percent of nuclear households surveyed contained minor kin who had been left with relatives, either temporarily or permanently. Another 20 percent contained grown unmarried children, adult nieces or nephews, or more distantly related adults for whom separate housing units were unavailable. They remained at home or lived with relatives until they married or left the region. Unmarried adults generally contribute what they can to household expenses, including paying for food, butane, or firewood.

Limited employment opportunities make it difficult for many families to commit permanently to the region, since prospects for steady, year-round work are virtually nonexistent. Nuclear families, aside from tapping resources of extended kin networks, employ various other tactics to minimize expenses while providing for themselves and family members. Strategies include living on church grounds, leaving the Choctaw Nation to find work elsewhere, and the most desirable remedy of mutual-help home construction supported by income derived from a mixture of wage labor, public assistance, and home-based subsistence activities.

The housing shortage is still alleviated in part by using church buildings as residences for some Choctaw families. Nearly every church had at least one family living permanently in one of the extremely small, often dilapidated outbuildings normally used for weekend church camp meetings. Families who own no land and cannot afford to purchase an acre of land occupy church buildings, since they can live rent-free as caretakers. These buildings are little more than shacks constructed fifty or more years ago, lacking indoor plumbing in most instances. This population segment is really the most deprived in terms of housing needs, since they lack the acre of land that would make them eligible for the mutual-help housing program.

One family living on church property was an extended family consisting of a husband and wife, several children, plus an unmarried daughter and her young child. All shared a two-bedroom home lacking running water or indoor plumbing. This family had purchased an acre of land for five hundred dollars to become eligible for the mutual-help housing program, only to be turned down by the Housing Authority when the lot was declared unbuildable.

Each of the fifty households surveyed engaged in at least some nonwage

Table 10.1. Common household nonwage subsistence activities, Choctaw sample

Activity	Families		Activity	Families	
	#	%		#	%
Woodcutting	36	72	Quilt making	25	50
Gardening	35	70	Canning/freezing	22	44
Fishing/hunting	32	64	Sewing	15	30
Raising chickens	28	56	Hogs/cattle	11	22
Gathering wild food	26	52	Beadwork/silver	3	6

subsistence, petty commodity production, or both to supplement wages and unearned income, ranging from "a little gardening" to extensive canning and freezing of fruits and vegetables sufficient to last an entire season. Cash incomes were supplemented through various activities, including gardening, gathering, woodcutting, raising of hogs and chickens, quilt making, and sewing. Nearly half of households, twenty-four families, indicated that nonwage subsistence activities contributed a "moderate" amount to their household subsistence, while eight households indicated a high degree of nonwage subsistence work. Thirteen households performed nonwage subsistence activities only minimally, although even they generally cut their own wood supply if they could, hunted and fished occasionally, and gathered one or two wild foodstuffs seasonally.

Table 10.1 shows the common forms of Choctaw subsistence and petty commodity production. Woodcutting and gardening were the most common subsistence activities undertaken by Choctaw families, and about 60 percent engaged in hunting or fishing. Although many families viewed hunting and fishing as leisure time activities or a form of sport, they also welcomed the game on the dinner table. Quite a few families fished at least once a week, particularly in the spring and summer months, when fish became an important supplement to the family's diet.

Many families took advantage of the tribe's policy of making seeds available for home gardens. Gardening is still subject to the prevailing climate, which at times can be harsh. During the especially dry, hot summer of 1980, many families complained that their gardens produced nearly nothing and simply "burned up."

Canning and freezing of home-grown, gathered, or purchased foods are common in rural Choctaw households. Several families canned as many as thirty pints of pokeweed in early spring. Huckleberries, blackberries, and muscadine are canned in large quantities, and wild onions are gathered. Fruits are commonly purchased by the bushel, either at retail grocery stores or from vendors who go door to door seasonally. Several households canned large quantities of fruits to be consumed throughout the year. Several informants remembered fruit trees in their yards, although most have been neglected or cut down. A couple of households claimed that pesticides used by Weyerhaeuser (formerly sprayed by air) contributed to the death of their fruit trees.

More than 50 percent of households sampled (twenty-eight) raised chickens, which produced from three to a couple dozen eggs per day. A valuable protein source, eggs are consumed by the household or shared with kin. Eleven households raised hogs, some as part of a church-sponsored program to introduce hog raising. Teenage household members cared for hogs and marketed offspring. Feed is provided for the first year, when it is hoped the family will become self-sufficient in its hog-raising operations. Although only a small number of families participated in hog raising, this venture could become a valuable subsistence activity. Pork is popular with Choctaw families and could provide an inexpensive source of meat for families who persist in their hog-raising efforts. Most families could not afford to purchase hogs and received them either as gifts or through this program. Choctaw families were generally receptive to small-scale hog-raising enterprises. Cattle are much less common in the timber region, and only one of the older nuclear households engaged in cattle raising. Cattle ranching demands greater cash outlays for feed and herd maintenance, as well as larger land resources for pasturage, which most households could not provide.

Choctaw households differentially undertake home-based subsistence activities depending on household composition, other demands on the family's time, and personal initiative. Families occupying more traditional, unimproved shacks were found to be more likely to engage in canning, gathering of wild fruits and vegetables, hunting, and fishing than were families who worked full-time in the wage laboring sector and inhabited modern, well-furnished contemporary homes. This traditionally oriented sector used nonwage subsistence activities in ways reminiscent of a former Choctaw lifestyle one or two generations ago, when the Choctaws were a more self-sufficient rural farm population. Intrafamily produce sharing is practiced extensively by this segment, particularly between parents and married children. Since household cash resources are limited, home-based subsistence activities supplement marginal cash resources.

Households composed of elderly or disabled members and families whose needs could be met with available cash (mainly where both spouses worked) were less likely to engage in extensive domestic subsistence activities. Also, those households struggling at distasteful jobs in the wage-earning sector, barely making ends meet, appeared simply to lack the physical and emotional energy necessary to undertake domestic subsistence activities, as evidenced by the Wilson household, above, where both parents worked nights at a local chicken plant. Garden produce would have been welcome, but the Wilsons said they simply did not have the energy to garden when they came home from work to face their five children and unpaid bills.

Choctaws depend extensively on unwaged household labor in subsistence and petty commodity production along with wages and various public-sector entitlement programs to meet their livelihood needs. Remnants of preindustrial reciprocity and sharing traditions, along with subsistence and craft commodity production, signify that Choctaws have managed to preserve viable indigenous elements within the wage-laboring context. Such traditions reflect both cultural survivals and cultural adaptations to conditions of externally imposed resource scarcity.

In the core/hinterland dialectic, Choctaws as a rural indigenous ethnic minority have faced the imperative of both economic and cultural adaptations to new modes and relations of production. Choctaw adaptations represent an indigenous struggle to retain political and economic sovereignty as a tribe while accommodating to a new reality as a rural hinterland proletarian labor force only marginally able to sustain and reproduce itself. Choctaws are accommodating to new economic realities by retaining some prior subsistence strategies and developing new economic survival strategies, to be discussed in a later chapter. The following chapter explores how Choctaws use a variety of income sources to eke out a living in a region that benefits substantially from this "reserve army" of cheap, readily available labor for resource extraction and food-processing industries.

ELEVEN

Maintaining and Reproducing
Choctaw Households, 2:
The Formal Economy

Choctaw subsistence and wage labor strategies are typical of working poor in the semiperiphery who rely on paid and unpaid labor to maintain and reproduce their families (see Stack 1974; Rapp 1978; Collins and Gimenez, eds., 1990; McGuire and Woodsong 1990; Collins 1990; Glazer 1990; Gimenez 1990). Although Choctaws are fully subsumed within the U.S. political economy, they are more accurately *semiproletarians* (see Gimenez 1990) who subsidize inadequate wages with informal economic strategies using kin reciprocity networks, labor exchange, petty commodity production, and nonwage subsistence activities. Regional towns such as Talihina, Idabel, McAlester, and Durant, Oklahoma, and Mena and Fort Smith, Arkansas, constitute the wider web of interaction spheres that Choctaw households tap as wage laborers and consumers to meet subsistence and reproduction needs.

HOUSEHOLD INCOME-PRODUCING STRATEGIES

Choctaws, like rural semiproletarians throughout the capitalist periphery, aim to produce a family wage adequate to maintain and reproduce their households. Households mobilize all potential workers when wage labor is available, performing a variety of jobs, some seasonal and many part-time. Eligible family members, particularly older persons, take advantage of unearned income such as food stamps, Social Security and veterans' benefits, and tribal entitlement programs when available. They and younger kinsfolk also serve as unpaid household workers, thereby maximizing the earning power of employed household members. As Rapp (1978) accurately notes, these households are "essentially living below socially necessary reproduction costs. They therefore reproduce themselves by spreading out the aid and the risks involved in daily life" (Rapp 1978:291). Choctaw household

Table II.I. Average per capita and household income by household
type, Choctaw sample, 1981–82

	Average household		Average per capita	
	Monthly	*Yearly*	*Monthly*[*]	*Yearly*[*]
Younger nuclear	$829.18	$ 9,950.16	$169.22	$2,030.64
Older nuclear	465.26	5,583.12	177.24	2,126.88
Extended	834.31	10,011.72	129.75	1,557.00
Average, all households	$714.16	$ 8,569.95	$147.45	$1,769.40

[*]Permanent residents only were used in computing per capita incomes.

economic strategies articulate with a wider economy controlled by outsiders, mainly private corporate producers, the largest being the multinational timber company Weyerhaeuser and the retail food producer Tyson
Foods, Inc. The current generation of Choctaws has emerged as a strategically available labor force for Weyerhaeuser's timber enterprises and for the
chicken-processing industry.

Choctaw household economic strategies vary according to household
composition, skills, employment options, household and family needs, and
willingness to relocate to other regions. Households surveyed earned anywhere from four thousand dollars or less per year to nearly twenty thousand
dollars for one of the extended households, which contained six wage earners supporting four separate family units. Typical of poor Choctaw families, this household was in extreme economic distress, inhabiting a dilapidated housing unit, unsuitable for the thirteen permanent residents who
awaited construction of a mutual-help home that would alleviate some of
their housing problems. The lack of full-time jobs remained a persistent unresolved problem for all family members, who relied on chicken processing,
seasonal timber work, Social Security, and food stamps for income.

Table II.I summarizes average household and per capita monthly and
yearly incomes of the fifty households surveyed. Household incomes, although varied, were consistent in per capita incomes. As the table shows,
per capita monthly incomes in extended households were the lowest, although these households actually had the largest average monthly incomes.
Choctaw sample incomes were far below McCurtain and Pushmataha
County average per capita incomes, shown in table II.2. The data show just

Table II.2. Per capita personal incomes, two-county and Choctaw samples

	Average monthly	Average yearly
Pushmataha County*	$365.50	$4,386.00
McCurtain County*	452.50	5,418.00
Choctaw sample	147.45	1,769.40

*Source: Employment Security Commission 1979, reported in Oklahoma IMPACT 1981; Choctaw sample, 1981–82.

how economically distressed timber region Choctaws are in their ability to earn a living.

Older nuclear and extended households relied far more heavily on public assistance than did younger nuclear households, as shown in table II.3. Of twenty-two households showing no earned income at all, nineteen were older nuclear or extended households. Twenty-one households received both earned and unearned income, while seven households relied exclusively on wage labor. All were younger nuclear households. Only two younger nuclear households relied exclusively on public-assistance income.

Many households were constrained by physical disabilities. Elderly couples, unmarried heads of household, and the disabled accounted for nearly 60 percent of households surveyed. One elderly couple, both in their sixties, although unable to work and relying solely on disability and public-assistance benefits, cared permanently for six children, including three grandchildren and three more distant kin. The elderly man was ineligible for Social Security benefits because he lacked five quarters for eligibility, having spent nearly all his life working as a subsistence farmer on the family's homestead.

This family supplemented public-assistance benefits with extensive subsistence and petty commodity production. The wife sewed quilts, made clothing and beadwork on consignment, and canned jellies, fruits, and vegetables for home consumption and for church meetings. The children cut and hauled wood for home heating, and family members hunted and fished regularly, two or three times per week. They also raised hogs and chickens for home consumption. Their three-bedroom home was furnished modestly with couches in the living room to accommodate some of the children. "We Choctaws don't look to be rich," said the woman, as she told of the hard work necessary to meet the family's subsistence needs. She was proud that all of her children had graduated from school and that her "second family" also attended school regularly.

Table II.3. Household income source by household type, Choctaw sample

	Solely earned	Mostly earned	Mostly unearned	Solely unearned	Total
Younger nuclear	7	8	3	2	20
Older nuclear	0	2	2	12	16
Extended	0	5	1	8	
Total	7	15	6	22	50

Households headed by disabled or elderly individuals tended to rely on public-assistance payments for their livelihoods, if the benefits were sufficient to meet household expenses. Frequently, young children shared a home with grandparents on a semipermanent basis. One elderly widow who cared for her great-grandson intermittently found it difficult to provide for the boy on a monthly income of $275, and she could not obtain public-assistance benefits for him at short notice. She was assisted by a daughter, although she, too, faced her own financial problems. "There are always peanut butter sandwiches, and beans and potatoes for dinner," she confided. She concluded, "We always manage to get by, and I guess we always will."

Employment opportunities for younger families were severely limited by the lack of full-time jobs. One option is for the principal wage earner to travel elsewhere for work. One younger nuclear household was able to earn about seventeen thousand dollars per year when the husband worked on an oil rig, returning home every two or three weeks. Travel expenses cut deeply into earnings, however, making the arrangement economically unfeasible. One man traveled about seventy miles to a construction site, returning home only on weekends, while his wife struggled to meet household expenses. He managed to earn only about thirty-five hundred dollars. Several local households had simply given up such arrangements as economically unprofitable and personally unworkable.

Education is another factor that restricts Choctaw employment options. Older Choctaws, most no longer in the work force, had only an average of five years of formal schooling. Approximately half of younger adults surveyed had completed high school, and another third had completed at least some high school; although few have taken advantage of opportunities available to Native Americans for advanced training, which require relocating for both training and later to find suitable work. About 15 percent had

Table II.4. Principal income source by average yearly
income, Choctaw sample

Average yearly income	Number of families	Income source		Both sources
		Earned	Unearned	
<$5,000	9	1	8	1
$5,000 to $10,000	26	9	17	9
>$10,000	15	12	3	10
Total	50	22	28	20

not gone beyond the eighth grade, while another 15 percent attended postsecondary schools. Women frequently completed more years of school than men, although men are generally the principal household wage earners.

Typical of peripheral economies globally, men tend to earn higher wages in a gender-stratified labor market. Women are overrepresented in lowerpaid "female" occupations, such as teaching and health services, while men work in better-paid unionized semiskilled and skilled jobs. Currently only about 15 percent of Weyerhaeuser's unionized work force is female, while Tyson's nonunionized and unskilled chicken-processing plant is 57 percent female. At the tribe's chemical finishing plant only two of approximately twenty workers are women. Women are also overrepresented in the informal unwaged sector earlier discussed (Ray 1993–96).

College-trained women contribute significantly to household earnings as teacher's aides or tribally employed community health representatives (CHR). Such jobs – scarce, unreliable, and frequently underpaid – are contingent upon federal and tribal entitlement programs and county education budgets.

Households were most successful that took advantage of multiple income sources rather than relying solely on wages or government entitlement programs. Table II.4 shows a breakdown of average yearly incomes based on principal income sources for all households surveyed. Those households with the lowest incomes, below five thousand dollars per year, represented individuals unable to work who depended solely on public-assistance benefits. At the highest levels of income, above ten thousand dollars annually, two-thirds of households had two income sources. Like the Jefferson family, where the husband was employed as a timber cutter while his wife worked as a teacher's aide, households benefited substantially from such an arrangement.

Higher incomes, as both tables II.3 and II.4 show, were not universally cor-

Table II.5. Younger nuclear household income by source and number
of wage earners, Choctaw sample

Income source*	# Households	Average yearly income	Wage earners/Household	
			One	More than one
Wholly earned**	9	$10,254	4	5
Mostly earned (≥50%)	6	11,022	1	5
Mostly unearned (<50%)	3	8,791	3	0
Wholly unearned	2	7,110	–	–

*Unearned income includes public assistance and food stamps.
**Figures include households with $20 or less unearned income per month.

related with wage labor. Often higher incomes resulted from households
taking advantage of public-assistance benefits, mainly food stamps, to supplement inadequate part-time wages. Younger nuclear household income
sources are analyzed in table II.5.

Employed individuals overwhelmingly held part-time jobs. Of thirty-
eight permanent household members sampled, thirty-two worked part-
time while only six worked full-time, as shown in table II.6. Timber work
was one common part-time occupation, while a nearly equal number
worked in the more distasteful chicken plants, all part-time. In fact, fourteen
workers in our sample worked at chicken plants part-time while fifteen –
thirteen part-time and only two full-time – worked in timber-related occupations.

Table II.6 summarizes occupations of the thirty-eight wage earners according to their status as part- or full-time workers. As this table shows, only
two workers were employed full-time by Weyerhaeuser directly, one of
whom was Mr. Chiders, the general laborer described above. Fourteen
worked at chicken plants approximately twenty-five to thirty hours per
week, nearly all on night shifts. Three worked as teacher's aides, and one was
a full-time teacher in a local school. Like most local jobs, the pay is low,
about $3.75 per hour for a teacher's aide employed thirty hours per week for
nine months.

A UNIQUE JOB-GETTING STRATEGY: SELF-EMPLOYMENT

The James family, a full-blood Choctaw couple in their thirties, devised a
unique strategy to accommodate to the dilemma of underemployment. This
nuclear family, consisting of a husband, wife, and several young children, re-

Table II.6. Part-time and full-time distribution of workers by
occupational categories, Choctaw sample

	# Workers	%
Part-time tree work and related occupations	13	34
Part-time chicken plant work	14	37
Part-time miscellaneous occupations	2	5
Part-time teacher's aide	3	8
Total	32	84
Full-time Weyerhaeuser employee	2	5
Full-time teacher	1	3
Full-time miscellaneous occupations	3	8
Total	6	16

turned to the region after the husband grew tired of intermittent layoffs at his job as a sawmill worker. Partners in an independent logging business, they maintain their own equipment, including a nearly twenty-year-old logging truck being paid for on time, and a chain saw, another essential item for their logging business. Both spouses cut timber together, making about one load per day, which they transport over unimproved roads to an area purchaser, earning about fifty dollars per truckload. They live a frugal lifestyle in a two-room unimproved shack rent-free, while attempting to save for a piece of land on which to put their trailer, occupied by a kinsman who is making the monthly payments of seventy-five dollars. They hoped to be given land by a family member.

The Jameses work every day, although weather and equipment problems hinder steady work. They reported that, "nearly every week one or the other – the chain saw or the truck – breaks down." They repaired their own equipment if they could, since they could not afford costly outlays for repairs. This household supplemented its earnings with about three hundred dollars in food stamps, free housing, and an extremely frugal lifestyle. They liked the independent life their work afforded, although they realized that their job was difficult and precarious. After interviewing the James couple, I met them on the road on their way to deliver a truckload of posts to a Talihina sawmill. Heavy with timber, the truck sat helplessly with a flat tire, with neither a usable jack nor a spare tire. Events such as this, a weekly occurrence by their estimate, extend their work day and cut deeply into profits. Facing no better employment alternatives and desperate to improve the lives of their children locally rather than in some distant community, they persevere.

Most timber workers provide their own equipment, and a couple of other families owned logging trucks. Costly repairs were a universal problem, and most timber cutters said that chain saws lasted only a year or two. One family had purchased a logging truck less than a year before from a logging company, which broke down after only the first payment had been made. It was irreparable and sat idle in the yard. The company refused to take the truck back, so the family ceased to make further payments. Timber workers who provide their own equipment and pay necessary maintenance costs find that these expenses cut deeply into their earnings.

Local chicken-processing plants offer a second important source of jobs, as noted earlier, particularly for unskilled minorities and women. Chicken plants, most located in nearby Arkansas towns, are the region's second largest private employer, second only to Weyerhaeuser. One informant said that many Arkansas chicken plant workers are minorities – blacks, Native Americans, and Spanish-speaking workers – who turn to the more unpleasant jobs when they cannot find employment elsewhere. The chicken-processing industry, notorious for its antiunion stance, has actively curbed employee unionization efforts, a topic to be discussed in a later chapter. One local chicken plant, Lane Company, employing from five to seven hundred workers, filed for bankruptcy and shut down temporarily in the late 1970s, following several acrimonious conflicts with employees over unionization efforts, costing at least thirty workers their jobs. This shutdown hit local Choctaws hard, since many families relied on chicken-processing jobs.

Rural families depend on a second type of work associated with the chicken business. This is night work catching chickens at local chicken houses, often performed by teenagers. Several families told how their children, as young as thirteen years of age, worked nights catching chickens, for which they were paid fifteen dollars per night. This work when performed by minor children is illegal, although it occurs because the families need the added income. Vans recruit nightly and transport workers to various chicken houses. Children are exploited, however, and in one instance family members were not paid for work performed over several months. When attempts were made to collect wages owed, the family learned that the contracting company had gone out of business and there was no way to collect the wages, amounting to three hundred dollars each. Children working nights often miss school, and authorities, including tribal officials, have sought to terminate these illegal labor practices, although the chicken-processing plants have resisted attempts to curb these exploitative practices.

HOUSEHOLD CASH FLOW

How do Choctaw households meet their basic expenses, given their limited cash resources? Recent research has shown how women's unpaid domestic labor subsidizes inadequate family wages (see Collins and Gimenez, eds., 1990). Close examination of Choctaw households shows how a similar process is at work where unpaid household labor – female and male – combined with other subsistence and welfare subsidy programs support inadequate Choctaw family wages.

Choctaws, as earlier noted, use multiple resource-deriving strategies, including kin networks, shared housing, gardening, and craft production. Choctaws often live on credit from month to month to extend their available cash. Others simply spend what little they do have for housing, food, and clothing. Nearly every household took advantage of credit to some degree and practiced a variety of economizing measures. Conspicuous consumption or lavishness is wholly absent from the rural poor Choctaw community. Simplicity in housing, dress, and eating habits enables Choctaws to live within their tenuous levels of spendable income. Household furnishings are extremely modest, except in households that benefit from full-time jobs or combined incomes from two or more sources. Automobiles are purchased secondhand, and several households did without a car because they could not afford to purchase even a used one.

Cash resources are generally managed by both spouses. Extended households often contain more than one bread-winning conjugal unit, and each typically manages their own cash resources to some degree. Pooling of resources in extended households is spontaneous rather than prescribed, often leading to friction when inhabitants do not contribute their share. Working children rely on parents to provide much of the household's food resources, the single greatest expense in nearly every household surveyed. Food stamps, when available, are shared, although purchases beyond food stamp allocations are common, since benefits typically do not meet household needs.

A trip to a regional center, such as Broken Bow, Idabel, or Fort Smith, for large food purchases is a family outing often occurring once or twice a month. Many households make periodic shopping trips to distant regional centers, fifty or more miles away, often around the time welfare, disability checks, or food stamps arrive. Some households spend their entire food stamp allotment at one time, purchasing large quantities of staples such as potatoes, pinto beans, salt, sugar, coffee, lard, and other nonperishable items. Frequently the entire household goes on the shopping venture, and others without transportation are brought along on treks to the "city."

Households benefited substantially from reduced housing costs and the use of firewood for home heating. Mutual-help home payments ranged from fifteen to fifty dollars per month, averaging about twenty-five dollars per month. Some households paid nothing for housing if they inhabited unimproved shacks, although they paid dearly in personal comfort. Fuel costs for hot water and electricity typically added fifty to sixty dollars per month to housing costs. More than 70 percent of households surveyed used wood for most of their home heating needs and relied on butane only when absolutely necessary. Households also economized in other ways, such as washing clothing by hand (or in the river, in one instance) or using the washer of kinsmen when available. Households also dispensed with unnecessary expenses such as telephones, which most viewed as luxury items. Many households took advantage of secondhand items, including clothing and furniture, when available. Visits to the city included stops at secondhand clothing shops, particularly around the time that children must be prepared for school with new clothing. Clothes were passed from household to household when possible. Cardboard boxes were often used as storage for clothing and personal items when bureau space was unavailable. Many households, as discussed earlier, also economized by making their own quilts, sewing their own clothes, and performing extensive gardening, stock raising, and hunting.

PUBLIC-SECTOR SUBSIDIES

Choctaws, in addition to relying on wage labor, family networks, and other economizing measures, tap the welfare state for livelihood maintenance. Public-assistance programs and tribal economic initiatives supplement locally inadequate wages, reducing the material desperation and sense of exploitation underemployed and poorly paid Choctaw workers might otherwise feel. As previously discussed, during the 1980s, an era of public budget-cutting frenzy, southeastern Oklahoma experienced a persistently high unemployment rate, and local communities remain mired in poverty.

Workers are supported when unemployed or underemployed by various sources of unearned income, including food stamps, supplemental security income (SSI), veteran's benefits, Aid to Families with Dependent Children (AFDC), and various Choctaw subsidy programs – costs increasingly shouldered by the Choctaw Nation as Reagan/Bush-era budget-cutting measures reduced federal subsidies to Native Americans, as a later discussion will show. In the study of fifty timber region households, forty-one households received public assistance, mainly food stamps. Incidentally, Oklahoma finances public welfare through sales tax revenues; thus recipients, in their role as consumers, actually pay for their own welfare benefits.

Choctaws also are beneficiaries of several federal and state programs owing to their status as Native Americans. These programs have emerged from longstanding federal obligations and commitments to Native American people, although funds for many federally sponsored programs, such as Community Health Representatives, were seriously curtailed or even eliminated during the Reagan/Bush era. Tribal members by blood and their dependents are entitled to free health care at local health clinics and hospitals, a program taken over by the tribe in 1985. The tribe now subsidizes the Community Health Representative program, designed to seek out rural people needing health-related assistance and information about available programs. In addition to the previously mentioned mutual-help housing program, the tribe, using its own funds and various federal grant monies, provides housing assistance, including cash for utility bills for the elderly and disabled, weatherization funds to insulate homes, cash to purchase home heating fuel, and occasionally eyeglasses and dental services for the elderly.

Native American children are beneficiaries of educational programs, from preschool Head Start programs to full tuition scholarships for college-bound Choctaws. These funds are available only to students willing to leave their communities, since specialized educational programs are not locally available, nor are the jobs for which they will most likely be trained.

These various federally and tribally sponsored programs have enabled Choctaws to remain in their local communities by compensating them for the lack of private-sector income-producing opportunities. The system obscures the actual role the private corporate sector plays in the immiseration of Choctaw workers, however. Entitlement programs, especially public welfare subsidies, are indirect and masked forms of "corporate welfare" that benefit corporate producers by supporting an underemployed, readily available local labor force. This is particularly evident in the program of mutual-help housing, which has attracted many young families back to the region because they could obtain housing locally, although few employment prospects await them (see Muga 1988; Ward, ed., 1990:5–7).

As the above discussion has shown, the strategies that benefited Choctaw families most were to limit family size, take advantage of public-assistance benefits, and implement noncash subsistence strategies to supplement wages. Childbirth rates have declined considerably during the current generation. Whereas adults indicated that they were raised in households of six or more children, the current generation has an average of three children per household. Younger families indicated that they did not want so many children, since they could not provide for them all. Mutual-help housing has also improved living conditions dramatically for many families, particularly those who could not afford home financing costs. Nearly all families who today occupy mutual-help housing inhabited unimproved homes during their childhood without indoor plumbing facilities and electricity.

TAPPING WHITE-SECTOR RESOURCES

We have already seen that Choctaws share the rural landscape with white and African American neighbors, and in fact whites are a highly visible local population segment. Rural unincorporated communities located near Choctaw churches are predominantly Choctaw, although the socially recognized incorporated towns are generally more than 50 percent white. Interaction with whites occurs at town centers, where children attend school and adults shop, get their mail, and occasionally congregate at the small markets.

Some Choctaws when pressed claimed that they were really no different from their white neighbors; they believed that whites were subject to the same economic constraints and that work was equally scarce for white and Choctaw youth alike. Choctaws generally did not feel discriminated against in the job market or in their communities, although some expressed the opinion that whites do have greater cash assets and better job opportunities than do most Choctaws. They pointed out that nearly all of the local chicken houses are white-owned, and most Choctaw families could never establish such a business because they simply do not have the cash resources to do so.

A former assistant chief, Robert Gardner, argued that a significant difference between whites and rural Choctaws was that many Choctaws are not aware of opportunities available to maximize their options and make the most of their limited cash resources or educational skills (Gardner 1982). Rural Choctaws, he observed, were more easily manipulated and exploited because they lacked knowledge of opportunities available and how to take advantage of resource entitlements.

Choctaws experience two types of economic exploitation. First, they are taken advantage of as consumers by white entrepreneurs and shopkeepers from whom they obtain their basic necessities, such as food and durable goods. Second and more importantly, Choctaws are embedded in an institutionalized system of labor exploitation as an underemployed, low-paid, and largely nonunionized labor force in timber and chicken-processing industries. Choctaw livelihood-gaining strategies, based on domestic household subsistence combined with wage labor and public assistance, become mechanisms through which the capitalist sector accrues substantial added profit, while the costs to produce and reproduce Choctaw labor are borne largely by the Choctaws themselves and the poor rural communities where they live.

CHOCTAWS AS CONSUMERS: MAINTAINING THE LOCAL ECONOMY

Choctaw consumers enter the wider market nexus locally and regionally to obtain essential retail commodities. Choctaw consumption patterns radiate out from their web of familiar space – neighborhoods and regional towns – to the wider web of less familiar space: the county seats of Idabel and Antlers, and nearby McAlester, Oklahoma, and Mena and Fort Smith, Arkansas. With entry into more distant, impersonal space Choctaws are vulnerable to exploitation, both as traditionally oriented Native Americans and as a captive rural enclave population.

Choctaw consumers participate in a paternalistic and opportunistic system of retail trade and credit at the small, retail shops located in the nearby village centers. Not only do Choctaws purchase durable consumer goods locally, but they often purchase much if not most of their food locally as well. Many Choctaw families, particularly less acculturated full-blood families, tend to purchase foodstuffs and other items at local family-owned grocery stores, where some of their families have done business for generations. They can trade food stamps with ease and feel comfortable in familiar surroundings dealing with a proprietor whom their family has known for many years. These stores offer produce at higher prices, with a poor selection of items. Fresh fruits and vegetables are often unavailable or in poor condition. Fresh and frozen items such as meats, cheese, and fruit juices are sometimes outdated and not infrequently spoiled.

Approximately 20 percent of rural households surveyed were found to make most of their food purchases at small local grocery stores serving local towns, where long-standing credit arrangements with the proprietor existed. The previous month's bill would be paid at the beginning of the month and new purchases made until current funds were depleted, at which time credit would again be extended to the household. Nearly every family took advantage of local credit, even those who shopped at more distant stores. Most households, at least 60 percent, purchased gasoline locally, and a few even purchased clothing, shoes, and other household items from local retailers. Local prices, as expected, were approximately 30 percent higher than for groceries purchased in larger communities thirty to forty miles distant. Although households paid substantially higher prices at local stores, they purchased locally because they were familiar with the proprietor and did not want to jeopardize these valuable credit arrangements. Most households whose members shopped locally, and even many who tried to shop at more economical regional centers, were forced to obtain credit each month, particularly at month's end, when cash and food stamps were depleted, when some lived only on "beans and potatoes" because they simply had nothing else in the pantry. One elderly informant said, "If I had biscuits and eggs in the house, that's food! At times I have less" (author's interview 3/25/81).

The practice of shopping locally appears to be a vestige of earlier times when travel was restricted to walking to the town center and trade at the local grocery was the norm. Most households who habitually shopped at local markets were the more traditionally oriented full-blood families who spoke Choctaw at home, the elderly who spoke no English at all, and those who still inhabited unimproved shacks on church grounds or family homesteads. This group, about 20 percent of our sample, also included some young families who had not yet relinquished the more traditional methods of dealing with white society.

Credit was a strong incentive to shop locally. Shopkeepers extended cash as well as foodstuff credit to families whom they knew. Because many households experienced shortages nearly every month, they depended on the local storekeeper for credit. Some storekeepers charged an additional ten dollars each time credit was extended, regardless of the amount borrowed, thus earning extra income as well as insuring a continuous business from the more poorly informed, traditionally oriented Choctaw households. Like their Third World counterparts, rural Choctaws were exploited as both consumers and laborers, either unaware of or choosing not to take advantage of alternative strategies (see Nash 1979:241).

Shopkeepers when asked about credit arrangements viewed extending credit as a costly act of benevolence, a cost of doing business locally. Shopkeepers claimed to have lost money on families who refused to pay debts on time. One owner of a very small grocery store on the outskirts of one town showed a log listing families with whom she had outstanding credit over the years. Of approximately twenty-five "open" accounts, about 80 percent were Choctaws, and the rest whites, she claimed. Over the years she claimed to have lost about thirty-five hundred dollars in "dead accounts" but continued to extend credit. "They couldn't survive without it," she said. Choctaws squandered their money on frivolities, she argued, such as chips and soda pop, although she admitted that she made the foods readily available and even extended credit for these "frivolous" purchases (author's interview 6/82).

Her attitude was typical of a latent attitude among many local whites, who viewed Choctaws as ineffective home managers, unable to help themselves out of their economic predicaments. When pressed, however, shopkeepers universally admitted that Choctaws were often taken advantage of by whites when they failed to pay debts. Although local shopkeepers incurred financial losses from Choctaw "dead" accounts, they also benefited substantially by these credit practices, which brought much-needed business to their shops. Most Choctaws paid their bills even if this meant that the household would again have to request credit the next month. Shopkeepers appeared to welcome Choctaw business and assisted Choctaw consumers in picking out purchases.

Many Choctaw households occasionally made large purchases with surplus funds of durable items, such as freezers, refrigerators, television sets, dinettes, lawnmowers, and tillers, at regional centers of commerce. They again sought out smaller stores rather than the large chain stores, since they knew the proprietor would more readily extend credit without complicated paperwork. Credit terms were often excessively high, and in a couple of instances interest was charged in excess of 25 percent on the outstanding balance. Most households did not appear to shop for the best bargains. Instead they were attracted to shops used by family members, where the proprietor knew them, regardless of the item's cost. None of the households took advantage of larger retail chains, such as Sears, where they might have purchased durable goods at a more reasonable cost. It appeared that they opted instead to purchase from retailers whom they knew and who had a long history of transacting business under easy credit terms, although sometimes at illegally high interest rates.

Personal savings were generally unheard of among rural Choctaws. Only one of the fifty households interviewed maintained a personal savings account, and nearly all of the families saw saving money as something absolutely beyond their means, since keeping up with monthly bills was marginal at best. Many households did borrow money, mainly through banks, loan companies, and personal loans from whites. Several families customarily went to the home of a prominent local white man and borrowed cash, one hundred dollars or more, to be repaid when they could for a ten-dollar fee. Several relied on one white individual who had a reputation as a moneylender of last resort.

Choctaw credit practices seemed to be remnants of earlier practices, prior to World War II or the 1950s, when many individuals worked exclusively for credit or were paid in commodities for their labor. Older Choctaws reported that until the Depression-era WPA programs, they did not work for wages. Many were hired by whites as common laborers and were paid in groceries. One local white man living in the vicinity of several Choctaw settlements, who today serves as a local moneylender, was an employer of several older Choctaws in earlier days. Families interviewed, particularly older and more traditionally oriented families, did not view these credit relationships as exploitative. Many were unaware of other options, and they felt they were doing the best they could in making purchases locally and obtaining much-needed credit.

Choctaws are a readily available captive labor force in the southeastern Oklahoma hinterland economy, serving as semiskilled and unskilled workers in local extractive and labor-intensive industries. Choctaw men and women maximize household resources by combining waged and unwaged labor, pooling, sharing, and distributing household resources efficiently.

Choctaws continue to be exploited because of their own unfamiliarity with prevailing systems of credit and finance, their lack of professional and educational skills, and their desire to return to and remain in their homeland rather than migrate elsewhere for jobs.

Today, facing serious quandaries in their quest for a livelihood in their native homeland, most Choctaws have turned to wage labor for jobs, to the very same corporations who today own their former tribal land base. The following chapter investigates the role Choctaws play as a strategically available labor force within the globally oriented Weyerhaeuser production strategy.

TWELVE

Tapping the Dependent Labor Force and Other Corporate Profit-Maximizing Strategies

Rural hinterland poverty can be best understood as a dialectical relationship between resource owners and local citizens, bound in intricate socioeconomic arrangements that, as Robert Coppedge and Carleton Davis (1977:ix) argue, tend to foster and perpetuate rather than mitigate rural underdevelopment, poverty, and labor exploitation. The southeastern Oklahoma timber region is just such a frontier (see Dunaway 1996; Hall 1995), "marginal enclave" (see Prattis 1980:313), internal colony, or what Joseph Jorgensen (1978:3) calls a "domestic dependent niche": a region that serves metropolitan-based production interests while perpetuating rural poverty and underdevelopment. As noted earlier, more than one-third of timber region Choctaws were unemployed in 1987 (*Bishinik* 5/87:2); and McCurtain and Pushmataha Counties recorded among Oklahoma's highest poverty and unemployment rates. These unemployment rates occurred while the two largest regional employers – Weyerhaeuser and Tyson Foods – were giants among Fortune 500 companies, each ranked among the nation's top revenue producers in their product areas.

Multinational corporations are especially subtle in how they use local communities and their inhabitants to their own advantage, since to do so is contrary to the ideology of U.S. private enterprise. However, a closer look at how Weyerhaeuser's and Tyson Foods' production strategies relate to systems of land and labor use, taxation, and public welfare in southeastern Oklahoma shows how private business grows at the expense of local residents and public-sector inputs.

WEYERHAEUSER'S PRODUCTION STRATEGY
Weyerhaeuser was a highly successful, multinational corporation with extensive landholdings in the United States, Canada, and as many as fifteen

foreign countries when it entered the southeastern Oklahoma region in 1969. Southeastern Oklahoma, like the Deep South generally in the postwar era, has attracted manufacturers and industries that have been historically nonunionized and hostile to unionization efforts and that are seeking unskilled workers accustomed to low wages (Colclough 1988:75–76; Flora et al. 1992:37–38, 136–37). Weyerhaeuser was just such a company (see Dierks 1972; Smith 1986).

Weyerhaeuser's 1969 purchase of Dierks's Oklahoma and Arkansas timberland was a strategic corporate move that fit well into its ideology of capital-intensive expansion. The purchase brought to Weyerhaeuser a substantial forest base situated in the heartland of the nation, accessible to both East and West Coast markets (Students 1975:49). According to Weyerhaeuser's own report,

With the acquisition of Dierks Forest, Inc., a $325 million purchase completed in 1969, Weyerhaeuser, for the first time, has a substantial raw materials base within a day's drive from most of its major midwest and eastern markets. The Dierks property is unique: 1.8 million acres of underutilized forestland in Arkansas and Oklahoma, ideally situated from our marketing standpoint.

The combination allows Weyerhaeuser to use its technical marketing and financial capabilities to expand Dierks' conversion facilities and product lines. At the same time, with expanding production facilities in the heart of the nation, the Company's tidewater mills could turn more and more to coastal and international markets. . . .

. . . In a single move, Weyerhaeuser management made it possible to serve its domestic markets more efficiently and to offer greater commitment to overseas customers. (Weyerhaeuser ca. 1975:38)

Weyerhaeuser, which already owned 3.8 million acres of land, raised its domestic landholdings by nearly one-third, to 5.6 million acres. Today more than 50 percent of Weyerhaeuser's exports are to Japan, which Weyerhaeuser supplies from its Pacific Coast and Canadian tree farms.

The largest private owner of timber resources in the United States today (Weyerhaeuser 1977), Weyerhaeuser's Oklahoma and Arkansas landholdings, about 1,841,000 acres, constitute about 17 percent of their worldwide acreage and is their largest region (Weyerhaeuser 1977). Weyerhaeuser currently owns 5.8 million acres of commercial forestland in the United States and has cutting rights on an additional 12 million acres in Canada and the Far East (Weyerhaeuser 1980, 1981, 1987).

THE MULTINATIONAL CORPORATE STRATEGY

Multinational corporations (MNCs), or transnational enterprises (TNEs), as they are sometimes called (Kumar 1980:2), are megaenterprises in the corporate business world today. This business segment uses a "coordinated global strategy" to implement horizontal and vertical integration of all entrepreneurial sectors (Roberts 1989:671; Gilpin 1975:10; Students 1975:53). A study of Weyerhaeuser by Evergreen State College research students states, "A corporation may be considered multinational if the scope of its operations is global, if its operations are integrated, and corporate and productive units are not operated independently. Accordingly, management must have a worldwide organizational orientation" (Students 1975:52).

The MNC strategy aims to monopolize all production components to maximize profits and reduce costs: raw materials, corporate financing, research and development, product marketing, and distribution. Corporate activities are vertically and horizontally integrated through centralized management, direct access to strategically accessible resources throughout the sphere of investment, and access to development capital, technology, and markets (Gilpin 1975:10; Bonilla and Girling 1973:50). Multinational corporate owners participate in interlocking directorships of allied banking, finance, and industrial institutions to enhance operations efficiency and maximize access to strategic natural resources, cash and markets. MNCs use foreign subsidiaries not only as sources of raw materials but also as markets for finished products, thereby taking advantage of locally available resources, cheap labor supplies, and local consumer demands while simultaneously enhancing the parent company's corporate profits (Students 1975:5–10).

Weyerhaeuser is an archetype of just such a multinational enterprise, which since the late 1950s has created an impressive, centrally coordinated worldwide timber products conglomerate (Students 1975:51; see also Smith 1986; Dierks 1972). Weyerhaeuser in 1965 owned manufacturing plants in twenty-seven states and twelve foreign countries in Central and South America, the Far East, Europe, and Canada (Students 1975:3; Weyerhaeuser, *Annual Report* 1966). Weyerhaeuser corporate directors sit on the boards of at least seven financial institutions, universities, the Burlington Northern Railroad, Boeing Company, and various insurance and real estate companies (Students 1975:5–8; Weyerhaeuser, *Annual Report* 1988).

Foreign investment has been crucial to Weyerhaeuser's corporate success.

Weyerhaeuser entered the foreign timber market during the early 1960s when its domestic market appeared stalled in opportunities for further corporate growth. Foreign investment brought Weyerhaeuser new opportunities to increase its productivity and corporate profits, which in 1974 exceeded $2.5 billion (Students 1975:51–53). In 1980 sales to customers outside the United States amounted to $1.5 billion, 34 percent of Weyerhaeuser's total sales for that year (Weyerhaeuser, *Annual Report* 1980:22). Weyerhaeuser's 1988 exports, mainly to Japan, totaled a record $1.8 billion, 70 percent as finished products shipped largely from company-owned docks on Westwood Shipping Lines, a Weyerhaeuser-owned subsidiary (Weyerhaeuser, *Annual Report* 1988).

Weyerhaeuser's corporate success, based on efficient, coordinated management to maximize marketing opportunities and profits, has been achieved using several strategic approaches, including: (1) intensive scientifically oriented research and development; (2) capital-intensive production; (3) high-yield forestry practice using clear-cutting; (4) product diversification; (5) complete product use, including wood chips and other residue; and (6) worldwide land acquisitions, production, and marketing (Weyerhaeuser, *Annual Report* 1980:2–3, 1981:7–10). All of these practices have made Weyerhaeuser among the top one hundred revenue-producing U.S. corporations and by far the most profitable timber company in the world. Within the U.S. timber industry, Weyerhaeuser has been consistently rated number one in income, profit margin, and return on investment, although it has a lower asset base and volume of sales figures than other domestic timber producers. Weyerhaeuser sales topped one billion dollars in 1968, and in just five years, in 1973, they topped two billion dollars. Corporate sales and revenues in 1988 for the first time topped ten billion dollars (Students 1975:4, 17, 53; Weyerhaeuser, *Annual Reports* 1968–94).

Weyerhaeuser views its forestry practices as an "agricultural enterprise," relying heavily on scientific research and development to produce high-yield species, develop faster-growing trees, and cultivate to maximum efficiency through clear-cutting and uniform harvesting methods. Said Weyerhaeuser's Wright City public relations officer, "We're farming the woods instead of cutting and letting nature take its course. We're cultivating" (Hankins 1982). This practice improved Oklahoma per acre yields from three to seven times since Weyerhaeuser entered the region in 1969. Weyerhaeuser can now harvest its genetically improved timber in thirty years or less, whereas previously the time frame was fifty to sixty years.

Vertical and horizontal integration has brought under Weyerhaeuser's corporate wing a wide array of enterprises that maximize production capacity, product use, and profitability in an unpredictable business. Wholly owned Weyerhaeuser subsidiaries include facilities for the growing and harvesting of timber; processing plants for producing building materials, pulp, paper, and packaging products; the Weyerhaeuser Real Estate Company; the GNA Corporation, an investment subsidiary; home construction and mortgage companies; six railroads; and a twelve-story office building in Tacoma, Washington (Weyerhaeuser, *Annual Reports* 1979–88; Students 1975; Weyerhaeuser 1980). Weyerhaeuser's integrated operations use forest products to maximum efficiency, providing not only raw materials but also end products in its own enterprises, thereby eliminating payments to middlemen as well as product waste. This strategy has enabled Weyerhaeuser to avoid cyclical changes in the construction industry, thereby minimizing losses during periods of market decline (Students 1975:30).

Weyerhaeuser owns in the Oklahoma/Arkansas region alone, in addition to 1.9 million acres of timberland, a wood fiberboard plant at Craig, Oklahoma; mills at Wright City and Valliant, Oklahoma; the Weyerhaeuser Townsite Company; the Weyerhaeuser Real Estate Company; and the Texas, Oklahoma, and Eastern Railroad. Its Valliant operation, built in 1972, produces paper and paperboard products solely from wood chips. This single mill has enabled Weyerhaeuser to meet its own needs for containerboard, which previously it had to purchase. Furthermore, according to the trade journal *Pulp and Paper* (1972:39), "the mill's centralized location will shorten virtually all lines of transportation for both foreign and domestic markets." The Valliant mill epitomizes the capital-intensive, technology-oriented nature of much of Weyerhaeuser's operations, in which six men operate the entire pulp mill portion of the Valliant mill from a central control panel (*Pulp and Paper* 1972:43).

Weyerhaeuser's corporate growth during the past two and one-half decades has been consistent and impressive. Since 1969 the corporation's total assets have more than tripled. The corporation's timberland base, which currently stands at 5.8 million acres domestically owned, has not increased substantially since 1969, when it owned about 5.6 million acres; in two decades, however, Weyerhaeuser doubled per acre yield by converting more than half of its domestic acreage to plantations planted in fast-growing shortleaf and loblolly pine species. Weyerhaeuser has further insured profitability by diversifying into new areas of production and investment. While

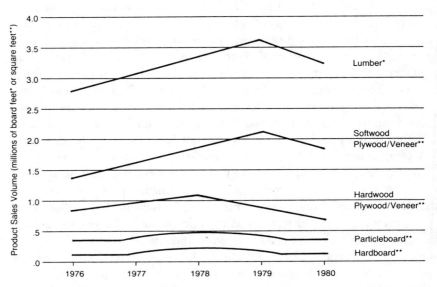

Figure 12.1. Sales of standard Weyerhaeuser products, 1976–80. *Source*: Weyerhaeuser, *Annual Report* 1980:13. *millions of board feet. **millions of square feet.

sales of Weyerhaeuser's traditional products, such as lumber, plywood, and particleboard, have declined during this period, the company has compensated by accruing greater revenues from diversified investments in soft disposable (mainly Sears-sold) diapers, chemicals, nursery supplies, and home construction and real estate subsidiaries, including the GNA Corporation and Republic Federal Savings and Loan Company (Weyerhaeuser, *Annual Reports* 1969–96). Additional revenues have been achieved through sales to foreign markets, particularly exports to Japan. Corporate profits in various Weyerhaeuser standard and diversified products between 1976 and 1980 are shown in figures 12.1 and 12.2.

EFFECTS OF CORPORATE DEVELOPMENT: HINTERLAND UNDERDEVELOPMENT

Multinational corporate development in the periphery, according to Dos Santos (1970:235), promotes underdevelopment as a result of three phenomena: "First, it subjects the labor force to highly exploitative relations which

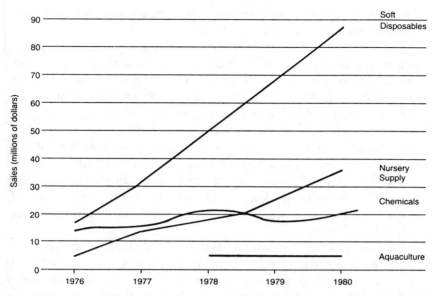

Figure 12.2. Sales of diversified Weyerhaeuser products, 1976–80. *Source*: Weyerhaeuser, *Annual Report* 1980:19.

limit its purchasing power. Second, in adopting a technology of intensive capital use, it creates very few jobs in comparison with population growth, and limits the generation of new sources of income. . . . Third, the remittance abroad of profits carries away part of the economic surplus generated within the country." In this form of what Dos Santo terms "technological-industrial dependence" the intrusive MNC relies on massive technological and capital inputs to produce an ever-increasing rate of return on investments. The "secondary labor market" (see Flora et al. 1992:42–43) provides cheap unskilled and semiskilled workers for extractive industries, who accrue substantial surplus value, both in the actual work performed and through unpaid household labor and public welfare subsidies.

Weyerhaeuser, since entering southeastern Oklahoma in 1969, has undergone several phases of "corporate restructuring" typical of contemporary global capitalism (Flora et al. 1992:37–38). First, Weyerhaeuser bought up smaller firms, including Dierks, eliminating competition and controlling the regional asset base. Second, as noted, it introduced highly capital-intensive technological innovations to streamline production. Third, it reintro-duced cheaper, more labor-intensive nonunionized peripheral production strategies, such as labor subcontracting.

These strategies, although enhancing corporate profits, severely limit local wages and opportunities for community economic growth. Weyerhaeuser claimed that it created one thousand new jobs since 1969 in southeastern Oklahoma (Weyerhaeuser 1977). In 1981 and 1982 it shut down a plant in Broken Bow and laid off 295 workers at its plant in Craig. During the same two years 400 workers out of a total work force of 1,800 in Oklahoma were laid off, including 65 salaried and nearly 350 hourly workers. Weyerhaeuser's unionized work force has declined by nearly one-half since the late 1970s, from a high of 2,800 to a current union membership of 1,224 (Ray 1996). "We have had to get lean and mean and competitive, and more profitable," said Weyerhaeuser's public relations officer in Wright City, Oklahoma (Hankins 1982).

The labor force and the households from which it is drawn are crucial elements in the hinterland production strategy. Laborers may be drawn to the region as a result of expropriation of their own land base and the absence of alternative employment opportunities as migrant laborers. Or, living as a captive labor force in close proximity to the industrial enterprise as rural traditional landowners, they become an essential source of unskilled, readily available labor for the MNC (see Laite 1981; Flora et al. 1992:42–44). The Choctaws are an example of the latter: a permanently based local population segment that has become an unskilled surplus labor force for the timber resource extraction industry.

Weyerhaeuser's timber cutting, harvesting, and tree maintenance activities, the heart of their local industrial enterprise, epitomize how the industry exploits and marginalizes laborers to achieve maximum economic advantage and accrue profits, paying little attention to the human needs of workers and leaving instead to the public sector the task of subsidizing inadequate salaries and benefits. Choctaw timber workers are part of a sophisticated labor-use system that has become increasingly common globally in peripheral MNC enterprises, based on nonunionized part-time contracted labor (see Roberts 1989:678–81ff.; Flora et al. 1992:42–43). Local Choctaw timber workers work mainly as part-time timber cutters and tree planters organized into independent (nonunionized) work crews of four to seven men employed by head contractors. The head contractor, or crew boss, obtains work contracts directly from Weyerhaeuser through competitive bidding and then hires his own crew for a particular job.

Timber cutting crews were generally composed of kinfolk. For example, one crew consisted of two brothers, two half-brothers, and one unrelated individual, most of whom were part-Choctaw. The head contractor supplies all heavy equipment, while the cutters supply their own chain saws. One contractor stated that he had $240,000 invested in heavy equipment in 1982, including a skidder (a truck used to drag logs to transport vehicles) and a logging truck, which he repaired himself to reduce operating costs.

This same contractor explained how he and his fellow contractors are able to turn a profit in a business directly tied to fluctuations in Weyerhaeuser's demand for timber. His crew consisted of five, including himself, although optimally he would hire two additional log cutters if sufficient work were available. He paid them $6 per hour each, and they averaged a three-day work week, with occasional weeks without work due to lack of contracts, inclement weather, or other factors. His profit margin depended on tax remuneration on depreciation allowances on his heavy equipment, which in 1981 amounted to $76,000 on equipment worth about $296,000. He claimed that he trades in his heavy equipment every two years to write off depreciation costs. In this way he paid nothing for his equipment and profited substantially more from his gross earnings than he would have under a different system of taxation. As this individual claimed, a successful contractor "must be foremost a good businessman" (author's interview 6/5/82). The timber slump of 1981–82 reduced logging activities for this particular crew to a three-day week, although it appears that even prior to the early 1980s housing crisis logging crews normally worked less than full-time.

Contractors typically provide only legally mandated worker benefits. The contractor interviewed said that his workers are eligible for worker's compensation, although they do not receive family health insurance benefits, nor are they paid for layoffs, holidays, or sick days.

Tree planting and tree maintenance, including thinning and insect control, are also performed by part-time crews hired through private contractors. Contractors hiring tree planting crews afford their workers even less job security and lower pay than do logging contractors, since the tree planting season is only about four and one-half months long, from January through mid-May. Tree planters are paid at piecework rates, an average of thirty-six dollars per thousand trees in 1982. Workers reported that they planted from one thousand to fifteen hundred trees per day, with women planting fewer than men and novice workers planting more slowly than experienced workers. Tree planting is physically rigorous, entailing trekking through recently clear-cut acreage rough with deep grooves and stumpage where seedlings must be set. Approximately half the tree planters are females and older workers who take advantage of the seasonally available work. Workers are told that if trees are planted too far apart or if the stand does not take, they must return to the site to replant, the cost of which is taken out of their wages.

Working as a contractor, crew member, or independent logger is a cyclical business dependent on Weyerhaeuser's demand for timber. Efforts to break into the logging business are not always successful. One individual claimed that at least three contractors had folded because demand for timber was low. He also claimed that "people buying [logging] trucks are barely surviving," a claim substantiated by the James family, which was barely subsisting on its logging income. Another summarized, "Fall used to be good. This year the industry is bad. This year is the worst! Lumber is not that much in demand. You're better off being able to draw unemployment than work for contractors" (author's interview 5/6/81).

Throughout the 1980s and 1990s Weyerhaeuser has increasingly relied on contractors to harvest timber and plant and maintain stands, while slashing its unionized work force dramatically, a strategy designed to reduce corporate costs and increase its competitive edge. Weyerhaeuser currently uses contract workers almost exclusively to harvest and transport timber. Only about 12 percent of timber brought to Weyerhaeuser's Wright City plant is carried by company trucks; the rest by contractors. Twenty-seven logging contractors, ten chipping contractors, two pruning contractors, and a couple of tree-planting contractors do the work formerly performed by Weyerhaeuser's permanent workers. An estimated two hundred men work for tree-cutting crews, one hundred in chipping operations, and about forty to sixty in seasonal tree planting. Weyerhaeuser has contracted road and mill maintenance jobs as well, further reducing its unionized work force by over half between the late 1970s and 1993, from approximately 2,800 to 1,224 members (Tharp 1990; Ray 1996).

Weyerhaeuser's tree-harvesting practices have made unionized timbermen a truly dying breed in southeastern Oklahoma. A single Weyerhaeuser logging crew of twelve men, the last remnants of what in 1978 was a company force of 278, has been threatened with elimination if it cannot remain competitive with contracted loggers. This followed corporate field assessments by a management team sent from Tacoma, Washington, which determined that company logging operations were not cost effective (Ray 1993).

This last remaining twelve-man logging crew is the most racially integrated Weyerhaeuser labor component, with five Native American and seven white members. The crew operates heavy equipment, including large cutters, limbers, skidders, and loaders, working side by side with contract crews who perform final tree felling and trimming with chain saws. Included in its ranks is Choctaw tribal councilman Billy Paul Baker from northern McCurtain County, a union shop steward and twenty-five-year Weyerhaeuser veteran.

Weyerhaeuser's contract labor system benefits the corporation substantially, reducing or eliminating various costs of production, borne instead by workers and contractors, including maintaining a permanent work force that may not be profitably used throughout the year and costly equipment such as skidders and limbers. Furthermore, the company reduces costs to transport workers to widely scattered worksites on their estimated 890,000 acres of active timberland in southeastern Oklahoma and Arkansas and costs to maintain tree-harvesting equipment, since these are borne by the contracted crews themselves. Fringe benefits, such as health insurance, vacation pay, and other employee benefits, are not paid by Weyerhaeuser, but rather by contractors or workers, or not at all, further eroding already substandard wages.

The Woodworkers Local W15, representing Weyerhaeuser's unionized workers, has vocally opposed Weyerhaeuser's use of contract labor throughout the 1980s and 1990s for several reasons. The contract labor system erodes jobs available to permanent workers and brings in outsiders, since several contracting crews have come in as roving contractors, taking jobs away from the local community. There is no Weyerhaeuser policy to insure that local workers are preferentially hired to prevent such practices. Furthermore, the union has objected to contractors' subunion wage scales, substandard benefits provided, and the lack of worker protection for job-related injuries (Rice 1982; Baker 1993; Ray 1993).

Weyerhaeuser has continued to reduce its work force by employing contractors at its mill sites and in timber transport, while reducing employee benefits, including eliminating time-and-a-half pay for overtime, in its most recent contract negotiated in 1993. Weyerhaeuser was called by one worker "a snake without a head" for its ruthless treatment of its rank-and-file workers both in the field and at the bargaining table. The company has also refused to entertain unionization of contract labor, a proposal advocated by union officials.

Weyerhaeuser's employment of ethnic minorities and women, the timber cutting crew notwithstanding, has also been unimpressive throughout the 1980s and 1990s, particularly in managerial sectors. Woodworkers Union data show that of its approximately fifteen hundred unionized workers in 1993, eleven hundred were white, eighty Native American (less than 5 percent), approximately three hundred African American (20 percent), and twelve Hispanic. No Native Americans work in managerial or supervisory positions at Weyerhaeuser's headquarters at Wright City, and longtime Choctaw workers claim that they have been overlooked in promotions to supervisory jobs for which they were qualified. Contract crews, on the other hand, hire illegal aliens, often exploiting them with subminimum wages paid under the table to do intermittent and dangerous work, such as insect control and limbing (Ray 1993; Baker 1993).

Statistics also show that women are overrepresented in lower-paid chicken-processing jobs and underrepresented in better-paid timber industry jobs. Weyerhaeuser's local unionized work force is currently only about 15 percent female, while women compose 57 percent of Tyson's local nonunionized work force (Ray 1996; Langford 1995).

CHICKEN PLANT WORKERS

Like Weyerhaeuser, Tyson Foods, Inc., with a regional work force of approximately sixteen hundred, is a fast-growing company that relies on product diversification, cheap labor, and technological innovations to process locally more than one hundred thousand chickens per hour. Tyson Foods opened a processing plant in Broken Bow, Oklahoma, in 1969, where approximately twelve hundred workers – 70 percent minority and nonunionized – process 1.3 million chickens a week. Twenty-five percent of the plant's workers are Native American, 30 percent African American, and 15 percent Hispanic. Approximately 57 percent of Tyson's local work force is female, as earlier noted. Tyson also supports approximately five hundred chicken breeder and broiler houses, some corporate owned (Langford 1995).

Tyson Foods, headed by the entrepreneur Don Tyson, recently purchased Louis Rich Foods, a Phillip Morris–owned subsidiary. In 1992 it bought Louis Kemp Seafood and Arctic Alaska Fisheries, Inc., to diversity its food production enterprises. Also in 1992 Tyson Foods expanded its operations in Mexico by linking with the Mexican poultry producer Trasgo SA Company (*Wall Street Journal* 6/24/92, B4; 8/28/92, B4; 6/11/93, B3; 3/2/92, B4).

Tyson and its predecessor operators in southeastern Oklahoma and southwestern Arkansas, including Lane Chicken Company, notorious for their antiunion views and union-busting practices, have persistently resisted unionization efforts throughout the 1970s, 1980s, and 1990s. One worker at a local chicken plant told that employee efforts to unionize a shop in Idabel, Oklahoma, in 1978 resulted in termination of about thirty workers. She quit as a result and was rehired only after she pledged to refrain from further unionization activities. She said, "I didn't want to go back there but I had no choice. There was no place else to work" (author's interview 2/23/81).

Tyson has not been reluctant to use illegal labor and marketing practices. In 1993 the National Labor Relations Board (NLRB) found Tyson guilty of illegal labor practices at an Arkansas poultry plant, following court decisions in 1992 that gave chicken growers rights to organize, efforts Tyson and other chicken processing companies actively resisted (*Wall Street Journal* 8/12/92, B6; author's interviews, Tyson plant workers, Broken Bow OK, 6/9/93; Ray 1993). Ongoing efforts to unionize the Broken Bow, Oklahoma, plant have met with intimidation and threats by Tyson management and so far have been unsuccessful.

The relationship between Choctaw laborers and these corporations is somewhat different from that between a company and a fully proletarianized urban industrial work force, however. Choctaws, like migrant laborers analyzed by Julian Laite (1981) or Claude Meillassoux (1981, 1983), move between the domestic subsistence sector and the wage laboring sector, rather than being wholly submerged in the wage sector as landless workers. By relying on diverse household-based subsistence activities, supplemented by public assistance, tribal assistance programs, and otherwise "making do," Choctaw households shoulder many of the costs to reproduce their own labor force, thus further reducing corporate costs. Furthermore, the community and its workers, rather than Weyerhaeuser or other private employers, bear the costs of low wages and seasonally available work, because workers collect unemployment or public assistance or resort to other subsistence strategies, such as gardening, hunting, odd jobs, even collecting aluminum cans, to compensate for low or erratic wages (see also Hedley 1993; Collins and Gimenez, eds., 1990).

Contract workers, particularly those employed in kin-based logging crews, expressed general satisfaction with their job situations; and the few remaining Weyerhaeuser loggers – most with over fifteen years of service – discussed with sadness Weyerhaeuser's threatened elimination of their crew. Several loggers said that they preferred to work under the contract system rather than as wage laborers directly for Weyerhaeuser. As one logger put it, "You're just a tool for them [Weyerhaeuser]. If you dropped dead they'll have a replacement in about an hour" (author's interview 5/28/81). Participation in logging crews composed of kinsmen permits workers to experience at the workplace the fellowship and support of kinsmen, generally absent in more depersonalized corporate worksites. Job security is ostensibly, but not always, higher, particularly if one is employed by one's sibling or in-law. Loggers shared a common sentiment that they are more in control of their lives as workers than they would be as wage earners at a Weyerhaeuser plant. They are not tied to a time clock, nor are they told when or where to work, and the reduced work week offers a more leisurely pace of life. Part-time work fits well into the seasonal ebb and flow of their lives, which some families accommodate to by moving from household to household, taking advantage of seasonally available jobs and public-assistance benefits during layoffs. When asked if they would prefer to hold down more steady jobs that paid higher wages, most loggers claimed they would not, opting instead for part-time work and greater leisure time.

Enduring commitments to the region, both culturally and historically, also contribute to Choctaws' becoming an easily exploitable work force, since they are willing to take jobs under almost any conditions of employment. Jobs are simply too scarce and dear to do otherwise. Although part-time wage earners experience exploitation directly, they don't perceive its full impact, in part because they don't have direct economic ties to Weyerhaeuser. Participation in household-based subsistence activities coupled with public-sector assistance benefits further shield workers from the full impact of an employment system characterized by seasonal layoffs and inadequate wages.

Choctaws were divided in their opinions of Weyerhaeuser's economic impact on them and their communities, and their own future prospects for well-being. Many expressed discontent with Weyerhaeuser and the economic system in general for placing their people at a low level of economic well-being. Several, particularly those with adult children unable to find full-time work, charged that jobs today are no more available than they were before Weyerhaeuser's takeover in 1969. One retired worker commented, "It seems jobs are worse now. A lot of young people are out of work. Seems there was more work in the 1950s and 1960s" (author's interview 5/7/81). Another individual nearing retirement age whose children have left the region to find work said, "I don't think there are more jobs today. You can't get a job around here. Some work in timber, but there isn't much work around. I think they should get more pay. For two years they haven't gotten a raise" (author's interview 5/11/81). One individual with children just entering the work force, whose husband worked in timber for many years on and off, said, "If Weyerhaeuser had more jobs for Indians they could help us, but they don't seem to care about Indians. They're destroying and taking away all of our hardwoods" (5/28/81).

Sentiments critical of Weyerhaeuser's clear-cutting practices, curtailed by the corporation in the early 1990s, were widely heard among local residents in the 1980s. Many expressed displeasure with clear-cutting, claiming that wildlife was endangered and wild game was no longer as plentiful. Others were displeased with the ugly appearance of the local landscape denuded of its timber cover. An older individual summed up Weyerhaeuser's impact on the local ecology, saying, "I don't think Weyerhaeuser is helping the situation. They're doing away with deer and turkey. Wildlife will suffer. At first they cut here and there. Now they're coming back and joining these clear-cuts. Dierks had a better system. They didn't do any clear-cutting" (author's interview 5/7/81).

Workers in the early 1980s readily admitted their dependence on Weyerhaeuser, regardless of inadequate wages, layoffs, and objectionable clear-cutting practices. One young full-blood Choctaw said, "If Weyerhaeuser were to pull out, this would be a depressed area. We have to admit jobs have been increased since they came here" (author's interview 6/12/81). Another full-blood said, "If Weyerhaeuser weren't here, people wouldn't have many jobs at all. People hate them, but they're down here. Might as well accept them because they're going to stay" (author's interview 6/18/81).

Little more than a decade later, the sentiment has changed drastically, particularly for Weyerhaeuser's full-time timber cutters, who have seen their comrades disappear into the ranks of nonunionized contract workers. Fearing the loss of their own jobs, they sullenly talk of Weyerhaeuser production quotas, speedups, watchful bosses, and the likelihood that today's paycheck will be their last.

Older retired workers expressed the underlying contradictions of the private enterprise/welfare-subsidized economy when they pointed out that their own lives actually improved only after they stopped working. Said one man in his midsixties,

Living improved after I stopped working. Now I have a steady income from my VA pension. When I worked I earned six dollars per day on the average doing odd jobs. I was laid off a lot. My kids missed school because I was laid off and I couldn't afford to send them. We went to Texas to pick cotton when we couldn't find work around here. The whole family helped the best they could. It was a harder life for us then. (author's interview 6/17/81)

Many recognized that their improved lifestyle was due not to better job opportunities but rather to increased public-sector benefits along with the mutual-help housing program. Many who experienced a lifetime of underemployment think – and rightly so – that conditions have improved, both for themselves and their children. Public-assistance benefits, mutual-help housing, and reliance on domestic subsistence provide most households with sufficient cash and material resources to meet their basic necessities, albeit below federally recognized poverty levels. Several individuals pointed out how the housing program had dramatically changed their lives. One said, "Life has definitely changed for us for the better. We lived in a two-room house growing up. We had no running water, an outdoor privy. If it weren't for the housing deal, we never would have been able to buy a home" (author's interview 5/28/81).

Many workers are unaware of how Weyerhaeuser's use of local laborers might exploit them. Most households do not perceive that their nonwaged activities in the domestic sector compensate their own inadequate wages in the timber or other industries. They do not blame Weyerhaeuser for hiring them only part-time or seasonally, since most do not actually work directly for Weyerhaeuser. Many, in fact, work for their own kinsmen who are responsible for managing work crews.

Many workers believe the opportunity to work full-time is potentially available (and some workers have in the past worked at Weyerhaeuser's or other timber mills). They declare that they have instead opted for greater personal freedom and independence. Many indicated, however, that an important factor was the distance to Weyerhaeuser's mills, seventy or eighty miles, and the excessive traveling costs that would entail.

The mixed subsistence economy, which offers the appearance of a system of Chayanovian "household economizers" (see Chayanov 1925; Sahlins 1972) opting for leisure time rather than material benefits, in fact shows the direct exploitation of wage laborers in the world economy. Householders, mainly women, subsidize underemployed and poorly paid wage earners with their informal unpaid labor in subsistence, commodity production, and resource sharing and exchanges. Women's unpaid work adds value to the household wage, thereby subsidizing inadequate family wages with domestically accrued resources (see also Shelton and Agger 1993:39; Ward 1990; Collins and Gimenez, eds., 1990).

Meillassoux, in analyzing the domestic subsistence sector, illuminated why workers such as the Choctaws do not perceive themselves as truly exploited and why they persist in their wage-laboring occupations. The wage laborer who leaves the domestic sector to participate in wage labor "has access to cash which is scarce and 'dear' in the domestic sector . . . [and] the prospect of a relatively higher income compared to that which is possible for him using the same labour power within the domestic mode of production" (Meillassoux 1981:128; see also McGuire and Woodsong 1990). As earlier data have revealed, wages accrue greater material wealth than do exclusive reliance on household subsistence strategies combined with public assistance, the only alternatives to part-time work. Even though the wage laborer in the capitalist sector is underpaid, Meillassoux concludes, "his immediate income is nevertheless raised, because, on average, the productivity of his labor has been increased" (1981:128). The wage earner, however, must contend with exploitation, lack of job security, and inadequate wages.

Choctaw lack of class consciousness is particularly evident in the course the tribe has taken under the leadership of Chief Hollis Roberts. Roberts, touting Reaganomics and using the Indian Self-Determination Act of 1975 as a vehicle for tribal economic development initiatives, has created in microcosm a capitalist, welfare state. Any self-conception of oppression at the hands of Weyerhaeuser or U.S. private enterprise is little evident today. As David Muga argues (1988:40), focusing on governmental hindrances to Indian self-determination "remove[s] attention away from the underlying forces based in private ownership of the means of production, and thereby, obscure[s] a class understanding of ethnic oppression." These contradictions in the emergent Choctaw political economy, rooted in the U.S. welfare-subsidized corporate capitalism, are explored further in a later chapter.

The Choctaw Nation represents a rural hinterland region dominated by two multinational corporations, Weyerhaeuser and Tyson Foods. Typical of internal colonies globally, southeastern Oklahoma only marginally benefits from the multinational corporate presence, while substantial profits accrue to corporate owners. Corporate strategies benefit from vertical and horizontal integration, product diversification, shrewd and sometimes ruthless management, and cheap labor.

A basic component of Weyerhaeuser's production strategy is subcontracting, which reduces corporate labor force maintenance costs and turns over to the workers themselves many costs to maintain and reproduce the local labor force. As a nonunionized work force, subcontracted labor generally receives lower wages, fewer employee benefits, and more unstable hours of employment. Weyerhaeuser has increased its reliance on nonunionized workers, thereby reducing corporate costs. The next chapter explores some of Weyerhaeuser's more subtle, indirect profit-making strategies and the forms "corporate welfare" takes in the southeastern Oklahoma timber industry.

THIRTEEN

Corporate Profit-Making Strategies: A Macroanalysis

Today southeastern Oklahoma's rural main streets – Idabel, Talihina, and Wright City – bear the face of rural poverty: dusty main streets and empty storefronts. These symptoms of malaise, caused by high unemployment, underemployment, and an inadequate tax base, are by-products of the local expression of a global development strategy that profits multinational corporations (MNCs) while it impoverishes local communities. As Brian Roberts has noted (1989:671), "Corporations operating in a world strategy have no strong commitment to place, relocating different divisions according to the most cost effective strategy – where certain types of labor are cheaper, are more available, or where favorable tax or other concessions are obtained." Although Choctaws have benefited from mutual-help housing, improved health care, and other subsidy programs, the poverty exhibited by these local communities demonstrates that the trickle-down benefits of welfare state corporate capitalism accrue only marginally to rural enclave communities.

The previous chapter explored Weyerhaeuser's highly efficient coordinated global production strategy to show how MNCs use local land and labor to accrue maximum profits at minimal costs. Weyerhaeuser was also shown to benefit from welfare subsidies and from household petty commodity and subsistence production, all features of peripheral economies. Rural extraction enterprises, such as Weyerhaeuser Corporation, also use county, state, and federal taxation structures to maximize profits, particularly in rural communities starved for tax dollars. These forms of "corporate welfare" reduce the corporate tax burden and increase corporate profit-making potential.

THE ENCLAVE POLITICAL ECONOMY: COUNTY LAND ASSESSMENT AND TAXATION POLICIES

If the more obvious effects of corporate development lie in local labor force exploitation and natural resource depletion, corporate profit-making strategies also involve indirect methods of bookkeeping, land assessment, and capital investment, not so readily comprehensible to outside observers. These strategies further deplete local resources and return vast profits to corporate producers, often unbeknownst to the local communities where production and profit making occur.

Local communities penetrated by MNCs rely on property and sales taxes revenues, which often entice local citizens to welcome corporate development schemes in their communities. Local property and sales tax and land assessments – the heart of the local revenue base – often favor corporate landowners, undermining revenues returned to local communities (see Flora et al. 1992:131–32). This process is particularly evident in the Choctaw Nation timber industry at the county level.

Weyerhaeuser is the single largest property tax payer in Pushmataha and McCurtain Counties, where the majority of its Oklahoma timberland is located. Evidence shows, however, that Weyerhaeuser has not paid its fair share of the county property tax burden, because appraisal methods assure that its property tax rates are extremely low when compared with the land's actual market value. For instance, Weyerhaeuser's timberland in both counties, amounting to about 808,600 acres, is assessed in a category similar to agricultural land, to compensate for periods of nonproductivity. But in fact, Weyerhaeuser paid a property tax rate of only $6.50 per acre in 1981, while agricultural producers in McCurtain County paid $17 to $25 per acre (figures from County Tax Assessor, Pushmataha and McCurtain Counties, Oklahoma, 1982). Weyerhaeuser's timberland was assessed at little more than 2 percent of its fair market value (assuming that timberland was worth a mere $300 per acre). Weyerhaeuser acknowledged this shrewd business advantage in its own corporate literature: "This massive asset [approximately 11 billion cubic feet of timber located on nearly 6 million acres] is valued on our books at only $614 million, its historic costs of acquisition, planting and growing, which is only a fraction of current market value" (Weyerhaeuser, *Annual Report* 1982:8).

Weyerhaeuser land in both Pushmataha and McCurtain Counties is appraised by the corporate landowners themselves, under the guidance of the county assessor's office, since the rural counties cannot afford to hire their own appraisers. Weyerhaeuser has succeeded in obtaining a tax structure extremely favorable to its own circumstances in both counties. Table 13.1 shows Weyerhaeuser's tax contributions to Pushmataha and McCurtain Counties

Table 13.1. Weyerhaeuser's two-county tax payments, 1980–89

		McCurtain County	Pushmataha County
Timberland acres		545,842	262,736
Total acres		1,210,000	910,720
Assessed value	1980	$3,550,200	$1,660,902
Taxes paid	1981	$ 274,720	$ 104,698
	1989	$2,563,647*	$ 150,086**
Avg assessed value/acre	1981	$6.51	$6.32
	1989	$9.00	$8.69
County tax revenue	1981	n/a	$ 994,632
	1989	$5,897,910	$1,580,570

Source: Pushmataha and McCurtain County Assessor's Office, Treasurer's Office.

*Taxes reported are on all Weyerhaeuser properties in the county.

**Taxes reported are only on timberland. Weyerhaeuser paid additional property taxes on industrial sites in both counties.

during selected years between 1980 and 1992. Weyerhaeuser's tax payments to Pushmataha County in particular (then the poorest county in the state) show that the corporation paid only slightly more than 10 percent of the county's total property tax revenue, at a time when Weyerhaeuser owned more than 25 percent of the county's land.

Weyerhaeuser's land value self-assessments are even more questionable because virtually its entire timberland base has been replanted with genetically improved stock as a result of extensive technological advances in the cultivation of superior pine species. Corporate spokespeople predicted in 1982 that once their entire 890,000 acres of Oklahoma timberland were cut and reseeded with genetically improved pine, they would enter into a predictable harvesting pattern over a thirty-year growing cycle, which would produce four times what they harvest from their unimproved acreage (Hankins 1982).

County taxation, land assessment, and land use practices do not adequately compensate local counties for these dramatic increases in Weyerhaeuser timberland values, what one analyst called the "hidden value of timber." This is how "most of the forest product companies' timber reserves are carried on their balance sheet at values below current market prices" (*Business Week* 2/23/81:125). This common practice permits timber companies to undervalue assets for tax purposes. Since 1966 Weyerhaeuser's average annual timberland growth rates have doubled owing to intensive technological innovations in clear-cutting and reforestation with genetically improved fast-growing species (Weyerhaeuser, *Annual Report* 1988). Weyerhaeuser's own calculations show that their timber and timberland are undervalued by more than two and one-half times when the value of assets is adjusted for changes in the purchasing power of the U.S. dollar (Weyerhaeuser, *Annual Report* 1981:47).

Federal tax laws benefit timber owners similarly, since growers are compensated for the extended period when their land is unproductive and for potential risks associated with their product, such as environmental disasters or other natural phenomena that could inhibit long-term productivity. Timber growers, like other corporations, are taxed on profits earned from their productive activities. Changes in federal tax laws in the early 1980s reduced tax rates on timber to compensate for its unique risks (Weyerhaeuser, *Annual Report* 1981:28, 39). While corporations routinely paid an overall profits tax rate of 46 percent in 1981, profits on timber revenues were charged at a rate of 28 percent, a rate that was further reduced by Weyerhaeuser to 24 percent in 1981 as a result of various corporate deductions (Weyerhaeuser, *Annual Report* 1981:39). Weyerhaeuser was, in fact, able to pay no federal corporate taxes in 1981, although the corporation's overall domestic earnings alone totaled $260.6 million (*Hartford Courant* 8/17/82:D1).

Attempts were made in 1982 to alter Pushmataha County's tax structure to bring in added revenue because, as one local newspaper claimed, "Pushmataha County is going broke" (*Talihina American* 4/8/82). One proposed solution was to increase all county land values to a uniform flat rate, a move that would have hit Weyerhaeuser hard. This solution, according to news accounts, "hit a snag called politics," since everyone was related and no one wanted a greater share of the tax burden than his neighbor (*Talihina American* 4/8/82). An alternative proposal, a two-cent sales tax, was more popular, although this regressive taxation policy burdens wage earners as consumers, while the corporate landowners remain largely unaffected.

In 1987 the Pushmataha County tax assessor appealed to the county and state equalization boards to revise how the county's managed timber is assessed, based on scientifically determined categories of soil type. The tax assessor sought to increase the assessed value of managed timberland to $10.45 per acre. Weyerhaeuser, along with Nakoosa Paper Company, filed suit in district court in 1990 challenging Pushmataha County's land reassessment efforts, and an out-of-court settlement was reached temporarily setting the value of managed timberland at $8.69 per acre. The court subsequently ruled in Weyerhaeuser's favor when it determined that the asset be classified as "waste timber" rather than in a higher "managed timber" category, a move that county spokespeople describe as "very unfair."

Pushmataha County is the only one of five counties where Weyerhaeuser owns managed timberland that is addressing the problem of land assessment equalization based on scientifically determined categories of evaluation, to more equitably distribute tax liabilities. Since 1990 Weyerhaeuser has sold off more than half of its Pushmataha County timber holdings, over 100,000 acres, to John Hancock Mutual Life Insurance Company and a company subsidiary called Forestree, with corporate offices in Birmingham, Alabama (author's telephone interviews, Pushmataha County Tax Assessor, 3/29/90, 8/14/96; Ray 1996). Weyerhaeuser's corporate strategy appears to be to consolidate its local forest base by dispensing with less-productive acreage.

These profit-maximizing strategies reflect the power and influence of private entrepreneurs, at the expense not only of the local community's labor force but also of the community at large. Weyerhaeuser can drastically undervalue its timber resources for tax purposes, a practice that is simply one manifestation of the systematic exploitation of satellite economies by metropolitan-based corporations. In the long run, local populations are deprived of revenues from their input both as a labor force and as a supplier of basic raw materials, while the wealth extracted from the community accrues to the corporate owners.

WEYERHAEUSER'S DIVERSIFICATION STRATEGY
Timber remains by far Weyerhaeuser's single greatest asset. The underlying key to Weyerhaeuser's success has been its ownership of 5.8 million acres of strategically located highly productive timberland in the United States and access to another nearly 11 million acres worldwide. In the words of corporate spokespeople, "The producers with the best matchups of wood, markets, and converting facilities have strategic and economic advantage. Where the resource/geography mix gives such an advantage, the economic values over time tend to flow back primarily to the resources, and thus to the landowners, whether public or private" (Weyerhaeuser, *Annual Report* 1981:6). Timber is the building block of many derivative Weyerhaeuser enterprises, including plywood manufacture, pulp and paper production, and

packaging enterprises. Building materials derived from raw wood constitu-ted more than half of corporate gross revenues in 1981. This included sales to outside customers as well as intracorporate commodity transfers. Weyer-haeuser's timber and timberlands alone were estimated to be worth $619.8 million in 1981 (Weyerhaeuser, *Annual Report* 1981:27).

Secondary to timber-based enterprises are Weyerhaeuser's more recent investments in real estate and investment companies, home construction, aquaculture, and soft disposable products. Figures 12.1 and 12.2, in the pre-vious chapter, chart Weyerhaeuser's sales of various traditional and diver-sified products during the half decade 1976–80. Product diversification, economies of scale, and multiple uses of its timberland have been effective Weyerhaeuser strategies to compensate for declines in revenues from its pri-mary wood-based products during the slumps in home construction of the late 1970s and early and mid-1980s (Weyerhaeuser, *Annual Report* 1980:13, 19, 1985, 1986). As sales of lumber and lumber-related products fluctuated, diver-sified product sales have steadily enhanced corporate revenues, as the previ-ously cited figures indicate.

Weyerhaeuser's diversification strategy is not new. In the early 1980s in Washington and Oregon, Weyerhaeuser entered the aquaculture business, which used heated water, a by-product of its own production process, as a salmon-spawning bed. Salmon, decimated when their natural habitats were destroyed by timber harvesting, are artificially inseminated and reintro-duced into their previous habitat on Weyerhaeuser's own timberland. Weyer-haeuser in 1983 entered into contracts with Standard Oil of Ohio (Sohio) to conduct oil and natural gas exploration surveys on approximately 810,000 acres of Pushmataha and McCurtain County timberland, making Weyer-haeuser's timberland potentially even more profitable (*McCurtain Gazette* 1/12/83).

Following a corporate reorganization and slimming of its work force dur-ing the mid-1980s, Weyerhaeuser increased its investments in subsidiary en-terprises, including banking, home finance, and real estate, while its timber-related production activities benefited from increased overseas markets, particularly Japan (Weyerhaeuser, *Annual Reports* 1986, 1988). In the early 1990s another slump in timber prices hit the timber industry hard. In a move to concentrate on its wood and paper business, Weyerhaeuser in 1992 pur-chased Proctor and Gamble's pulp and sawmill operations and timberland, to become the world's largest producer of wood pulp (*Wall Street Journal*

8/21/92:3). The company in 1993 divested its annuity investment subsidiary, GNA Corporation, which it sold to General Electric Capital Corporation (*New York Times* 1/7/93:D4).

CUTTING THE COST OF LABOR

Another Weyerhaeuser cost-reduction strategy has been to economize its labor force. As discussed earlier, Weyerhaeuser solved its problem of more costly unionized workers by simply eliminating many and subcontracting the work, a trend increasingly popular in the competitive business marketplace of the 1990s (see Flora et al. 1992:37–50). Weyerhaeuser has also implemented other strategies to reduce labor costs, including tough union negotiating, introduction of capital-intensive equipment, and work force cuts. Weyerhaeuser's local labor force has declined by nearly 25 percent, while the company's potential for timber harvesting has increased dramatically. This fact points to the degree to which Weyerhaeuser is a capital- rather than a labor-intensive business. In concrete terms, the number of employees nationwide declined between 1979 and 1982 from a high of nearly 48,000 to 40,760 in Weyerhaeuser's forestry operations (Weyerhaeuser, *Annual Report* 1982:60). The timber component of Weyerhaeuser's southeastern Oklahoma/Arkansas labor force was reduced from more than 2,000 in 1982 to about 1,500 in 1993. In its containerboard and other production mills, both locally and nationally, Weyerhaeuser significantly reduced its labor force by adding technologically advanced equipment, requiring fewer, although more highly skilled, workers to perform essential production tasks.

Local plans to introduce labor-saving heavy equipment into tree-harvesting operations during the 1980s were not implemented, since the company found that subcontracting labor was more cost effective. Instead, the company drastically cut its own tree-harvesting crews, as noted above, and threatens to reassign its last remaining tree-harvesting crew if it cannot remain competitive with contractors (Hankins 1982; Tharpe 1990; Ray 1993).

Weyerhaeuser has coupled its orientation toward capital-intensive mill production and timber contracting with a view that it will not tolerate "wage inflation." In response to deteriorating housing starts and reduced overall timber products demand nationwide, the corporation implemented various wage-freezing measures nationwide, laid off workers, and sought to negotiate union contracts with scaled-down union demands (*McCurtain Sunday Gazette* 7/11/82; Weyerhaeuser, *Annual Reports,* 1985–88; Tharpe 1990;

Ray 1993). Weyerhaeuser sought to rewrite union contracts containing auto-matic cost-of-living increases, to place on the workers more of the financial burden of an unpredictable timber products market. A contract negotiated in 1982 by more than two thousand members of the International Wood-workers of America (now an affiliate of the International Association of Ma-chinists and Aerospace Workers) in Oklahoma and Arkansas reflected this trend, and the union finally accepted a contract twice rejected by its mem-bership to avoid a costly strike. This contract contained provisions for smaller annual pay raises and rejected the union's demand to represent non-unionized logging crews in contract negotiations (*McCurtain Gazette* 7/30/82). Contracts negotiated in 1988 contained no provisions for wage in-creases, and workers were granted bonuses in lieu of wage increases. Union-ized workers fared no better in contract negotiations in 1993 and faced con-tracts with salary reductions and reduced overtime benefits (Tharpe 1990; Ray 1993).

These labor practices, which emanate from the center of Weyerhaeuser's corporate structure (from the desk of then- president George Weyerhaeuser himself), permit Weyerhaeuser to exploit its timber workers and accrue added value from workers who perform the backbone of their overall timber operations. Not only are workers viewed as dispensable, but their ever-increasing productive potential derived from technological innovations also reduces negative effects of market fluctuations and insures continued corpo-rate profitability. This is especially significant in light of earlier discussions, which showed that timber and timberland are in fact accruing ever-increas-ing wealth to the corporation in forms that are not reported as corporate earnings on Weyerhaeuser's balance sheet. The capitalist tax structure in fact permits Weyerhaeuser to write off its capital expenditures for capital im-provements, including roads, research, and development, while it simul-taneously reduces its labor force.

Weyerhaeuser's production strategy is not unique to southeastern Okla-homa but is replicated in communities throughout the United States and globally. Workers are called upon to perform unskilled or semiskilled jobs as migrant farm laborers, in urban manufacturing and industrial jobs, and in maintenance and service occupations. This peripheral labor force, often eth-nic minority, sometimes women, is drawn from poverty enclaves through-out the United States. Often the corporate sector takes advantage of such workers by rejecting unionization attempts, paying only minimum or slightly above minimum wages, and failing to provide employee benefits (see Fernández Kelly 1989; Roberts 1989; Flora et al. 1992). Since workers are readily available and jobs scarce, workers accept the substandard working conditions.

The timber industry is a beneficiary of a variety of local and federal tax incentives programs, perhaps a legacy of the long-standing power of railroad, mining, and timber interests historically. Local and federal tax policies and various corporate profit maximization strategies substantially enhance corporate profits. "Corporate welfare" benefits have long been a popular component of corporate profit-making strategies, using various cost-accounting methods and tax incentive programs to reduce corporate tax liabilities. Southeastern Oklahoma counties, inadequately poised to counter the influential timber lobby, have only recently begun to increase Weyerhaeuser's tax obligations by reassessing the corporation's valuable land assets. Local communities, however, remain impoverished, while its local industries thrive. The next chapter examines Choctaw development initiatives, as the Choctaws grapple with their own efforts to provide economic self-sufficiency while retaining cultural integrity in the twenty-first century.

FOURTEEN

The Choctaw Crossroads:
Reconciling Politics, Economics, and
Culture in the Choctaw Nation

Choctaw transformation from nation to tribe to ethnic minority occurred as stages toward assimilation and accommodation to a new social order, as shown in chapter 2 (see figure 2.1). First, as an independent native collectivity in the lower Mississippi Valley, Choctaws lived in kin-based neighborhoods headed by influential "big men," relying on mixed subsistence. In the second phase, Choctaws were converted from a nation into a semiautonomous domestic dependent tribe and ghettoized on a reservation to permit more effective direct access to and control over Choctaw land. Interactions with Euro-Americans intensified through external trade, political control, and intermarriage. In the third phase, the Choctaws faced land allotment and termination, converting the tribe into just another ethnic minority citizenry to be assimilated into the U.S. cultural mainstream. They were allowed what George Castile (1993:273) called only "limited 'autonomy,'" similar to ethnic enclaves in socialist settings.

CHOCTAW TRIBALISM AND ETHNICITY
Our story, although not always explicit, is about defining and contesting what it has meant historically and what it means today to be Choctaw: politically, economically, and culturally. It is about "nation," "tribe," sovereignty, cultural persistence, resilience, encroachment, resistance, and co-optation. Public discourse labels Choctaws a "tribe"; however, like all Native Americans so designated, the tribe faces the perennial ambiguity of a historically constructed and historically contingent meaning of Native American sovereignty, ever at the behest of U.S. assimilationist and hegemonic agendas.

Like Native Americans generally, Choctaws are unique among U.S. ethnics and therefore have consternated both U.S. hegemonically oriented policymakers and assimilationist agendas. Through the eras of allotment, Indian "New Deal," termination, and most recently resurgent Indian self-determination, Native Americans have negotiated, contested, and renegotiated indigenous rights, entitlements, and identities (see Wilkins 1993; Cornell 1988, 1990; Muga 1988:38; Hall 1988). Although transformed long ago from independent nations to rural ethnic enclaves, First Nations people have managed to retain at least some unique features, including reservation land, language, independent political structures, and various cultural traditions.

To comprehend the indigenous perspective, non-Indians must critically analyze such terms as *tribalism* and *ethnicity* in the context of Native American history, culture, contact, and change. Indigenous people, like other ethnics, have always had a sense of who they are, based on a sense of peoplehood, sovereignty, and geography, rooted in commonalities of language, transgenerationality, shared cultural practices, leadership, land, and history. As discussed earlier, the U.S. government in effect created "tribes" out of native "nations" by redefining in the service of its own aggrandizing agenda what were formerly rather fluid band- or kin-based entities (see D. Smith 1994:181ff.; Cornell 1988:101–5, 1990a:380–81). As Stephen Cornell states (1988:101), "The tribe was reduced to an administrative category in a program of enforced culture change. Tribalization now occurred not as a native response to invasion, but as the by-product of a particular formal structure of dominant/subordinate group relations."

Native American tribal and ethnic persistence do not merely reflect external forces, however, but are produced through a dialectic between majority and minority cultures (Wilkins 1990:405; Cornell and Kalt 1990:105–8; Dunaway 1994). Native Americans, including the Choctaws, have persistently worked to remain viable. Kin-based residential communities, exchange networks, nonmarket subsistence strategies, and tribal political and cultural traditions, drawn in part from the Choctaw past, set Choctaws apart from their rural non-Indian neighbors and have allowed Choctaws to perpetuate a sense of transgenerational boundedness – albeit increasingly rooted in ethnic rather than "nationhood" criteria.

The history and legacy of past conquest, ghettoization, expropriation, racism, and marginalization have made tribalism particularly ambiguous for land-depleted tribes such as the Choctaws, who no longer have the geographic contiguity of a reservation or the sense of communal boundedness that attachment to land brings. Nor does the tribe benefit by being in a numerical majority locally or regionally. Even Choctaw "blood" and language have become imperfect measures of tribal membership, as more and more Choctaws have dispensed with their native language and intermarried with whites. As noted earlier, today only 8 percent of Choctaws are full-bloods, and of a population estimated nationwide at 98,000, only about 730 Choctaws speak their native language with any fluency. In the context of this homogenization process – culturally, linguistically, racially – wherein, then, lies the substance of Choctaw culture from which the Choctaw people can derive a sense of their own identity as a collective entity?

Ethnic groups, such as tribes, share a common history, language, and culture. Unlike indigenous tribes, however, other U.S. ethnic minorities are "politically encapsulated within the larger state"; their group identification is "no longer . . . a matter of self-identity, but . . . increasingly subject to external definition" (Hall 1987:12–13). Native Americans, too, have had to negotiate their status as domestic "nations," existing largely "subject to external definition." Indians, argues Ronald Takaki (1993:240), were resurrected from near-extinction in the 1934 New Deal Indian Reorganization Act and redefined in an "ethnic experiment" aimed to "social engineer" (see Jiobu 1990:20) a new definition of "tribalism" within a U.S.-sanctioned New Deal "melting pot" framework. Tribes were permitted limited sovereignty and economic self-determination, "modeled on dominant-group political forms" rather than indigenous cultural practices (Cornell 1988:95; Cornell and Kalt 1990:101–4; see also Buffalohead 1986; Wilkins 1993). New Deal self-determination policies sought to resolve persistent endemic poverty and successfully assimilate Indians into the majority culture, so long as they conformed to the majority culture's views of "appropriate" tribalism (see Buffalohead 1986; Muga 1988; Mohawk 1991; Stuart 1990; Mundt 1967). In this process some Native American tribes – particularly nonreservation tribes such as the Choctaws – have become more like other U.S. ethnics, whose status is not linked to national sovereignty, a land base, or long-standing treaty rights. U.S. ethnic status is rooted in voluntary tradition building and maintenance, rather than any legislated or treaty-based institutional structures. In the arena of U.S. state and federal jurisdictional battles over Native American tribes, which have heated up in the 1990s, and in light of conflicts between Congress, the courts, and executive branches over issues of tribal sovereignty and self-determination, Native American tribalism, as perennially, is at best a contested status.

CHOCTAW TRIBAL PERSISTENCE: CHURCH COMMUNITIES

For seventy years, between official termination and the mid-1980s, timber region Choctaws lived in large part in church-based impoverished rural communities, with weak links to a near-extinct political apparatus. This era represented an intermediate stage between traditionally oriented village life rooted in "nation" or "tribe" and modern ethnic group status. Neil Smelser (1967:41–42), investigating processes of political modernization, showed that "in a typical pre-modern setting, political integration is closely fused with kinship position, tribal membership, control of the land or control of the unknown. . . . As social systems grow more complex, political systems are modified accordingly." Oklahoma Choctaws showed a similar process of increasing internal differentiation in the twentieth century. Rural Choctaw communities preserved kin-based socioreligious life, while ties to the tribe's political sector weakened considerably as the tribe took on a modern face as a bureaucratic state in microcosm (see Cornell and Kalt 1990:101–3).

Modeled on the majority culture's ideology of church/state separation, the tribal leadership structure today is a wholly independent entity, with tribal activities headquartered at its Durant, Oklahoma, tribal complex. The role of church elder, unlike indigenous village leaders, is now restricted to the church sphere. The elder's wisdom and leadership capabilities are generally not brought to bear in the secular domain of tribal government, except incidentally where an individual may occupy elected tribal and church positions simultaneously. Then-Assistant Chief Robert Gardner alluded to this split when he noted that tribal meetings are never held in church buildings because Choctaws "don't like to mix religion and politics" (Gardner 1982).

The Choctaw people, however, turn to local-level church communities as fundamental units of social interaction and vehicles for cultural expression. Choctaw membership and active participation in Choctaw church activities were found to be far more extensive than was participation in tribal activities in the early 1980s. While more than thirty of fifty households surveyed reported very active membership in a Choctaw church, only about four or five families expressed even a moderate degree of participation in tribal affairs. Many complained that the tribal complex was too far away. Others said they could not afford to travel to Tuskahoma or Durant, where most tribal business is conducted. Some mentioned that they stay out of tribal politics altogether, claiming that it is too acrimonious or simply irrelevant.

In the early 1980s Choctaws faced the problem of reconciling this split between tribal secular and religious domains. This problem was crucial because the leadership skills of church elders were not tapped to address broader tribal issues. Furthermore, the underlying Choctaw social institution at the heart of Choctaw ethnic expression – the Choctaw church community – did not interface effectively with the secular tribal entity, the tribal government.

NEW U.S. GOVERNMENT ECONOMIC STRATEGIES

These quandaries have persisted as the Choctaws entered a new era of tribal self-determination with Congress's passage of the Indian Self-Determination and Education Assistance Act of 1975 (PL93-638). Responding to persistent economic and social malaise throughout Native American communities, this legislation was aimed to redefine Native American sovereignty and self-determination to give tribes tools necessary to build viable economies, retain some degree of cultural expression, and resolve astronomical unemployment rates, diminished health status, and persistent social welfare dependence (see U.S. Joint Economic Committee 1969).

This legislation proposed that by dealing with Indians on a government-to-government basis, providing block grant seed money for private-sector business initiatives, and reducing bureaucratic meddling in tribal decision making (i.e., turning over many BIA functions to recognized tribes), Native Americans could begin to develop economically self-sustainable tribal economies, thereby alleviating extreme poverty and cultural and social malaise endemic to Native American life (see Cornell 1988; Muga 1988; Stuart 1990; Mohawk 1991; Castile 1993). The federal position, according to Rob Williams (1983:4), was that "only by reducing their dependence on federal funds can Indian people be successful in forcing the federal government to move away from the 'surrogate role' which it has played in reservation life."

REAGAN'S TRIBAL SELF-SUFFICIENCY POLICIES:
FACT AND FICTION

In 1983 Ronald Reagan unveiled a new policy initiative to promote tribal development and self-determination, reduce bureaucratic waste and excessive federal regulation in Indian administration, and cut federal costs to administer tribal programs. The Reagan policy stressed two fundamental goals: first, reduce federal funding significantly by substituting private-sector development initiatives; and second, scale down bureaucratic structures that, although designed to protect Native Nations' trust rights, fostered serious trust abuses. According to the White House Indian Policy Statement of January 24, 1983,

Excessive regulations and self-perpetuating bureaucracy have stifled Tribal decision-making, thwarted Indian control of reservation resources, and promoted dependency rather than self-sufficiency. . . . This Administration will reverse this trend by removing obstacles to self-government and by creating more favorable environments for development of healthy reservation economies. (Quoted in *Indian Truth* April 1983:6)

Tribal self-sufficiency would be achieved through "free market forces," which would "provide the bulk of the capital investments required to develop tribal energy and other resources" (Williams 1983:15; see also White 1990:275–76; Stuart 1990).

A series of "Social and Economic Development Strategies" (SEDS) were proposed to bring self-sufficiency and economic autonomy to Native American communities, while reducing federal expenses and "excessive federal control" of tribal decision making (see U.S. Administration for Native Americans 1985). Policies enabled entitled tribes to apply for federally funded block grants under Title XX to finance housing, employment training, and other services previously administered through the BIA. Another by-product of the "new Federalism" is a recent proposal that tribes be given an alternative to tribal trust status and receive a proportional share of the federal Indian budget, called a Tribal Self-Governance Grant (TSGG), to run their own programs independently (Biard and Craven 1990:17; see also *Akwesasne Notes* 22(1):26; Jorgensen 1984, 1986a).

Many Indian leaders responded optimistically to "new Federalism," with its emphasis on tribal sovereignty and self-determined development. In response, a variety of entrepreneurial ventures – some involving private corporate partnerships – in Indian gaming, tourism, resource extraction, electronics, and production industries have been initiated on reservations throughout the United States (see Mohawk 1991:499–500; Vizenor 1989; D. Smith 1994; Faiman-Silva 1993; White 1990:270–78; Cornell and Kalt 1990, 1992b; Cornell and Kalt, eds., 1992). Reporting on several successful economic initiatives, Richard White concluded (1990:273), "To spend any time among the Passamaquoddies, Mississippi Choctaws, Ak-Chin or Warm Springs is to believe that the private sector indeed offers Native

America a better way out of poverty and powerlessness than does the public sector."

Others, taking a more skeptical view, called Reagan's policies nothing more than another attempt to terminate the federal government's historic trust relationship – what one analyst called "sophisticated termination" (Winslow 1983:8). Others termed the Reagan policies "termination by accountants" (Morris 1988:731).[1] One undisputed effect was to drastically downsize federal budget expenditures to Native Americans, reduced by 22 percent in one year, from $3.4 billion in fiscal year 1982 to $2.7 billion in the fiscal year 1983 budget. Essential Native American programs including health-related Community Health Representatives (whose entire appropriation was cut in 1983 but later reinstated), CETA jobs programs, mutual-help home construction monies, and BIA-funded education entitlements were all targets of Reagan-era budget cuts (*Bishinik* 5/87:2; see also Means 1983).

Tribal sovereignty and economic self-determination efforts were given a boost when California and Florida courts in the 1980s affirmed Indian rights to initiate organized gaming on reservation lands (*Federal Reporter*, 2d ser., vol. 658 F. 2d. [1983]; *New York Times* 7/1/86; *Boston Globe* 9/29/93:1, 24–25). Congress in 1988 passed the Indian Gaming and Regulation Act (U.S. Title 25, S441), which created the National Indian Gaming Commission to regulate reservation Indian gaming activities. Against various state protests, Indian gaming has taken off as a "new buffalo," bringing jobs and revenues to resource-poor tribes. By 1993 more than half of federally recognized tribes ran sixty-eight casinos and 174 high-stakes bingo games in twenty-four states, with gross incomes estimated in 1993 at between $2 billion and $5.8 billion (*Boston Globe* 9/29/93:24). Bingo dollars are infusing tribal communities with cash and benefits, subsidizing federal welfare programs, housing assistance, health care, and infrastructural improvements (*Boston Globe* 9/29/93:1, 24–25; *Bishinik* 1985–95; Faiman-Silva 1992; Folwell 1988).

1. Reagan- and Bush-era policymakers have used yet another strategy to terminate tribes: designating tribes as "historic" or "nonhistoric," thereby terminating so-called nonhistoric tribal groups. The U.S. Congress in May 1994 passed a "Technical Corrections to Native Americans Laws Act" (PL 103-263, 108 Stat. 707), which added language to the 1934 Indian Reorganization Act "prohibiting regulations that classify, enhance or diminish privileges and immunities of an Indian tribe relative to other federally-recognized Indian Tribes." This most recent maneuver again points to the ever-present vulnerability of Native Americans as "domestic dependent nations" (Slagle 1994:1).

REINVENTING CHOCTAW "TRIBALISM"

Choctaws today, under the leadership of an economically innovative, politically conservative chief, Hollis Roberts, are at the forefront among Native Americans "reinventing" (see Sahlins 1993:381) indigenous culture and tribal community life in the context of these new political economic realities, "participat[ing] in their destinies by ordering the global 'reality' in their own terms" (Borofsky 1993:477). In doing so they are walking a familiar triangular tightrope that links Indians, states, and federal agencies vying for a gold mine of gaming industry and other entrepreneurial dollars while they hammer out jurisdictional and tribal sovereignty issues. What hangs in the balance is again the future of Indian sovereignty, self-determination, and Native American cultural integrity (see Stuart 1990; D. Smith 1994).

Until officially terminated in 1906, the tribe was organized along the lines of the federal system under the Choctaw Constitution of 1860. After more than a half century of attenuated existence as a result of Allotment Act provisions, the Choctaw Nation was reorganized in an act of June 26, 1936 (49. Stat. 1967), and a tribal government was reinstituted in 1971. That year the tribe held its first elections since allotment, electing Jimmy Belvin as chief. In a special election in 1978, following the untimely death of then-Chief C. David Gardner, Hollis E. Roberts was elected (Morrison 1987:preface).

Again revised in 1983, the tribal government consists of an elected chief, assistant chief, an elected Tribal Council drawn from the nation's twelve districts, and a judiciary branch, which serves as a court in legal matters. The tribe also has regional planning committees, which draw representatives from throughout the nation. The tribal government makes and enforces tribal laws, manages tribal assets, undertakes various revenue-producing activities, and serves as an intermediary with various entitlement programs available to Native Americans. The tribe offers job counseling services, programs for juveniles and the aged, employment programs, and financial assistance programs. A major employer of Choctaws, the tribe increased its work force from four hundred to seven hundred during the 1980s, most of whom work at the large tribal office complex at Durant.

The tribe's chief, Hollis Roberts, during his nearly two decades in office, has transformed definitions of Choctaw tribalism and tribal culture, as he has worked to change a vaguely sovereign tribe into a highly successful corporate economic entity. The Choctaws took advantage of both the 1975 Indian Self-Determination legislation and the 1988 Indian Gaming Act to build impressively successful tribal economic initiatives. Choctaws overwhelmingly reelected Roberts, with his youthful, charismatic style, with more than 80 percent of the vote in the 1995 tribal election. Still evident is the personalistic relationship between the chief and his constituency, reminiscent of ancient *mingoes*, who were not only kinsmen but also spiritual and political mentors. Chief Roberts affirmed that many Choctaws still expect him to be personally accessible, seeking his guidance pertaining to personal issues, large and small. Choctaws still go to the chief for counsel and guidance in matters pertaining to land, jobs, or personal finances. They viewed their relationship with the chief as part of their personal extended kinship network, as for many it actually is (Roberts 1993; Gardner 1982).

Roberts since the early 1980s has worked to turn around the image and reality of distance between the tribe and its people, using his leadership skills to build a remarkable record of tribal growth, numerically, economically, and culturally. The Oklahoma Choctaw story since Roberts's election in 1978 is similar to that of their Mississippi counterparts, the five thousand descendants of a band who remained in Mississippi following the Trail of Tears, and whose economic accomplishments in the past two decades have also been impressive (see White 1990:55–113; Bordewich 1996).

Roberts in the early 1980s faced a tribal membership that appeared only marginally connected to their tribal roots. Informants in the early 1980s generally expressed weak allegiance to the tribe as it operated politically and economically from its modern office complex in Durant, in the extreme southwestern corner of the Nation. In fact, even the tribal headquarters' location belied the tribal government's quandary in working to promote Choctaw cohesiveness. Many complained, as earlier noted, that Durant was difficult to reach because it was so far away. Many also complained that the tribe did not provide enough activities, either informative or entertaining, and most wanted to be better informed about tribal affairs. The yearly tribal gathering at Tuskahoma, the Choctaw capital, over Labor Day weekend was attended by only a small percentage of families in the Choctaw sample. Most claimed that they could not afford gasoline to travel to that distant part of the nation. Few informants read or even received the tribal newspaper, *Bishinik*, on a regular basis. This paper, the one link to rural communities, temporarily ceased publication in the mid-1980s owing to lack of funds, although publication was soon resumed.

The tribe in the early 1980s began to construct Choctaw community centers throughout the nation, including ones at Bethel, Poteau, Coalgate, Antlers, and recently Oklahoma City. Today a modern community center building stands in each of the ten Choctaw Nation districts. These buildings provide much-needed centralized meeting places for secular tribal gatherings, including business meetings, social gatherings, educational events, and casual gatherings. Tribally owned buildings may offer the essential links between the tribal entity and village communities missing since the reinstitution of a formal elected tribal government in the early 1970s. The assistant chief summarized the role these community centers can play in rebuilding a sense of tribal cohesiveness for the Choctaw people:

ASSISTANT CHIEF: We now have some community centers. . . . Four of them. Those were really needed because before that whatever county we met in, we would have to beg, borrow, or steal a place to meet in and it was kind of an embarrassing thing. We always had to beg for a place, but now we have a place.

QUESTION: That should help to establish some sort of Choctaw feeling, then?

ASSISTANT CHIEF: Right, that's what we wanted. People could come in and meet and say, "This place is mine, and I want to take care of it. I feel free to say what I want to in here and have a sense of well-being." We used to meet in courtrooms. I don't like courtrooms. To me that wasn't a good fellowship meeting at all, sitting in a courtroom. But they were nice to let us use it. Again, that was not the place you could feel fellowship, though. (Gardner 1982)

CHOCTAW DEVELOPMENT STRATEGIES IN THE 1980S

With many of his people languishing in poverty in the early 1980s, a centerpiece of Roberts's evolving vision of a modern Choctaw Nation was to solve his tribe's persistent poverty and unemployment problems. Roberts faced a fundamental challenge of providing his members with a sustainable economy while working to achieve three crucial cultural goals: (1) accommodate to a decentralized, nonreservation Choctaw community lifestyle; (2) preserve some viable forms of Choctaw self-identity; and (3) promote national self-sufficiency and sovereignty. Choctaw leaders have worked to promote two major economic objectives: creating jobs in Choctaw-owned and -run enterprises, and taking over BIA-contracted programs and services under the Indian Self-Determination Act. To accomplish these ends, the tribe developed an elaborate corporate structure that manages tribal assets and serves as intermediary between the Choctaw people and various opportunities available to them through federal government programs, the BIA, the private corporate sector, and local communities.

The Choctaw Nation's major assets, aside from Choctaws' potential as a labor force, are its collective landholdings and income derived therefrom; trust income; and federal subsidies, mainly in the areas of health, education, and jobs. National assets in June 1981 amounted to approximately $14,568,000, compared to a whopping $6 billion for their neighbor, Weyerhaeuser (*Talihina American* 7/23/81; Oklahoma State Corporation Commission Certificate of Authorization, 1981). These assets included land estimated to be worth about $10.8 million, and a tribal trust fund of approximately $3.6 million. The Choctaw annual tribal budget in 1988 was $27.5 million (*Bishinik* 3/88:3). In 1991 the tribe had more than doubled its trust fund assets, to an estimated $7.6 million, with another $2.9 million in its general fund. In that year total tribal assets, including monies, land, buildings, and equipment, were worth an estimated $35 million (*Bishinik* 12/91:5). Today the tribe's net worth is an estimated $65 million (Hollis E. Roberts, promotional flyer 1995).

The Choctaws receive approximately 65 percent of their income from several federal agencies, including the BIA, Department of Agriculture, Department of Labor, Housing and Urban Development, Indian Health Services, and Community Development Block Grants, to finance various programs. Assets derived from these programs amounted to an additional income of nearly $5.4 million in fiscal year 1981 (*Talihina American* 7/23/81; *Bishinik* 12/91:5).

Shortly after Roberts's 1978 election, the tribe began to tackle its economic woes when feasibility studies were undertaken to construct a fiberglass boat fabrication plant in Broken Bow, Oklahoma. This project and its eventual demise after four years of planning is a revealing example of how BIA mismanagement, ineptitude, and failure to adequately advise the Choctaws worked against collective goals, complaints commonly heard throughout Native American communities during the 1970s and 1980s (see Champagne 1983:3–28; Biard and Craven 1990:17).

The proposal for the boat plant was itself of questionable merit, given economic conditions at the time. The plant would have had to gross an estimated $300,000 per month just to meet operating expenses. Interest payments, then at their highest level in several years, would have cost nearly $150,000 annually. Feasibility studies or market assessments were never made to determine local demand for pleasure boats. Later in the project's planning stages the tribal council proposed diversifying the plant's productive capacity into other areas, such as fiberglass oil-drilling bits and transport pipeline, a strategy crucial to this venture's possible success (*Talihina American* 2/11/83; *McCurtain Gazette* 11/15, 11/28, 12/9, 12/13/82, 1/10, 3/14/83).

Despite the project's serious drawbacks, Donald Moon, at that time the local BIA agency superintendent, called the project a good opportunity for the Choctaws, claiming that demand for pleasure craft was high (Moon 1982). The BIA, however, within six months placed the project on hold in light of its serious drawbacks and shortly thereafter demanded the Choctaw's trust money as collateral, a potentially devastating option. The two agencies, the Choctaw Nation and the BIA, were not working in concert, but the BIA was placing unreasonable demands on the Choctaws while failing to offer necessary information about the project's real risks.

This enterprise, although backed by the BIA and federal development agencies, typified the supervision of Native American entrepreneurial development by agencies with little regard for or understanding of fundamental Native needs. This enterprise would have offered jobs to perhaps thirty Choctaws, a paltry number given the costs for construction and project implementation. The Choctaws, after four years of struggle and having spent $183,000, abandoned the proposal in 1983 (*McCurtain Gazette* 1/10/83).

CHOCTAW RESPONSE TO "NEW FEDERALISM"

Beginning in 1985 the Choctaws implemented Reagan-era "new Federalism" policies in earnest when they took over the fifty-two-bed Talihina Indian Hospital, renamed the Choctaw Nation Indian Hospital, and three outlying health clinics, which together employed over two hundred people. The Choctaws were the first Native Nation to act on their newly acquired right under provisions of the 1975 Indian Self-Determination Act to contract what were formerly BIA-run services in the area of full hospital administration. Since takeover, the outpatient census has tripled, and in 1990 Chief Hollis Roberts announced plans to seek federal funds to build a new hospital facility at Talihina.

A second tribal initiative was the 1986 acquisition of the 256-acre Arrowhead Lodge, located in the northern Choctaw Nation, which was renovated to provide beach accommodations and an amphitheater, again with the goal of providing additional jobs for Choctaws. The lodge complex employed over 140 people in 1987, three-quarters of whom were Choctaws. A capstone to the lodge is a recently completed 12,000-square-foot convention center that accommodates eight hundred people (*Bishinik* 5/87:2, 2/92:1).

The boldest and potentially most controversial Choctaw undertaking was in 1987, when the Choctaw Indian Bingo Palace opened at Durant, creating about 140 additional jobs and promising to be a significant revenue producer. The bingo concession attracts approximately 160,000 people per year, 80 percent from Texas. In its second year of operations bingo netted more than one million dollars in profits, and the Choctaws expected to earn twelve million dollars annually when they took over full ownership after seven years. The complex has been expanded to include a full-service travel center, the Choctaw Nation Travel Plaza, which in 1992 grossed over $1.4 billion per month (*Bishinik* 2/92:3).

Bingo profits subsidize health-related services not funded by Indian Health Service appropriations, including specialized medications for diabetes and arthritis (*Talihina American* 12/21/89:1), funds drastically curtailed during the Reagan years, as a later discussion reveals. Revenues have also been used to construct community centers throughout the Choctaw Nation and to fund higher-education scholarship programs, elderly nutrition programs, emergency assistance programs, and even road maintenance (tribal news release, Durant, OK, June 1991; *Bishinik* 1987–95).

The Choctaws, with a 1988 annual budget of $27.5 million and an estimated worth of over $34 million, continued to undertake additional development projects, including takeover and renovation of a nursing home facility at Antlers in 1987, and a 230-acre pine plantation at Tuskahoma on tribal ranch property. In 1989 the nation obtained a $249,000 BIA Indian Business Development Grant to subcontract chemical finishing operations from Texas Instruments, Inc., under Defense Department contracts (*Bishinik* 11/89:1), and the tribe began courting Boeing, General Dynamics, and other companies to entice them to site industrial development enterprises in the Choctaw Nation (*Bishinik* 3/88:3). In 1988 Choctaws gained added managerial leverage when they established the Choctaw Nation Tax Commission and passed a Sales Tax Act, which would permit them to collect tax revenues on their various business operations, a right denied since the Curtis Act termination legislation of 1898 (*Bishinik* 2/88:3).

Under Chief Roberts's leadership, the tribe has become a corporation with only a minimal cultural facade. Committed to an entrepreneurial corporate profit-making model, Roberts built his tribe's economic initiatives on the very same cornerstones as Tyson Foods and Weyerhaeuser: shrewd, efficient entrepreneurial business practice. Choctaws also took advantage of a favorable national political climate to build their economic centerpiece: the Choctaw Nation Bingo Palace. Choctaws currently own a bingo palace, two travel plazas, shopping centers, smoke shops, and several other business ventures, as well as a six-passenger tribal airplane, and recently introduced their own "Choctaw Visa" credit card (*Bishinik* 8/91:1, 9/96:1). Tribal general fund revenues, along with federal entitlement monies, provide supplementary medical, dental, and optical services; home maintenance and upkeep programs; Head Start, WIC, and food distribution programs; energy assistance, nutrition, and support for the elderly; and low-interest business and personal loan programs.

Not only is the tribe subsidizing federal entitlement programs, but it recently agreed to contribute one million dollars through its Tribal Improvement Program to pave and modernize State Highway 144, which the state of Oklahoma threatened to abandon and the county refused to accept in its unpaved condition. The highway links the McCurtain County Choctaw settlements of Honobia and Bethel to the Choctaw Nation Indian Hospital, located in Talihina, north of Honobia. In response to the tribe's offer, the Oklahoma Department of Transportation agreed to a cost-sharing plan for the road project (*Bishinik* 2/1995:1).

These aggressive economic initiatives brought more than three hundred jobs to Choctaws during the 1980s, and by 1990 the tribe employed more than seven hundred people. Choctaws currently have taken over the contracting of all BIA services, although about 65 percent of operating funds still come from the federal government.

Choctaw Nation economic development during the "new Federalism" era under Chief Roberts – a staunch political conservative – has been stunningly successful, transforming the tribe into a highly efficient quasi-corporation with a net worth that has grown from $2.6 million when Roberts took office to more than $68 million in 1995 (Hollis E. Roberts, campaign literature, 1995). Like their Mississippi counterparts (see White 1990:78; Bordewich 1996), this "bootstrap" approach has brought Roberts praise from constituents. At appreciation dinners held throughout the Choctaw Nation, his followers consistently laud his development efforts. Said Randle Durant, a Tribal Council member:

He has helped all of our communities – Honobia, Summerfield – with water systems, road work and community centers. Bingo has brought in new money and the Chief is using it to get new jobs and bring more money into southeastern Oklahoma. He got us the Lodge, the hospital and Jones Academy. I am proud of these.

The greatest thing is that all of this is helping our people. Helping ourselves. (*Talihina American* 1/3/90:1)

Chief Roberts himself predicted that "within four years we will be able to put every Choctaw Indian to work in southeastern Oklahoma," and the tribal trust fund, currently worth $7.6 million, will be worth $20 million (*Talihina American* 1/3/90:1).

These development efforts have directed the Choctaw Nation's focus away from BIA dependency and toward its national headquarters at Durant, which Chief Roberts envisions as the Nation's present and future nerve center, at "the four-way crossroads created by U.S. 70 and U.S. 69-75" (*Bishinik* 5/87:1). This contemporary crossroads, where Choctaw visions of development and progress intersect, symbolizes a new direction taken by the chief and other elected officials to bring Choctaws into direct contact with the wider society, through ties to business, trade, and the service economy, explicit "new Federalism" goals.

Tribal economic growth, built largely on highly successful bingo and travel plaza enterprises, has provided an economic cushion to Choctaws during the 1980s and 1990s, when federal entitlement programs were slashed, allowing the tribe to pick up the slack where federal and state monies were unavailable. The Choctaw Nation has become in effect a branch of the U.S. welfare state bureaucracy, channeling substantial profits into what were previously federal- and state-mandated programs. Indeed, the tribe's entrepreneurial initiatives have brought significant improvements to the lives of local Choctaws, through a myriad of tribally sponsored subsidy programs, jobs, housing, and health care.

Chief Roberts reasoned that as federal entitlement programs decline and tribal takeover is complete, the Choctaw Nation will in effect become obsolete as we know it. His vision is to wean his people from entitlement dependence through education, self-discipline, and hard work, just as he raised himself from poverty to relative affluence. Roberts views traditional Native American culture as "regressive." "Why do beadwork for four dollars per hour when you can get a real job and earn fifteen or even fifty dollars per hour?" he posed (H. Roberts 1993). Roberts has eliminated blood quantum mandates for tribal membership and lauds the tribe's national membership of over 98,000, of whom only about 18,000 live in the ten and one-half counties of the Choctaw Nation, about 75 percent are less than one-quarter Choctaw by blood, and only about 780 speak Choctaw fluently.

Roberts's charismatic leadership and his personal and economic philosophy are cornerstones of the contemporary Choctaw Nation success story, built around several key philosophical and operational features: (1) individual initiative as the key to success; (2) traditional culture as "regressive"; (3) an orientation to the present and future as preferable to cultural "sentimentality"; (4) long-term stable but aggressive leadership; and (5) moderate economic risk taking. Roberts has little patience with failure – personal or institutional – and his individualist philosophy lays the blame for personal failure on individuals themselves. Expressing little patience for fellow tribesmen who squander resources, allow their homes to deteriorate, or don't take advantage of educational opportunities available to them, Roberts said: "We educate. We don't dictate to people what they will do with their land" and resources. The tribe provides the opportunities; it is up to individuals to take the initiative to use them to their best advantage, he argued. "If you can't afford to purchase one acre of land [for a mutual-help home], you can't afford to own an Indian home," he reasoned. Choctaws, he said, must take responsibility for their own choices, actions, and initiatives, and for their own success or failure. Tired of bailing out his countrymen, Roberts argues that economic success is achieved the old-fashioned way: through self-discipline, education, and hard work (H. Roberts 1993).

His tribal vision is corporate: tribal shareholders/members will earn shares/profits from corporate investments. The tribe's director of economic development, Wilma Robinson, reiterated Roberts's vision: economic success in the marketplace, she said, is Native America's "truest form of revenge." "The true form of revenge is [Indian] success!" Rather than wallowing in the past, the tribe has found its "new buffalo": shrewd private sector development initiatives and *bingo*! (Robinson 1993).

SOME IMPLICATIONS OF "NEW FEDERALISM": NATIONAL
AND INTERNATIONAL PERSPECTIVES

Choctaw efforts to increase tribal revenues have been laudable, but at what cost? Placing the Choctaw Nation's development strategy into national and international contexts reveals that Choctaws continue to be subject to exploitation and dependency, veiled in self-determination rhetoric, which compromise fundamental moral, ethical, and economic considerations in favor of singularly economic strategies.

Contrary to Stephen Cornell and Joseph Kalt's assertion that "economic development is a *social* problem" requiring that tribes consider a range of "opportunities and constraints" in their pursuit of successful development outcomes (1992a:228 [emphasis in original]; see also Cornell and Kalt 1990, 1992b), tribal economic development remains foremost a problem that is simultaneously structural and political-economic, rooted in historic and contemporary indigenous sovereignty issues and class exploitation. Native Americans remain subsumed within the U.S. political economy, governed by externally created and externally enforced rules, competing with non-Indians who largely control tribal assets, whether natural resources or human labor. Just as in prior eras, Indian economic and political sovereignty exist at the will of U.S. interests (see Swenson 1982).

Three significant problem areas emerge in a closer examination of Choctaw development strategies and remain as persistent obstacles to full national sovereignty and economic and cultural viability. First is the very nature and implications of the asymmetrical relationship between Native American enclave ethnicities and the U.S. political economy. As tribes compete increasingly with private corporations, they are at the mercy of formidable development interests, which may sacrifice human, environmental, and social well-being in favor of corporate profits. Native American communities, including the Choctaw Nation, now compete in a global economy for multinational corporate investment dollars with foreign locations little regulated and often politically unstable. Choctaw workers replace cheap, readily available, unskilled foreign workers in the MNC formula for corporate profit making (see Wolf 1982; Wallerstein 1976; Flora et al. 1992:37–38, 135–55).

Texas Instruments was just such an investor when it contracted a branch of its chemical finishing operations with the Choctaw Nation in 1989. The company was forced to close its El Salvadoran chemical facility in 1985, then the largest chemical plant in Central America, because of that war-torn country's ongoing civil unrest (Barry and Preusch 1986:221). Texas Instruments was attracted to southeastern Oklahoma because it offered many advantages at greatly reduced costs compared with its former Central American site, including a relatively cheap, docile, and readily available labor force willing to perform routine jobs using often dangerous chemicals in a setting free of the volatility of a nation embedded in the turmoil of civil war. Native American communities seeking valuable investment dollars, which translate into jobs and income for their citizens, are ripe for such domestic corporate entrepreneurial investments, which entail heavy costs in both personnel and tribal resources. Like foreign laborers and illegal aliens, Native American workers are willing to perform hazardous, distasteful jobs American-born white laborers often refuse.

A second area of heavy Choctaw investment, again with an ambiguous history and potentially volatile future, is high-stakes gambling. Since 1980 dozens of tribes have invested in high-stakes bingo operations, which offer the lure of substantial revenues with minimal costs for capital outlays or technological expertise. Currently about half of U.S.-recognized tribes sponsor high-stakes gambling, a particularly attractive option for resource-poor tribes (Sockbeson 1987:4; Folwell 1988:69; Cordeiro 1992; Cozzetto 1995).

Debates over high-stakes bingo and other gaming operations on Native American land – at times acrimonious – have pitted factions opposed to gaming against members who favor such enterprises. Factional disputes among Canadian and New York State Mohawks led to violence that left two dead and brought local and Canadian mounted police intervention (see *Akwesasne Notes* midwinter 1989–90; Folwell 1988). Mohawk factions for and against organized gambling have been likened to "two irreconcilable visions of the future – one based on greed and profit and the other on collective ownership and the extended family" (*Akwesasne Notes* midwinter 1989–90:4), according to one native spokesperson.

Not only does gaming precipitate intracommunity factional disputes, but tribes vie among themselves, with private entrepreneurs, and with states for gaming revenues. Several states, including California, Arizona, North Dakota, and Florida, have challenged Indian gaming in court, although recent Supreme Court rulings have protected Native American sovereignty on this issue. This right is by no means secure, however, being ever vulnerable to legislative and judicial definitions and national whim (Sockbeson 1987:3–5; *Los Angeles Times* 2/26/87: sec. 1, p.3; *New York Times* 7/23/90: sec. A, p.10; Cordeiro 1992:214–16; Vizenor 1990:22–24, 1992; *New York Times* 1/13/94; Begay and Leung 1994; Cozzetto 1995).

Gaming is a problematic jackpot for both tribes and states. Throughout the nation, states have turned to what has become "America's . . . No. 1 growth industry," to recoup revenues lost in the 1990s federal and state budget-cutting frenzy. The push for gaming revenues – states' "golden goose" and tribes' "new buffalo" – increases in direct proportion to federal spending cuts, in an effort to subsidize cash-depleted local aid programs. Gaming, a highly regressive revenue-producing strategy, preys on poor consumers, easily co-opted by gambling enticements and not infrequently trapped into addiction. Gaming "plays like Robin Hood in reverse, taking from poor communities and giving to rich," write the commentators Mitchell Zuckoff and Doug Bailey (*Boston Globe* 9/27/93:1). Furthermore, jobs created in gambling are typical of the secondary service sector: low paid and unskilled. As poor communities and their citizens fall prey to gambling enticements, corporate sponsors, including industry giants such as Ramada, MGM, and Hilton, are enriched, making $1.2 billion in profits in 1992 alone. Gaming also attracts organized crime and promotes addiction and family violence (*Boston Globe* 9/26/93:1, 18–19, 9/27/93:1, 8–9, 9/28/93:1, 16–17, 9/29/93:1, 24–25, 9/30/93:1, 18; Vizenor 1990:18–24, 1992; Cozzetto 1995:126–28).

A third by-product of Choctaw development has been the unresolved problem of unemployment. Continuing unemployment is perhaps a symptom of the private entrepreneurial strategy, based on a free-market economic model, in which Native American tribes operate like corporations; competing with states for federal and private investment dollars to implement development strategies that, while profitable, are not necessarily consistent with Native American cultural visions or needs. As earlier noted, the centerpiece of Choctaw economic development – gaming – is a highly competitive business where not only Indian tribes but also states and private entrepreneurs vie for whimsical gambling dollars. Tribes face both industry competition and federal and state government supervision of a highly politicized industry. As states lobby to curb Indian gaming to protect their own gaming industries, tribes may be shut out of the industry altogether if Indian sovereignty over this issue is not protected and maintained. Given the history of U.S. Indian policy, sovereign rights to Indian gaming are highly ambiguous and vulnerable (see Cordeiro 1992; Begay and Leung 1994; Cozzetto 1995:119–21).

Also, although the Choctaws and other Indian tribes have built impressive and diversified economic infrastructures, unemployment, at astronomical levels throughout Native American communities, including the Choctaw Nation, increased steadily during the "new Federalism" era:

In 1981, at the height of one of the most severe recessions in U.S. history, the unemployment on the Rosebud Reservation in South Dakota stood at fifty percent. In 1986, after what has been described as the longest and strongest economic recovery this country has ever experienced, the unemployment rate at Rosebud was eighty-six percent, an increase of seventy-two percent in five years. (*Indian Affairs* 115 [spring 1988]: 6)

Choctaw Nation unemployment, currently estimated at 37 percent, has risen steadily since the early 1980s, while elsewhere Native American unemployment is a shocking 80 to 90 percent (Cornell and Kalt 1990:90–95). Current development schemes persistently compromise the most abundant Native American resource: the members themselves. Many remain unemployed and often unemployable, owing to a lack of marketable skills. Those businesses attracted to reservations and rural Indian communities are often not labor intensive but capital intensive; and where labor is needed it is unskilled, as in virtually all the Choctaw tribal development initiatives so far undertaken.

Some tribes have benefited substantially from organized gaming, such as the Fort McDowell (Arizona) Yavapais, the Prairie Islands Sioux, and the Mashantucket Pequots; however, jobs created in gaming are frequently unskilled, service oriented, and poorly paid. The Yavapais receive forty thousand dollars per capita annually from gaming, but Begay and Leung (1994:6–7) acknowledge that the tribe now faces the problem of "educat[ing] tribal members in the value of work." Tribal gaming profits frequently replace federal dollars lost during the governmental downsizing of the 1980s and mid-1990s, providing day care and Head Start programs, home weatherization programs, dental and health benefits, and food commodities for local Indians. In effect, Indian-sponsored private-sector investment initiatives now maintain the tribal welfare state the federal government has abrogated to them (see Cozzetto 1995).

Choctaw self-sufficiency initiatives have been laudable during the 1990s;

however, federal privatization and self-determination initiatives in Native American communities, disguised as private-sector development and self-sufficiency agendas, may signal yet another attempt to abrogate the sacred trust relationship between the federal government and tribes, thereby resolving the Native American sovereignty dilemma once and for all. If indeed the "new Federalism" is a disguised policy to abrogate long-standing federal trust obligations and extinguish Native sovereignty along with cultural integrity, as some Native American spokespeople fear, then Native Nations indeed remain in jeopardy (see McGuire 1990).

The Choctaw Nation, after its near-demise in the postallotment era, was reinstituted in 1971. Under the leadership of the current chief, Hollis Roberts, the tribe has undertaken a variety of economic development initiatives based on the Indian Self-Determination Act of 1975 and the Indian Gaming and Regulatory Act of 1988. These bold economic initiatives have brought substantial tribal revenues, which compensate for revenues lost in federal downsizing during the 1980s and 1990s.

As the tribe experiences solid economic successes, persistent questions loom about tribal sovereignty, self-determination, and cultural survival. What will become of tribal sovereignty and Indian self-determination in a gaming context? Already states are challenging Indian gaming rights, seeking to tap into the gold mine of potential revenues. The Choctaws have so far avoided antagonistic confrontations both within their tribal borders and in the wider region, perhaps because they are creating jobs, generating tribal income, and providing appealing entertainment for a widely dispersed, largely non-Indian, constituency.

The tribe has opted to embrace a private entrepreneurial capitalist development model, with little or no debate over the cultural costs or benefits. The tribe, embedded in an externally determined majority culture's definition of "appropriate tribalism," has skirted the issue of tribal culture and embarked on a path toward nearly full cultural assimilation and amalgamation. As the twenty-first century looms, will Choctaw culture survive as more than a distant memory played out at the annual Labor Day tribal gathering? These and other questions are addressed in the epilogue.

Epilogue:
The Past and Future of Choctaw Culture

The Choctaw story is both global and local: it is about hinterland incorporation into a larger political economy and a tribe's culturized responses to that process of incorporation. Choctaw contact history began as a negotiated and contested relationship between European colonizers and autonomous Choctaw tribalists, each opportunistically accessing resources, technologies, and political-economic alliances. Choctaw cultural features were modified to accommodate new and powerful agents interested in accessing local resources and a potentially profitable labor force.

The aggrandizing economic imperative of global capitalism was the driving force behind colonization in the western hemisphere. John Moore (1993b:15) writes:

Native American history is best understood not as a *cultural* conflict between Indians and European invaders, but as an *economic* conflict between precapitalist or communal modes of production and capitalist modes. That is, the important fact about the invasion of North America is not so much that the invaders were European foreigners, but that they were *capitalist* foreigners. It was the capitalist mode of production which determined the form of the conflict, not religion, culture, or ethnicity. (emphasis in original)

Choctaws, like Native Nations throughout the Western Hemisphere, were not merely passive casualties of global political, economic, and cultural transformation. They were agents and actors who mediated the contact situation with their own cultural tools, albeit politically, technologically, and economically disadvantaged against formidable weapons, both ideological and technological. Choctaws situated the emerging relationship between colonizing agents and colonized people within their own cultural reality rooted in egalitarian partnerships, respect-based clan hierarchies, and gender complementarity. Intermarriage and alliance building permanently intertwined the Choctaws with their new European and Euro-American neighbors, transforming a racially homogeneous, culturally balanced, and ethnically autonomous nation into a culturally and racially amalgamated community of tribalists obliged to negotiate every aspect of their rightful place in the emerging United States.

The Choctaws, like Native Americans generally, bring a unique and problematic perspective to the ethnic, racial, and cultural diversity that is the United States. Historically, First Nations peoples had prior legitimate rights and entitlements to land that was aboriginally theirs. Powerless to counter externally driven hegemonic economic interests and political-economic aggrandizing tendencies, Native Americans at every stage had to negotiate rights and entitlements in political and legal jurisdictional arenas. Often inadequately informed and poorly protected from encroachments and exploitation, Native Americans were easy targets of land grabbing and cultural annihilation.

Perhaps the most formidable challenge to the Choctaws has been to retain tribal sovereignty and cultural integrity in the face of culture contact, change, and political and economic deterioration. Native national sovereignty is realized by collective resource control, independent tribal decision making, and cultural integrity. Throughout the postcontact era Choctaw sovereign rights have weighed in delicate balance with national and global political-economic interests. While the wider polity chipped away at the tribe's sovereign status, the Choctaws worked to retain a sense of collective community life and tribal identity throughout the nineteenth and twentieth centuries. The Choctaws confronted economic challenges to their livelihood-maintaining abilities, including land allotment, tribal termination, and the land-grabbing frenzy of the early twentieth century. Ongoing political encroachment on Choctaw sovereign status as a Native Nation ended when the tribal government was reinstated in 1971. Choctaws accommodated to tribal cultural deterioration brought by intermarriage, reservation termination, and cultural transformation into a rural marginal enclave of the global economy, negotiating their reentry as a modern nonreservation tribe.

Rural Choctaw life from the late nineteenth to the mid-twentieth century was a struggle to eke out a living amid a dominating white presence, a struggle that became increasingly difficult as Choctaws sold their allotted land to meet subsistence needs, thus depriving themselves of their means of subsistence. Weyerhaeuser Corporation's entry into the region in 1969 marked the full participation of the Choctaws as a wage-laboring class in the local corporate sector, albeit as an underutilized, underpaid, and easily exploitable semiproletarian labor force.

The capitalist sector, in its relationship with Choctaw producers, derives maximum returns from the Choctaws both as wage laborers and as domestic semiproletarians who help to maintain their own means of livelihood, thereby reducing capitalist-sector production costs. The capitalist sector has also benefited substantially from various federal and local taxation practices and from corporate production practices, such as vertical and horizontal integration of its various production activities. All of these factors have permitted Weyerhaeuser to make substantial profits from the local timberland and laborers drawn from the local communities. Profits, however, do not remit significantly to the local population as wages, taxes, or community benefits; rather, the region remains a rural poverty pocket with a dependent enclave economy, where profits are remitted outside the community rather than infused into it.

The Choctaw Nation typifies the core/periphery relationship, not only in external control of local productive resources but also in the peripheral workplace's racial, ethnic, and gender stratification. A workplace stratified by race and gender is a by-product of job scarcity, where elites, predominantly white males, secure the most financially remunerative jobs and leave to minorities and women jobs in the secondary and unskilled sectors. As noted by Kathryn Ward (1990:50–51), women are frequently marginalized under capitalism by being denied access to technologies controlled by males, relegated to less remunerative occupational strata, or eliminated altogether as new technologies are introduced.

Choctaws – males and females – are overrepresented in menial semiskilled and unskilled occupations in the logging and chicken-processing industries locally, and virtually absent from managerial jobs in Weyerhaeuser's local corporate headquarters, as earlier noted. Many rely on more poorly paid and less secure nonunionized contracted jobs in Weyerhaeuser's operations.

Choctaw women still occupy a prominent place in Choctaw households, although full gender complementarity and economic gender equality appear to have diminished. Men have privileged access to remunerative skilled occupations in both unionized and nonunionized work forces and in managerial jobs. Choctaw women enter skilled logging industry jobs such as

221

heavy-equipment operators only infrequently, such as in the family timber business alluded to earlier. Women work in seasonal and secondary occupations, such as tree planting, and are overrepresented in more distasteful chicken-processing work. Women also work in typically female occupations, such as seamstressing and the social service sector. Education, as earlier noted, does not necessarily advantage women, since many jobs are part-time, unskilled or semiskilled, and uncertain. Both men and women subsidize household wages with informal subsistence activities and home work, thereby reducing their own immiseration and adding surplus value to the inadequate family wage.

CHOCTAW CULTURE IN THE TWENTY-FIRST CENTURY

As the Choctaws approach the twenty-first century, the tribe has made new accommodations to global hegemonic forces framed within the ongoing debate between tribal, federal, and state jurisdictions in U.S. political-economic life. Choctaws, as noted, have discovered a "new buffalo" in Indian gaming, dealing what the tribe's economic development coordinator, Wilma Robinson, called "the tribe's best revenge" on the wider community: true economic success. "We are beating them at their own game!" she declared (Robinson 1993).

Many Native Nations are winning in truly grand style in their gaming-based economic development initiatives. Both in the political-economic arena of tribal politics and in the global marketplace of capitalist entrepreneurship, gaming has become the centerpiece of economic development and sovereignty-focused self-determination movements on reservations and in Native American communities from Connecticut to California. With American enthusiasm for gambling seemingly insatiable and unabated, Native Americans have entered an economic niche that could enrich them for decades to come. Gaming-based economic development initiatives are not without serious problems and detractors, however, as noted in the last chapter, not the least of which is the core quandary of conflicts over state, federal, and tribal legal and political rights rooted in the imperfect definition of tribal sovereignty itself.

Culturally, the Choctaws face new tribal challenges as they redefine what it means to be Native American in the twenty-first century, accommodating to a rural enclave economy controlled by external agents and a lifestyle only marginally distinguishable from rural communities nationwide. Does tribal sovereignty linked to economic self-sufficiency signal eventual cultural anni-hilation for Native Americans such as the Choctaws? Smith (1994) and Cornell and Kalt (1990, 1992a, 1992b) maintain that it is just this mix of effective leadership, shrewd business entrepreneurship, and cultural preservation that spells the formula for Native American cultural and social persistence. Smith (1994:177), however, notes the inherent tension in the mix: "Only when the individual tribe both controls its own resources and sustains its identity as a distinct civilization does economic development make sense; otherwise, the tribe must choose between cultural integrity and economic development."

As noted, the capstone of the Choctaw economic success story – gaming – grew out of protected rights rooted in Native national sovereignty and economic self-determination. The Indian Gaming and Regulatory Act of 1988 gave Native Americans an opportunity to further assert sovereign rights as independent entities to develop their own profit-making initia-tives. Indian gaming has brought sovereignty and economic agendas to-gether. The "truest form of revenge," however, may be yet another round of tribal assimilation and termination as Choctaws face a twenty-first-century ideological and cultural crossroads.

Economic success such as the Choctaws' contains the seeds of an uncer-tain cultural future for Native American communities, a future that will re-cast Native Nationhood yet again. Previous pages have documented the his-tory of Choctaw life in Mississippi, the brutal process of tribal removal to Indian Territory, and the final establishment of a new tribal community in Oklahoma. Factors that prevented the Choctaws from establishing a perma-nent tribal homeland in Indian Territory were examined, particularly the in-tense desire by whites – locally, regionally, and nationally – to dispense with tribes altogether and expropriate tribal land for their own use.

The most recent phase of Choctaw cultural history, built around a corpo-ratist model of economic development not unlike Weyerhaeuser's corporate success story, appears to have minimized the cultural in favor of the eco-nomic, gambling on economic success to bring Choctaws a new vision of cultural reality. The vitality of Choctaw community culture still resides in decentralized church- and community-based residence enclaves, which the tribal political entity has penetrated by constructing regional community centers. Enhanced service and entitlement programs, charismatic leadership, and a spectacular public relations component are bringing Choctaws into the twenty-first century.

The Mississippi Choctaws, the tribal remnant that remained in Mississippi subsequent to the Trail of Tears, have embarked on a similar path toward modernity via sustained economic development efforts. And like their Oklahoma counterparts, they are, says Fergus Bordewich (1996:82), "reinventing" themselves in typically U.S. fashion. They are creating jobs in tribally owned enterprises and "educating" people to a work ethic, out of which has come a Choctaw "middle class" of teachers, engineers, and professionals. This is the new Native American "adaptation process," argues Bordewich: unromantic, pragmatic, and realistically geared toward sustainable economic opportunities.

As they enter the twenty-first century, the Choctaws' ability to survive as a cultural entity may serve as a benchmark for an evolving ethnic subcultural reality among Native Americans throughout the United States and indigenous people globally in the context of nation-states and global communities. Choctaws, from a cultural perspective, have turned a corner toward "melting pot" assimilation by embracing urban-based U.S. values, political-economic agendas, and individualistic norms. One lesson of Choctaw success is that the twenty-first century is likely to strengthen global culture, where subcultural variations are veneers superimposed on a substratum of political-economic homogeneity. Indigenous cultural practices, rooted in communal lifestyles, collective ownership and decision making, ritual life, and subsistence production, will be modified to accommodate to a global marketplace. Tribalism as we know it, as Chief Roberts* has predicted, is becoming extinct in the modern era, as Choctaws transform into a rural ethnic minority community. Tribal culture persists as a superstructural bas relief over a base driven by world economic forces in a global marketplace.

---

*On June 6, 1997, Chief Hollis Roberts unexpectedly resigned as chief of the Choctaw Nation of Oklahoma, after being convicted on sexual assault and sex abuse charges. Assistant Chief Gregory E. Pyle was sworn in as chief on June 9. In a June 13th letter to the Choctaws, Chief Pyle stated that he intends to continue tribal business as usual during this difficult time in Choctaw history.

I. Household data: Family   Code #

Household head: (Full name)   Date of Birth: Age:

Spouse: (Full name)   Date of Birth: Age:

Education: Hu   Wi

% Choctaw: Hu   Wi   Duration of Marriage: # Marriages: Hu   Wi

Address: Phone:

Location: (How to get there)

II. Residents of household   Total #:   Permanent   Temporary

A. Permanent members (Put addl. info. on reverse)

1. Full name   Age   Reln. to Hu/Wi (Explain on reverse if needed)

2. Full name   Age   Reln. to Hu/Wi

B. Temporary members (Put addl. info. on reverse)

1. Full name   Age   Reln. to Hu/Wi

Duration of stay (How long have they/will they stay?)

2. Full name   Age   Reln. to Hu/Wi

Duration of stay (How long have they/will they stay?)

III. Description of dwelling

A. General description (exterior/interior):

B. # Rooms: Separate kitchen?   Year built:

Plumbing? (in/out)   Electricity?   Refrigerator?   Stove? (gas/wood)

TV?   Washer? (wringer/electric?)   Other appliances?

Autos? (Yr/type/running?) (Who owns it?)

Other property: Chain saw? Sewing machine? Tiller?

Is home owned? Rented? Monthly payment (Rent/mortgage/date due)

Who owns home?

Value of home (if owned)

Amount of original mortgage   Date bought

Years to pay   Bought from: (BIA, private, etc.)

IV. Household income: Earned   Amount reported on W2:

1. Husband: Occupation (firm/name)   Hrs/wk (current est.):

Earnings/wk: Addl. jobs? (Name/hrs/earnings)

Seasonal/yearly changes?

2. Wife: Occupation (firm/name)   Hrs/wk (current est.):

Earnings/wk: Addl. jobs? (Name/hrs/earnings)

Seasonal/yearly changes?

3. Other household members: (Name)   Occupation?   Hrs/wk (current est.):

Earnings/wk: Addl. jobs? (Name/hrs/earnings)

Seasonal/yearly changes?

V. Household income: Unearned

1. Name of household member   Type income   Amount   When received (date)
(AFDC, SSI, BIA, lease income)
How long received? Since when?

2. Name of household member   Type Income   Amount   When received (date)

VI. Household savings:

Hu: $ Where located (Bank? Home?)
List each on a separate line
   $

Explain income if necessary
(ex: nature of BIA income; lease income – name of company, nature of lease – oil, gas, etc.)

Wi: $ Where located?

Others (name) $

Any other savings/stocks/etc.? (Describe type/whose/amt.)

Expenses: Elec.:   Food:

                      Gas: Where shop?

                      Phone: How often?

                      Other: How far?

Food customarily purchased: (/mo, etc.)

Credit anywhere?

Other significant expenses? (Feed, expenses for school, traveling, etc.)

VII. Household debts: (House payments, auto, cash, loans, stores, etc.)

To whom: (Bank/ personal/store/etc.?)   In whose name? (household member?)

Amount of dept: (orig./current)   Payment schedule: (amt/mo? when?)

VIII. Lands owned/ rented/ leased

acres owned by husband & wife   Est. cash value

Type of acreage   Orig. allotment?

How was land obtained? (elaborate) (In whose name?)

Taxes paid on property: (amt.)   Location of lands owned:

Who owns adjacent lands?

Have others tried to buy your lands?

Who?   When?

Do you lease/rent land to others? How much? (acres)   Where?

To whom?   Est. income:

Do you rent from others?   How much? (acres)   Where?

Cost to you?	Use of land?

IX. Livestock owned

Do you own cattle? #	Pigs? #	Sheep? #	Horses? #

Other livestock?	Estimated value of lifestock:

Chickens? #	Estimated value of chickens:

Other poultry?	Do you produce hay, grain, or feed?

Acreage in hay?	Estimated value of hay acreage:

Taxes paid on livestock or hay acreage?	Amt. paid: $

X. Other income-producing household activities

Type	By whom?	Time/wk, day, or month	Amt. earned/wk or piece
(Quilt, crafts?)			
(Hunting/fishing?)			
(Babysitting/carpooling?)			
(Food gathering/gardening?)			
Canning? # last season?			
(Woodcutting/hauling?)			

XI. Open-ended questions

1. How many people sleep here each night?

2. How many generally eat with you? Who cooks? Who purchases food?

3. Do other household members help with expenses? How? Are resources shared in any way?

4. Where did your family grow up?

5. How much land did your family own when you were a child? What happened to it?

6. How have living conditions changed since you were a child?
   Are things better or worse for you now?

7. How often do you see your brother/sisters? Where do they live? How often do you see aunts/ uncles/ cousins? Where are they?

8. How important is it to be near family/relatives?   Very   OK but not necessary   Doesn't matter

9. Work history: What did your father/mother do for a living?   Wage work? (elaborate):   Farming?

10. Husband's/Wife's work history?

11. Jobs in the area. Are you satisfied with what is available?   Income. Do jobs pay enough? Assistance. Does it provide enough to be comfortable?

12. How often do you do things with other Choctaws?   Every day?   Once/week   Seldom   Never

13. What activities do you do with other Choctaws, including family members?
    a. Visit with family members almost exclusively
    b. Church, where?
    c. Other activities? Read "Bishinik"; Attend tribal council meetings; OU Extension homemakers; Tribal committees; active participant

14. If you could, would you rather work for the tribe or for a private company such as Weyerhaeuser or Lane Chicken? Would you like to see the tribe provide more jobs, such as the fiberglass plant?   Very much   Doesn't matter at all

15. Do you try to keep up with tribal activities? Do you encourage your family to keep up with tribal activities? Do your children/grandchildren speak Choctaw? Is this worthwhile?

16. How important is the land as an asset? Would you sell it to move to any area that had more job opportunities?

17. What do you think of Weyerhaeuser's presence in the area?

_____

_____

_____

_____

_____

_____

_____

SOURCES CONSULTED

Adair, James C.

1930 [1775]   *History of the American Indians*. Johnson City TN.

Albers, Patricia C.

1993   "Symbiosis, Merger, and War: Contrasting Forms of Intertribal Relationship among Historic Plains Indians." In *The Political Economy of North American Indians*, ed. John H. Moore, 94–132. Norman: University of Oklahoma Press.

Albers, Patricia C., and William R. James

1986   "On the Dialectics of Ethnicity: To Be or Not to Be Santee (Sioux)." *Journal of Ethnic Studies* 14.1:1–27.

Althusser, Louis, and Etienne Balibar

1979   *Reading Capital*. (*Lire le Capital*, 1968.) Trans. Ben Brewer. New York: Schocken; London: New Left/Verso.

Anders, Gary C.

1980   "Theories of Underdevelopment and the American Indian." *Journal of Economic Issues* 14.3:681–701.

Asad, Talal, ed.

1975   *Anthropology and the Colonial Encounter*. London: Ithaca.

Baber, Willie L.

1987   "Conceptual Issues in the New Economic Anthropology: Moving beyond the Polemic of Neo-Classical and Marxist Economic Theory." In *Beyond the New Economic Anthropology*, ed. John Clammer. New York: St. Martin's.

Bailey, Ronald

1973   "Economic Aspects of the Black Internal Colony." In *Structures of Dependency*, ed. Frank Bonilla and Robert Girling, 161–88. Stanford CA: Stanford University Press.

Bailey, Ronald, and Guillermo Flores

1973   "Internal Colonialism and Racial Minorities in the United States: An Overview." In *Structures of Dependency*, ed. Frank Bonilla and Robert Girling, 149–60. Stanford CA: Stanford University Press.

Baird, W. Daniel

1972   *Peter Pitchlynn: Chief of the Choctaws*. Norman: University of Oklahoma Press.

Sources Consulted

Baker, Billy Paul
1993   Tribal Council, Choctaw Nation of Oklahoma, Weyerhaeuser Shop Foreman. Personal interview, 6/8–9/93.
Barnett, Tony
1975   "The Gezira Scheme: Production of Cotton and the Reproduction of Underdevelopment." In *Beyond the Sociology of Development*, ed. Ivar Oxaal, et al., 183–207. London: Routledge & Kegan Paul.
Barry, Tom
1987   *Roots of Rebellion: Land and Hunger in Central America*. Boston: South End.
Barry, Tom, and Deb Preusch
1986   *The Central America Fact Book*. New York: Grove.
Barth, F., ed.
1969   *Ethnic Groups and Boundaries*. London: Allen & Unwin.
Baum, Laura Edna
1940   "Agriculture among the Five Civilized Tribes, 1865–1906." Master's thesis. University of Oklahoma.
Bee, Robert, and Ronald Gingerich
1977   "Colonialism, Classes and Ethnic Identity: Native Americans and the National Political Economy." *Studies in Comparative International Development* 12:41–56.
Begay, Manley A., and Wai-Shan Leung
1994   *One Bribe Beats the Odds: The Experience of the Fort McDowell Indian Gaming Center*. Harvard Project on American Indian Economic Development, Project Report Series, no. PRS94-7. Cambridge MA: John F. Kennedy School of Government.
Benson, Henry C.
1860   *Life among the Choctaw Indians and Sketches of the South-West*. Cincinnati: Swormstedt & Poe.
Berkhofer, Robert J., Jr.
1978   *The White Man's Indian*. New York: Random House/Vintage.
Bernstein, Henry
1988   "Capitalism and Petty-Bourgeois Production: Class Relations and Divisons of Labour." *Journal of Peasant Studies* 15.2:258–71.
Biard, Dorothy, and Sarah Craven
1990   "Washington Watch: Special Report on Native American Issues," *Practicing Anthropology* 12.2:17.

Binford, Leigh, and Scott Cook

1991   "Petty Production in Third World Capitalism Today." In *Marxist Approaches in Economic Anthropology*, ed. Alice Littlefield and Hill Gates, 65–90. Society for Economic Anthropology, Monographs in Economic Anthropology, no. 9. New York: University Press of America.

Bloch, Maurice, ed.

1975   *Marxist Analysis and Social Anthropology*. New York: Wiley.

Blu, Karen I.

1993   "'Reading Back' to Find Community: Lumbee Ethnohistory," in *North American Indian Anthropology: Essays on Society and Culture*, ed. Raymond J. DeMaille and Alfonso Ortiz. Norman: University Oklahoma Press.

Bonilla, Frank, and Robert Girling, eds.

1973   *Structures of Dependence*. Stanford CA: Stanford University Press.

Booth, David

1975   "Andre Gunder Frank: An Introduction and Appreciation." In *Beyond the Sociology of Development*, ed. Ivor. Oxaal, Tony Barnett, and David Booth, 50–85. London: Routledge & Kegan Paul.

Bordewich, Fergus M.

1996   "How to Succeed in Business: Follow the Choctaws' Lead," *Smithsonian* 26.12 (March): 70–82.

Borofsky, Robert, ed.

1993   "Assessing the Field," in *Assessing Cultural Anthropology*, ed. Robert Borofsky, 468–91. New York: McGraw-Hill.

Boserup, Ester

1970   *Women's Role in Economic Development*. London: Allen & Unwin.

Brown, Loren N.

1931   "The Dawes Commission." *Chronicles of Oklahoma* 9:71–105.

1944   "The Appraisal of the Lands of the Choctaws and Chickasaws by the Dawes Commission." *Chronicles of Oklahoma* 22:177–91.

Bryce, J. Y.

1928   "About Some of Our First Schools in Choctaw Nation." *Chronicles of Oklahoma* 6:354–94.

Buffalohead, W. Roger

1986   "Self-Rule in the Past and the Future: An Overview." In *Indian Self-Rule*, ed. Kennerty R. Phillip, 265–77. Salt Lake City UT: Howe.

Sources Consulted

Campbell, T. N.
1959   "Choctaw Subsistence: Ethnographic Notes from the Lyncenum Manuscript." *Florida Anthropologist* 12.1:9–24.

Cardoso, Fernando, and Enzo Faletto
1979   *Dependency and Development in Latin America.* (*Dependencia y dessarrollo en America Latina*, 1971). Trans. Marjory M. Urquidi. Berkeley and Los Angeles: University of California Press.

Castile, George P.
1993   "Native North Americans and the National Question." In *The Political Economy of North American Indians*, ed. John H. Moore, 270–87. Norman: University of Oklahoma Press.

Champagne, Duane
1983   "Organizational Change and Conflict: A Case Study of the Bureau of Indian Affairs." *American Indian Culture and Research Journal* 7.3:3–28.
1989   *American Indian Societies: Strategies and Conditions of Political and Cultural Survival.* Cambridge MA: Cultural Survival.

Chase-Dunn, Christopher, and Thomas D. Hall, eds.
1991   *Core/Periphery Relations in Precapitalist Worlds.* Boulder CO: Westview.

Chayanov, A. V.
1966 [1925]   *The Theory of Peasant Economy.* Homewood IL: Irwin.

Chevalier, Jacques M.
1983   "There Is Nothing Simple about Simple Commodity Production," *Journal of Peasant Studies* 10.4:153–86.

Choctaw Nation
1875   *Annual Report.* Washington DC: GPO.
1973a [1897–99]   *Acts and Resolutions of the Choctaw Nation, Passed at Regular Sessions, October 1897, 1898; Special Session, 1899.* Wilmington DE: Scholarly Resources.
1973b [1903]   *Acts and Resolutions of the General Council of the Choctaw Nation, 1903.* Wilmington DE: Scholarly Resources.
1973c [1894]   *Constitution and Laws of the Choctaw Nation: Together with the Treaties of 1837, 1855, 1865, and 1866.* Wilmington DE: Scholarly Resources.

Choctaw Nation of Oklahoma
1980   *Comprehensive Plan of the Choctaw Nation of Oklahoma.* Durant OK: Choctaw Nation Planning Dept.

Christian, Emma Ervin
1931   "Memories of My Childhood Days in the Choctaw Nation." *Chronicles of Oklahoma* 9 (June): 155–65.

234

Clammer, John

1987   *Beyond the New Economic Anthropology*. New York: St. Martin's.

Clammer, John, ed.

1978   *The New Economic Anthropology*. New York: St. Martin's.

Clapham, Christopher

1985   *Third World Politics: An Introduction*. Madison: University of Wisconsin Press.

Cohen, Ronald

1978   "Ethnicity: Problem and Focus in Anthropology," *Annual Review of Anthropology* 7:379–403.

Colclough, Glenna

1988   "Uneven Development and Racial Composition in the Deep South, 1970–1980." *Rural Sociology* 53.1:73–86.

Collins, Jane L.

1990   "Unwaged Labor in Comparative Perspective: Recent Theories and Unanswered Questions." In *Work without Wages: Comparative Studies of Domestic Labor and Self-Employment*, ed. Jane L. Collins and Martha Gimenez, 3–24. Albany: State University of New York Press.

Collins, Jane L., and Martha Gimenez, eds.

1990   *Work without Wages: Comparative Studies of Domestic Labor and Self-Employment*. Albany: State University of New York Press.

Conlan, Czarina

1926   "David Folsom." *Chronicles of Oklahoma* 4 (December): 340–55.

Cook, Scott

1990   "Female Labor, Commodity Production, and Ideology in Mexican Peasant-Artisan Households." In *Work without Wages: Comparative Studies of Domestic Labor and Self-Employment*, ed. Jane L. Collins and Martha Gimenez, 89–115. Albany: State University of New York Press.

Cook, Scott, and Leigh Binford

1986   "Petty Commodity Production, Capital Accumulation, and Peasant Differentiation: Lenin vs. Chayanov in Rural Mexico." *Review of Radical Political Economy* 18.4:1–32.

Coppedge, Robert O., and Carlton G. Davis

1977   *Rural Poverty and the Policy Crisis*. Ames: Iowa State University Press.

Cordeiro, Eduardo E.

1992   "The Economics of Bingo: Factors Influencing the Success of Bingo Operations on American Indian Reservations." In *What Can Tribes Do?: Strategies and Institutions in American Indian Economic Develop-*

ment, ed. Stephen Cornell and Joseph P. Kalt, 206–38. American Indian Manual & Handbook Series, no. 4. Los Angeles: UCLA American Indian Studies Center.

Cornell, Stephen

1988   *The Return of the Native: American Indian Political Resurgence.* New York: Oxford University Press.

1990   "Land, Labour and Group Formation: Blacks and Indians in the United States." *Ethnic and Racial Studies* 13.3:368–88.

Cornell, Stephen, and Joseph P. Kalt

1990   "Pathways from Poverty: Economic Development and Institution-Building on American Indian Reservations." *American Indian Culture and Research Journal* 14.1:89–125.

1991   *Where's the Glue? Institutional Bases of American Indian Economic Development.* Harvard Project on American Indian Economic Development, Project Report Series no. PRS91-1. Cambridge MA: John F. Kennedy School of Government, Harvard University.

1992a   "Culture and Institutions as Public Goods: American Indian Economic Development as a Problem of Collective Action." In *Property Rights and Indian Economies*, ed. Terry L. Anderson, 215–52. Landham MD: Lowman & Littlefield.

1992b   "Reloading the Dice: Improving the Chances for Economic Development on American Indian Reservations," in *What Can Tribes Do?: Strategies and Institutions in American Indian Economic Development*, ed. Stephen Cornell and Joseph P. Kalt, 2–59. American Indian Manual & Handbook Series, no. 4. Los Angeles: UCLA American Indian Studies Center.

Cozzetto, Don A.

1995   "The Economic and Social Implications of Indian Gaming: The Case of Minnesota." *American Indian Culture and Research Journal* 19.1:119–31.

Cushman, Horation B.

1962 [1899]   *History of the Choctaw, Chickasaw and Natchez Indians.* New York: Russell & Russell.

D'Amico-Samuels, Deborah

1991   "Undoing Fieldwork: Personal, Political, Theoretical, and Methodological Implications." In *Decolonizing Anthropology: Moving Further toward an Anthropology for Liberation*, ed. Faye Harrison, 68–87. Washington DC: American Anthropological Association/Association of Black Anthropologists.

Davis, Shelton H.

1977   *Victims of the Miracle: Development and the Indians of Brazil*. Cambridge: Cambridge University Press.

Dawson, Susan E.

1992   "Navajo Uranium Workers and the Effects of Occupational Illnesses: A Case Study." *Human Organization* 51.4:389–97.

Debo, Angie

1934 [1961]   *The Rise and Fall of the Choctaw Republic*. Norman: University of Oklahoma Press.

1940 [1972]   *And Still the Waters Run*. Princeton NJ: Princeton University Press.

1951   *The Five Civilized Tribes of Oklahoma: Report on Social and Economic Conditions*. Philadelphia: Indian Rights Association.

Deloria, Vine, Jr.

1969   *Custer Died for Your Sins*. New York: Macmillan.

DeRosier, Arthur H., Jr.

1967   "Andrew Jackson and Negotiations for the Removal of the Choctaw Indians." *Indian Historian* 29.2:343–62.

1970   *The Removal of the Choctaw Indians*. Knoxville: University of Tennessee Press.

Dierks, F. McD (Don), Jr.

1972   *The Legacy of Peter Henry Dierks, 1824–1972*. Tacoma WA: Mercury.

Dillman, Don A., and Daryl Hobbs, eds.

1982   *Rural Society in the U.S.: Issues for the 1980's*. Rural Studies Series. Boulder CO: Westview.

Dos Santos, Theotônio

1970   "The Structure of Dependence." *American Economic Review* 60:231–36.

Dunaway, Wilma A.

1994   "The Southern Fur Trade and the Incorporation of Southern Appalachia into the World-Economy, 1690–1763." *Review* 17.2:215–42.

1996   "Incorporation as an Interactive Process: Cherokee Resistance to Expansion of the Capitalist World System, 1560–1763." *Sociological Inquiry* 66.4:455–70.

Dunn, Dana, Elizabeth M. Almquist, and Janet Saltzman Chafetz

1993   "Macrostructural Perspectives on Gender Inequality." In *Theory on*

Gender/Feminism on Theory, ed. Paula England, 69–90. New York: Aldine De Gruyter.

Dupré, Georges, and Pierre Phillippe Rey

1978   "Reflections on the Pertinence of a Theory of the History of Exchange." In *Relations of Production*, ed. David Seddon, 171–208. London: Cass.

Edwards, John

1932   "The Choctaw Indians in the Middle of the 19th Century." *Chronicles of Oklahoma* 10:392–425.

Eggan, Fred

1937   "Historical Changes in the Choctaw Kinship System." *American Anthropologist* 39:34–52.

Faiman-Silva, Sandra

1992   "The Native Americans' Struggle for Economic Self-Sufficiency." *Bridgewater Review* 2.4:6A–8A.

1993   "Multinational Corporate Development in the American Hinterland: The Case of the Oklahoma Choctaws." In *The Political Economy of North American Indians*, ed. John H. Moore, 214–39. Norman: University of Oklahoma Press.

Ferguson, Robert B.

1985   "Appendix: Treaties between the United States and the Choctaw Nation." In *The Choctaw before Removal*, ed. Carolyn Keller Reeves, 214–30. Jackson: University Press of Mississippi.

Fernández Kelly, M. Patricia

1989   "Broadening the Scope: Gender and International Economic Development." *Sociological Forum* 4.4:611–35.

Fitzgerald, Richard

1982   Member, Choctaw Nation Planning Department. Personal interview, Tulsa OK, 5/30/82.

Flora, Cornelia Butler, et al.

1992   *Rural Communities: Legacy and Change*. Boulder CO: Westview.

Folsom, Joseph P.

1869   *Constitution and Laws of the Choctaw Nation: With the Treaties of 1855, 1865, and 1866*. New York.

Folwell, Elizabeth

1989   "High Stakes in the Land of Flint: The Mohawks of Ganienkeh Claim the Adirondacks without Reservation." *Adirondack Life* 25.5:40–45, 68–69.

Forbes, Jack D.

1990   "Envelopment, Proletarianization and Inferiorization: Aspects of Co-
        lonialism's Impact upon Native Americans and Other People of Color
        in Eastern North America." *Journal of Ethnic Studies* 18.4:95–122.

Foreman, Carolyn

1932   "Journal of a Tour in the Indian Territory." *Chronicles of Oklahoma* 10
        (June): 364–74.

Foreman, Grant

1934   *Indian Removal: The Emigration of the Five Civilized Tribes.* Norman:
        University of Oklahoma Press.

Foreman, Grant, ed.

1930   *A Traveler in Indian Territory: The Journal of Ethan Allen Hitchcock, Late
        Major-General in the United States Army.* Cedar Rapids IA: Torch.

Foster-Carter, Aiden

1978   "Can We Articulate 'Articulation'?" In *The New Economic Anthropology,*
        ed. John Clammer, 210–49. New York: St. Martin's.

Frank, André Gunder

1969   *Capitalism and Underdevelopment in Latin America.* New York:
        Monthly Review/Modern Reader.

Gardner, Robert

1982   Assistant Chief, Choctaw Nation. Personal interview, Durant OK,
        5/25/82.

Gates, Paul W.

1936   "The Homestead Law in an Incongruous Land System." *American His-
        torical Review* 41:652–81.

Geography Extension Division

1975   *Choctaw Census, 1975: Results of the 1975 Census of the Choctaw Nation of
        Oklahoma.* Robert E. Norris, Project Director. Stillwater: Oklahoma
        State University.

Gibson, Ariel M.

1973   "The Indians of Mississippi." In *A History of Mississippi,* vol. 1, ed. Rich-
        ard A. McLemore, 69–89. Hattiesburg MS: University and College
        Press.

Gilpin, Robert

1975   *U.S. Power and the Multinational Corporation: The Political Economy of
        Foreign Direct Investment.* New York: Basic.

Gimenez, Martha E.

1990   "The Dialectics of Waged and Unwaged Work: Waged Work, Domestic Labor, and Household Survival in the United States." In *Work without Wages: Comparative Studies of Domestic Labor and Self-Employment*, ed. Jane L. Collins and Martha Gimenez, 25–45. Albany: State University of New York Press.

Girvan, Norman

1970   "Multinational Corporations and Dependent Under-Development in Mineral-Export Economies." *Social and Economic Studies* 19:490–526.

Glazer, Nona

1990   "Servants to Capital: Unpaid Domestic Labor and Paid Work." In *Work without Wages: Comparative Studies of Domestic Labor and Self-Employment*, ed. Jane L. Collins and Martha Gimenez, 142–67. Albany: State University of New York Press.

Godelier, Maurice

1972   *Rationality and Irrationality in Economics.* (*Rationalite et irrationalite en economie*, 1966.) Trans. Brian Pearce. New York: Monthly Review.

1977   *Perspectives in Marxist Anthropology.* (*Horizon, trajets marxistes en anthropologie*, 1973.) Trans. Robert Brain. Cambridge: Cambridge University Press.

Goodman, David, and Michael Redclift

1982   *From Peasant to Proletarian, Capitalist Development and Agrarian Transitions*. New York: St. Martin's.

Graebner, Norman Arthur

1943   "History of Cattle Ranching in Eastern Oklahoma." *Chronicles of Oklahoma* 21 (September): 300–11.

1945   "Pioneer Indian Agriculture in Oklahoma." *Chronicles of Oklahoma* 23:232–48.

Gudeman, Stephen

1978   *The Demise of a Rural Economy*. Boston: Routledge & Kegan Paul.

Gunning, I. C.

n.d.   *"A Royal Family of Choctaws," or The Choctaw Story*. Stillwater: Eastern Oklahoma Historical Society.

Hall, Thomas D.

1987   "Native Americans and Incorporation: Patterns and Problems." *American Indian Culture and Research Journal* 11.2:1–30.

1988   "Patterns of Native American Incorporation into State Societies." In
            Public Policy Impacts on American Indian Economic Development, ed.
            C. Matthew Snipp. Native American Studies Development Series, no.
            4, Albuquerque: University of New Mexico, Institute for Native Amer-
            ican Development.

1995   "Seeing the Global in the Local: World-Systems Theories and Local
            Analyses." Paper presented at Social Science History Association meet-
            ing. Chicago IL, November.

1996   "The World-System Perspective: A Small Sample from a Large Uni-
            verse." *Sociological Inquiry* 66.4:440–54.

Hankins, David

1982   Public Relations Officer, Weyerhaeuser Corporation. Personal inter-
            view, Wright City OK, 6/2/82.

Hargett, Jay L.

            Manuscript collection. Western History Collection, University of
            Oklahoma, Norman.

Harris, Betty J.

1990   "Ethnicity and Gender in the Global Periphery: A Comparison of
            Basotho and Navajo Women." *American Indian Culture and Research
            Journal* 14.4:15–38.

Harrison, Faye

1991   "Anthropology as an Agent of Transformation: Introductory Com-
            ments and Queries." In *Decolonizing Anthropology: Moving Further to-
            ward an Anthropology for Liberation*, ed. Faye Harrison. Washington DC:
            American Anthropological Association/Association of Black Anthro-
            pologists.

Harrison, Faye, ed.

1991   *Decolonizing Anthropology: Moving Further toward an Anthropology for
            Liberation*. Washington DC: American Anthropological Association/
            Association of Black Anthropologists.

Hedley, Max J.

1993   "Autonomy and Constraint: The Household Economy on a Southern
            Ontario Reserve." In *The Political Economy of North American Indians*,
            ed. John H. Moore, 184–213. Norman: University of Oklahoma Press.

Heerwagen, P. K.

1963   "A Logger Remembers." *Oklahoma's Orbit*, November 17, 12–13.

Hernandez, Juan A. Avila

1994   "How the Feds Are Pushing Nuclear Waste on Reservations." *Cultural Survival Quarterly* 17.4:40–42.

Hidy, Ralph W., Frank Ernest Hill, and Allan Nevins

1963   *Timber and Men: The Weyerhaeuser Story*. New York:Macmillan.

Hiemstra, William L.

1949–50   "Presbyterian Mission Schools among the Choctaws and Chickasaws, 1845–1861." *Chronicles of Oklahoma* 27:33–40.

Hindess, Barry, and Paul Q. Hirst

1975   *Pre-Capitalist Modes of Production*. Boston: Routledge & Kegan Paul.

Hodge, Frederick Webb, ed.

1912   *Handbook of American Indians North of Mexico*. Smithsonian Institution/ U.S. Bureau of American Ethnology, Bulletin 30, pt. 1. Washington: Government Printing Office.

Holford, David M.

1975   "The Subversion of the Indian Land Allotment System, 1887–1934." *Indian Historian* 8:11–21.

Hoxie, Frederick E.

1984   *A Final Promise: The Campaign to Assimilate the Indians, 1880–1920*. Lincoln: University of Nebraska Press.

Hudson, Peter J.

n.d.   "A Story of Choctaw Chiefs." Unpaged typed ms. #19457A, box 47, folder 49, Western History Collection, University of Oklahoma, Norman.

1932   "Recollections of Peter Hudson." *Chronicles of Oklahoma* 10 (December): 501–20.

1934   "Reminiscences by Peter J. Hudson." *Chronicles of Oklahoma* 12 (September): 294–304.

1939   "A Story of Choctaw Chiefs." Chronicles of Oklahoma, 17:7–16.

Indian Archives

            Oklahoma Historical Society, Oklahoma City.

Ise, John

1920   *The United States Forest Policy*. New Haven CT: Yale University Press.

Ismaelillo and Robin Wright, eds.

1982   *Native Peoples in Struggle: Cases from the Fourth Russell Tribunal and Other International Forums*. Bombay NY: Anthropology Resource Center and Emergency Response International Network.

Jacobsen, Cardell K.

1984   "Internal Colonialism and Native Americans: Indian Labor in the United States from 1871 to World War II." *Social Science Quarterly* 65:158–171.

Jeltz, Wyatt F.

1945   "A Study of the Choctaw and Chickasaw Indians as Slaveholders." Master's thesis. Kansas State Teacher's College, Pittsburgh ᴋs.

Jiobu, Robert Masao

1990   *Ethnicity and Inequality*. Albany: State University of New York Press.

Jones, W. N.

n.d.   Manuscript collection. Western History Collection, University of Oklahoma, Norman.

Jorgensen, Joseph

1971   "Indians and the Metropolis." In *The American Indian in Urban Society*, ed. Jack O. Waddell and O. Michael Watson, 67–113. Boston: Little, Brown.

1978   "A Century of Political Economic Effects on American Indian Society, 1880–1980." *Journal of Ethnic Studies* 6.3:1–82.

1984   "The Political Economy of the Native American Energy Business." In *Native Americans and Energy Development*, vol. 2, ed. Joseph G. Jorgensen. Boston: Anthropology Resource Center.

1986a   "Federal Policies, American Indian Polities, and the 'New Federalism.'" *American Indian Culture and Research Journal* 10.2:1–13.

1986b   "Sovereignty and the Structure of Dependency at Northern Ute." *American Indian Culture and Research Journal* 10.2:75–94.

Jorgensen, Joseph, et al.

1978   *Native Americans and Energy Development*. Cambridge ᴍᴀ: Anthropology Resource Center.

Julian, George W.

1883a   "Our Land-Grant Railways in Congress." *International Review* 14:198–212.

1883b   "Railway Influence in the Land Office." *North American Review* 136:237–56.

Keesing, Felix M.

1958   *Cultural Anthropology: The Science of Custom*. New York: Holt, Rienhart & Winston.

Kehoe, Alice Beck

1992 *North American Indians: A Comprehensive Account*. 2d ed. Englewood Cliffs NJ: Prentice Hall.

Kelley, Jean Margaret

1991 "The Choctaw Economy: Reciprocity in Action." Master's thesis. University of Arizona.

Kidwell, Clara Sue

1987 "Choctaws and Missionaries in Mississippi before 1830." *American Indian Culture and Research Journal* 11.2:51–72.

Kincaid, Harold

1982 Private contractor. Telephone interview, 6/5/82.

Kingsbury, Cyrus

n.d. Papers. Western History Collection, University of Oklahoma, Norman.

Klein, Alan M.

1993 "Political Economy of the Buffalo Hide Trade: Race and Class on the Plains." In *The Political Economy of North American Indians*, ed. John H. Moore, 133–60. Norman: University of Oklahoma Press.

Knight, Oliver

1953 "Fifty Years of Choctaw Law, 1834 to 1884." *Chronicles of Oklahoma* 31:76–95.

Kumar, Krishna

1980 "Social and Cultural Impact of Transnational Enterprises: An Overview." In *Transnational Enterprises: Their Impact on Third World Societies and Cultures*, ed. Krishna Kumar, 1–43. Westview Special Studies in Social, Political, and Economic Development. Boulder CO.: Westview.

La Clau, Ernest

1977 "Feudalism and Capitalism in Latin America." *New Left Review* 68:19–38.

LaDuke, Winona

1994 "Breastmilk, PCB's, and Motherhood: Native Environmentalism." *Cultural Survival Quarterly* 17.4:43–48.

Laite, Julian

1981 *Industrial Development and Migrant Labour in Latin America*. Austin: University of Texas Press.

Langford, Art

1995 Personnel Director, Tyson Foods, Inc. Telephone Interview, Broken Bow OK, 8/2/95.

Sources Consulted

Laws Relating to the Five Civilized Tribes, 1890–1914
1915   Washington DC GPO ·
Littlefield, Alice
1991   "Native American Labor and Public Policy in the United States." In *Marxist Approaches in Economic Anthropology*, ed. Alice Littlefield and Hill Gates, 219–32. Society for Economic Anthropology Monographs in Economic Anthropology, no. 9. New York: University Press of America.
Locke, Victor M.
1926   "Coleman Cole." *Chronicles of Oklahoma* 4:229–32.
Lomnitz, Larissa
1977   *Networks and Marginality: Life in a Mexican Shantytown.* Orlando FL: Academic.
Long, Norman
1975   "Structural Dependency, Modes of Production, and Economic Brokerage in Rural Peru." In *Beyond the Sociology of Development*, ed. Ivar Oxaal, et al., 253–82. Boston: Routledge & Kegan Paul.
Lovejoy, Stephen B., and Richard S. Krannich
1982   "Rural Industrial Development and Domestic Dependency Relations: Toward an Integrated Perspective." *Rural Sociology,* 47.3:475–95.
McGuire, Randall H., and Cynthia Woodsong
1990   "Making Ends Meet: Unwaged Work and Domestic Inequality in Broome County, New York, 1930–1980." In *Work without Wages: Comparative Studies of Domestic Labor and Self-Employment*, ed. Jane L. Collins and Martha Gimenez, 168–92. Albany: State University of New York Press.
McGuire, Thomas R.
1990   "Federal Indian Policy: A Framework for Evaluation." *Human Organization* 49:206–16.
McKee, Jesse O.
1971   "The Choctaw Indians: A Geographical Study in Cultural Change." *Southern Quarterly* 9:107–41.
McKee, Jesse O., and Jon A. Schlenker
1980   *The Choctaws: Cultural Evolution of a Native American Tribe.* Jackson: University Press of Mississippi.
McLoughlin, William G.
1985   "The Missionary Dilemma." *Canadian Review of American Studies* 16.4:395–409.

Masterson, V. V.

1952   *The Katy Railroad and the Last Frontier*. Norman: University of Oklahoma Press.

Means, William A.

1983   "Reagan Policies Force Indians to Give Up Traditional Views." *Indian Truth* 250 (April): 7.

Meillassoux, Claude

1981 [1975] *Maidens, Meal and Money: Capitalism and the Domestic Community*. Cambridge: Cambridge University Press.

1983   "The Economic Bases of Demographic Reproduction: From the Domestic Mode of Production to Wage-Earning," *Journal of Peasant Studies* 11.1:50–61.

Memmi, Albert

1965   *The Colonizer and the Colonized*. Trans. Howard Greenfeld. New York: Orion.

Meserve, John Bartlett

1936   "Chief Coleman Cole." *Chronicles of Oklahoma* 14 (March):9–21.

1941   "Chief Allen Wright." *Chronicles of Oklahoma* 19.4:314–32.

1942   "Chief George Hudson and Chief Samuel Garland." *Chronicles of Oklahoma* 20:9–17.

Meyer, Melissa L.

1994   *The White Earth Tragedy: Ethnicity and Dispossession at a Minnesota Anishinaabe Reservation, 1889–1920*. Lincoln: University of Nebraska Press.

Mills, Lawrence

1919   *The Lands of the Five Civilized Tribes: A Treatise upon the Law Applicable to the Lands of the Five Civilized Tribes*. St. Louis: Thomas Law.

Miner, H. Craig

1976   *The Corporation and the Indian: Tribal Sovereignty and Industrial Civilization in Indian Territory, 1865–1907*. Columbia: University of Missouri Press.

Mohanty, Chandra Talpade

1991   "Introduction: Cartographies of Struggle: Third World Women and the Politics of Feminism." In *Third World Women and the Politics of Feminism*, ed. Chandra T. Mohanty, Ann Russo, and Lourdes Torres, 1–47. Bloomington: Indiana University Press.

Mohawk, John C.

1991   "Indian Economic Development: An Evolving Concept of Sover-eignty," *Buffalo Law Review* 39.2:495–506.

Moody's *Industrial Manual*

1936+   Moody's *Manual of Industrials*

1910–15   Moody's *Manual of Investments*

1909–51   Moody's *Manual: Steam Railroads*

1908+   Moon, Donald

1982   Superintendent, Talihina Agency, Bureau of Indian Affairs. Personal interview, Talihina OK, 6/7/82.

Moore, John H.

1993a   "How Giveaways and Pow-Wows Redistribute the Means of Subsistence." In *The Political Economy of North American Indians*, ed. John H. Moore, 240–69. Norman: University of Oklahoma Press.

1993b   "Political Economy in Anthropology." In *The Political Economy of North American Indians*, ed. John H. Moore, 3–19. Norman: University of Oklahoma Press.

Morris, C. Patrick

1988   "Termination by Accountants: The Reagan Indian Policy." *Policy Studies* 16:731.

Morrison, James D.

1954   "Problems in the Industrial Progress and Development of the Choctaw Nation, 1865–1907." *Chronicles of Oklahoma* 32:70–91.

1978   *Schools for the Choctaws*. Durant: Southeastern Oklahoma State University, Choctaw Bilingual Education Program.

1987   *The Social History of the Choctaw Nation: 1865–1907*. Ed. James C. Milligan and L. David Norris, Durant OK.: Creative Infomatics.

Muga, David

1984   "Academic Sub-Cultural Theory and the Problematic of Ethnicity: A Tentative Critique." *Journal of Ethnic Studies* 12.1:1–51.

Mundt, Karl E.

1967   "Indian Autonomy and Indian Legal Problems." *Kansas Law Review* 15:505–11.

Nader, Laura

1969   "Up the Anthropologist: Perspectives Gained from Studying Up." In *Reinventing Anthropology*, ed. Dell Hymes. New York: Random House/Vintage.

Nagel, Joane, and C. Matthew Snipp

1993   "Ethnic Reorganization: American Indian Social, Economic, Political and Cultural Strategies for Survival." *Ethnic and Racial Studies* 16.2:203–35.

Nash, June

1979   *We Eat the Mines and the Mines Eat Us, Dependency and Exploitation in Bolivian Tin Mines.* New York: Columbia University Press.

Nelson, George

n.d.   Manuscript collection. Western History Collection, University of Oklahoma, Norman.

Noley, Grayson

1985a   "1540: the First European Contact." In *The Choctaw before Removal*, ed. Carolyn Keller Reeves, 55–72. Jackson: University Press of Mississippi.

1985b   "The Early 1700s: Education, Economics and Politics." In *The Choctaw before Removal*, ed. Carolyn Keller Reeves, 73–119. Jackson: University Press of Mississippi.

Norcross, Charles P.

1907   "Weyerhaeuser: Richer than John D. Rockefeller." *Cosmopolitan* 42:252–59.

O'Brien, Philip J.

1975   "A Critique of Latin American Theories of Dependency." In *Beyond the Sociology of Development*, ed. Ivar Oxaal, Tony Barnett, and David Booth, 7–27. London: Routledge & Kegan Paul.

Oklahoma Department of Human Services

1989   *Annual Report.* Oklahoma City: Oklahoma Dept. of Human Services.

Oklahoma Employment Security Commission

n.d.   Miscellaneous Documents. Research Department, Oklahoma City.

Oklahoma IMPACT

1981   *Profile: Poverty in Oklahoma.* Oklahoma City: Legislative Information Action Network of the Oklahoma Conference of Churches.

Oklahoma State Corporation Commission

          Miscellaneous Documents. State Capitol, Oklahoma City.

Olson, James S., and Raymond Wilson

1984   *Native Americans in the Twentieth Century.* Urbana: University of Illinois Press.

Peach, W. N., and Richard W. Poole

n.d.   *Human and Material Resources of Pushmataha and McCurtain Counties:*

A Profile for Growth and Development. Durant: Southeastern Oklahoma State College, Technological Use Studies Center.

Peregrine, Peter

1991   "Prehistoric Chiefdoms on the American Midcontinent: A World-System Based on Prestige Goods." In *Core/Periphery Relations in Precapitalist Worlds*, ed. Christopher Chase-Dunn and Thomas D. Hall. Boulder CO: Westview.

Phillips, Richard Hayes

1982   "The Ouachita Timberlands of Southeastern Oklahoma: Unextinguished Choctaw-Chickasaw Indian Title and Unconditional Corporate Real Estate Holdings." Master's thesis. University of Oklahoma.

Poor's *Manual of Industrials*

1910–15

Poulin, Betty Jeanne Ward

1981   *Choctaw Heritage*. Heavener OK: privately printed.

Prattis, J. Iain

1980   "Modernizaton and Modes of Production in the North Atlantic: A Critique of Policy Formation for the Development of Marginal Maritime Communities." *American Journal of Economics and Sociology* 39.4:305–19.

1987   "Alternative Views of Economy in Economic Anthropology." In *Beyond the New Economic Anthropology*, ed. John Clammer. New York: St. Martin's.

Quinton, B. T.

1967   "Oklahoma Tribes, the Great Depression, and the Indian Bureau." *Mid-America* 49:29–43.

Rapp, Rayna

1978   "Family and Class in Contemporary America: Notes toward an Understanding of Ideology." *Science and Society* 42.3:278–300.

Ray, Wayne

1993–96   President, Local 5-15, International Wood Workers of America. Personal and telephone interviews, DeQueen AR, 6/8/93, 8/5/95, 8/14, 8/17, 8/18/96.

Rice, Randall

1982   President, Local 5-15, International Wood Workers of America. Telephone interview, 6/5/82.

Robbins, William G.

1994   *Colony and Empire: The Capitalist Transformation of the American West*. Lawrence: University Press of Kansas.

Roberts, Brian R.

1989   "Urbanization, Migration, and Development." *Sociological Forum* 4.4:665–91.

Roberts, Hollis E.

1993   Chief, Choctaw Nation of Oklahoma. Personal interview, Durant OK, 6/7/93.

Robinson, Wilma J.

1993   Director of Tribal Development, Choctaw Nation of Oklahoma. Personal interview, Durant OK, 6/7/93.

Sacks, Karen

1979   *Sisters and Wives: The Past and Future of Sexual Equality*. Reprint, 1982. Urbana: University of Illinois Press.

Sahlins, Marshall

1972   *Stone Age Economics*. Chicago: Aldine.

1993   "Goodbye to Tristes Tropes: Ethnography in the Context of Modern World History," in Assessing Cultural Anthropology, ed. Robert Borofsky, 377–95. New York: McGraw-Hill.

Satz, Ronald N.

1975   *American Indian Policy in the Jacksonian Era*. Lincoln: University of Nebraska Press.

Savage, David G.

1987   "Supreme Court Rules States Can't Regulate Indians' Bingo Games." *Los Angeles Times*, 2/26/87, sec. 1, p. 3.

Schusky, Ernest L.

1994   "The Roots of Factionalism among the Lower Brule Sioux." In *North American Indian Anthropology: Essays on Society and Culture*, ed. Raymond J. Demaille and Alfonso Ortiz, 258–77. Norman: University of Oklahoma Press.

Scott, Alison MacEwen

1986   "Women and Industrialization: Examining the 'Female Marginalization' Thesis." *Journal of Development Studies* 22:649–80.

Searcey, Margaret Zehmer

1985   "Choctaw Subsistence, 1540–1830: Hunting, Fishing, Farming, and

Gathering." In *The Choctaw before Removal*, ed. Carolyn Keller Reeves, 32–54. Jackson: University Press of Mississippi.

Seddon, David

1978   "Economic Anthropology or Political Economy? (II): Approaches to the Analysis of Pre-Capitalist Formations in the Maghreb." In *The New Economic Anthropology*, ed. John Clammer, 61–109. New York: St. Martin's.

Seddon, David, ed.

1978   Relations of Production, Marxist Approaches to Economic Anthropology. Trans. Helen Lackner. London: Cass.

Shabecoff, Philip

1990   "Indian Gaming Spreads Upsetting Some States." *New York Times*, 7/23/90, sec. A, p. 10.

Shelton, Beth Anne, and Ben Agger

1993   "Shotgun Wedding, Unhappy Marriage, No-Fault Divorce? Rethinking the Feminism-Marxism Relationship." In *Theory on Gender/Feminism on Theory*, ed. Paula England. New York: Aldine De Gruyter.

Slagle, Allogan

1994   "Recognized Tribes Must Stay Recognized: Ending the Threat of Administrative Termination by Recognized Indian Tribes." *Indian Affairs* 130 (spring): 1.

Smelser, Neil J.

1967   "Toward a Theory of Modernization." In *Tribal and Peasant Economies: Readings in Economic Anthropology*, ed. George Dalton, 29–48. Austin: University of Texas Press.

Smith, C.

1982   "Planning Development Impacts on Indian Reservations." In *Indian SIA: The Social Impact Assessment of Rapid Resource Development on Native Peoples*, ed. C. Geiser, 41–55. Ann Arbor: University of Michigan, Natural Resource Sociology Lab.

Smith, Carol A.

1983   "Regional Analysis in World-System Perspective: A Critique of Three Structural Theories of Uneven Development." In *Economic Anthropology: Topics and Theories*, ed. Sutti Ortiz, 307–59. Society for Economic Anthropology, Monographs in Economic Anthropology, no. 1. New York: University Press of America.

Smith, Dean

1994   "Commentary: The Issue of Compatibility Between Cultural Integrity
            and Economic Development among Native American Tribes." *Ameri-
            can Indian Culture and Research Journal* 18:2:177–205.

Smith, Gavin

1985   "Reflections on the Social Relations of Simple Commodity Produc-
            tion." *Journal of Peasant Studies* 13.1:99–108.

Smith, Kenneth L.

1986   *Sawmill: The Story of Cutting the First Great Virgin Forest East of the
            Rockies.* Fayetteville: University of Arkansas Press.

Smith, Louis Roycraft

1988   "A History of Sumpter County, Alabama, through 1886." Ph.D. diss.
            University of Alabama.

Snipp, C. Matthew

1986a   "The Changing Political and Economic Status of American Indians:
            From Captive Nations to Internal Colonies." *American Journal of Eco-
            nomics and Sociology* 45:145–57.

1986b   "From Captive Nations to Internal Colonies: American Indians and
            Natural Resource Development." *American Journal of Economics and So-
            ciology* 45:457–64.

1988   "Public Policy Impacts and American Indian Economic Development."
            In *Public Policy Impacts on American Indian Economic Development*, ed.
            C. Matthew Snipp. Native American Studies Development Series, no.
            4. Albuquerque: University of New Mexico, Institute for Native Amer-
            ican Development.

Sockbeson, Henry

1987   "Highlights of Indian Legislation in the 99th Congress." *Native Ameri-
            can Rights Fund Legal Review* 12.1:3–5.

Spaulding, Arminta Scott

1974   "Cyrus Kingsbury, Missionary to the Choctaws." Ph.D. diss. Univer-
            sity of Oklahoma.

Stack, Carol B.

1974   *All Our Kin: Strategies for Survival in a Black Community.* New York:
            Harper & Row.

Strong, Pauline Turner, and Barrik Van Winkle

1993   "Tribe and Nation: American Indians and American Nationalism." *So-
            cial Analysis* 33:9–26.

Stuart, Paul H.

1990   "Financing Self-Determination: Federal Indian Expenditures, 1975–1988." *American Indian Culture and Research Journal* 14.2:1–18.

Students of the Multinational Corporation Group Contract

1975   *A Study of the Weyerhaeuser Company as a Multinational Corporation.* Olympia WA: Evergreen State College.

Swanton, John R.

1918   "An Early Account of the Choctaw Indians." (Trans. of old French ms. from Mississippi.) *Memoirs of the American Anthropological Association* Lancaster PA 5.2. Reprint, 1964. New York: Kraus.

1928   *Aboriginal Culture of the Southeast.* 42d Annual Report of the Bureau of American Ethnology. Washington DC: GPO.

1931   *Source Material for the Social and Ceremonial Life of the Choctaw Indians.* Smithsonian Institution, Bureau of American Ethnology Bulletin 103. Washington DC: GPO.

Swenson, Sally, ed.

1982   *Native Resource Control and the Multinational Corporate Challenge: Aboriginal Rights in International Perspective.* Background documents. Boston: Anthropology Resource Center.

Takaki, Ronald

1993   *A Different Mirror: A History of Multicultural America.* Boston: Little, Brown.

Talbot, Steve

1981   *Roots of Oppression: The American Indian Question.* New York: International.

Tambiah, Stanley J.

1993   "The Politics of Ethnicity." In *Assessing Cultural Anthropology,* ed. Robert Borofsky, 430–41. New York: McGraw-Hill.

Terray, Emanuel

1972   *Marxism and "Primitive" Societies.* New York: Monthly Review.

Tharp, Darrell

1990   President, Local 5–15, International Wood Workers of America. Telephone interview, 1/25/90.

Thompson, John

1986   *Closing the Frontier: Radical Response in Oklahoma, 1889–1923.* Norman: University of Oklahoma Press.

Tishkov, Valery.

1993   "Inventions and Manifestations of Ethno-Nationalism in Soviet Academic and Public Discourse." In *Assessing Cultural Anthropology*, ed.
Robert Borofsky, 443–52. New York:McGraw-Hill.

Tucker, Hampton

n.d.   Manuscript collection. Western History Collection, University of
Oklahoma, Norman.

Ulin, Robert C.

1991   "Critical Anthropology Twenty Years Later: Modernism and Post-
modernism in Anthropology. *Critique of Anthropology* 11.1:63–89.

U.S. Administration for Native Americans

1985   "Pathway to Self-Sufficiency: Social and Economic Development Strategies for Native American Communities." In *Report*. DHHS publ. no.
(OHDS) 86–10013. Washington DC: GPO.

U.S. Board of Indian Commissioners

1869+   *Annual Reports*. Department of the Interior. Washington DC: GPO.

U.S. Bureau of Indian Affairs

1973   *The Choctaw Nation: Its Resources and Development Potential*. Planning
Support Group Report no. 213. Billings MT: U.S. Department of the
Interior.

U.S. Census Bureau

1982+   *Statistical Abstract of the United States*. Washington DC: GPO.

U.S. Commissioner of Indian Affairs

1836+   *Annual Reports*. Departments of War and Interior. Washington DC:
GPO.

U.S. Commission to the Five Civilized Tribes

1900+   *Annual Reports*. Department of the Interior. Washington DC: GPO.

U.S. Congress

1882+   *Serial Set Index*. Washington DC: GPO.

U.S. Department of Commerce and Labor

1913   *The Lumber Industry*. Vol. 1, *Standing Timber*. Washington DC: GPO.

U.S. Department of the Interior

1898–1920   *Annual Reports*. Washington DC: GPO.

U.S. Inspector for Indian Territory

1900+   *Reports*. Department of the Interior. Washington DC: GPO.

U.S. Joint Economic Committee

1969   *Toward Economic Development for Native American Communities.* 91st Cong., 1st sess. Washington DC: GPO.

Valentine, Charles

1975   "Voluntary Ethnicity and Social Change: Classism, Racism, Marginality, Mobility, and Revolution." *Journal of Ethnic Studies* 3.1:1–27.

Vizenor, Gerald

1989   "Minnesota Chippewa: Woodland Treaties to Tribal Bingo." *American Indian Quarterly* 13.1:31–57.

1990 [1976]   *Crossbloods, Bone Courts, Bingo, and Other Reports.* Minneapolis: University of Minnesota Press.

1992   "Gambling on Sovereignty." *American Indian Quarterly* 16.3:411–13.

Wallerstein, Immanuel

1976   *The Modern World System.* Vol. 1, *Capitalist Agriculture and the Origins of the European World-Economy in the Sixteenth Century.* New York: Academic.

1980   *The Modern World System.* Vol. 2, *Mercantilism and the Consolidation of the European World-Economy, 1600–1750.* New York: Academic.

1984   *The Politics of the World-Economy: The States, the Movements, and the Civilizations.* New York: Cambridge University Press.

1989   *The Modern World System.* Vol. 3, *The Second Era of Great Expansion of the Capitalist World-Economy, 1730–1840s.* New York: Academic.

Waltman, Henry George

1962   "The Interior Department, War Department, and Indian Policy, 1865–1887." Ph.D. diss. University of Nebraska.

Ward, Kathryn

1993   "Reconceptualizing World System Theory to Include Women." In *Theory on Gender/Feminism on Theory*, ed. Paula England, 43–68. New York: Aldine De Gruyter.

Ward, Kathryn, ed.

1990   *Women Workers and Global Restructuring.* Ithaca NY: Cornell University, School of Industrial and Labor Relations.

Weinberg, Daniel H.

1987   "Rural Pockets of Poverty." *Rural Sociology* 52.3:398–408.

Wells, Samuel James

1985   "Federal Indian Policy: From Accommodation to Removal." In *The*

Choctaw before Removal, ed. Carolyn Keller Reeves, 181–213. Jackson: University Press of Mississippi.

1987　　　"Choctaw Mixed Bloods and the Advent of Removal." Ph.D. diss. University of Southern Mississippi.

Weyerhaeuser Corporation

ca. 1975　　*Weyerhaeuser Company History*. Tacoma WA.

1977　　　"Weyerhaeuser in Oklahoma." April. Tacoma WA.

1978–89　　*Annual Reports*. Tacoma WA.

1980　　　"Weyerhaeuser Handy Facts." June. Tacoma WA.

1981　　　"Weyerhaeuser Handy Facts." October. Tacoma WA.

White, Richard

1983　　　*The Roots of Dependency: Subsistence, Environment, and Social Change among the Choctaws, Pawnees, and Navajos*. Lincoln: University of Nebraska Press.

White, Robert H.

1990　　　*Tribal Assets: The Rebirth of Native America*. New York: Holt.

Wilkins, David E.

1993　　　"Modernization, Colonialism, Dependency: How Appropriate Are these Models for Providing an Explanation of North American Indian 'Underdevelopment'?" *Ethnic and Racial Studies* 16.3:390–419.

Williams, Rob

1983　　　"Reagan's Initiatives Lead to More Questions than Answers." *Indian Truth* 250 (April): 4.

Williams, William Appleman

1966 [1961]　*The Contours of American History*. Chicago: Quadrangle.

Winslow, Art

1983　　　"Speaking with Forked Tongue." *Indian Truth* 250 (April): 8, 15–16.

Wolf, Eric R.

1982　　　*Europe and the People without History*. Berkeley and Los Angeles: University of California Press.

Wood, Peter

1985　　　"You Would Have Made Such a Good Indian: Passages from the Autobiography of Gideon Lincecum." *Southern Exposure* 13.6:62–66.

Worsley, Peter

1970 [1964]　*The Third World*. 2d ed. Chicago: University of Chicago Press.

Wright, Allen

1921　　　"Wheelock Seminary." *Chronicles of Oklahoma* 1.2:117–20.

Wright, J. B.

1959   "Ranching in the Choctaw and Chickasaw Nations." *Chronicles of Oklahoma* 37 (fall): 294–300.

Wright, Muriel H.

1927   "Old Boggy Depot." *Chronicles of Oklahoma* 5:4–17.

1928   "The Removal of the Choctaws to the Indian Territory, 1830–1833." *Chronicles of Oklahoma* 6.2:103–28.

Young, Mary E.

1958   "Indian Removal and Land Allotment: The Civilized Tribes and Jacksonian Justice." *American Historical Review* 64:31–45.

Zuckoff, Mitchell, and Doug Bailey

9/26/93   "US Turns to Betting as Budget Fix." *Boston Globe*, 1, 18.

9/27/93   "Poor Communities Lose Big in Lottery." *Boston Globe*, 1, 8–9.

9/28/93   "Gaming's New Face Has Corporate Profile." *Boston Globe*, 1, 16–17.

9/29/93   "Indians Pursue a Golden Chance." *Boston Globe*, 1, 24–25.

9/30/93   "Cities Weigh Quick Cash vs. Social Costs." *Boston Globe*, 1, 18.

NEWSPAPERS

Akwesasne Notes (Mohawk Nation NY), 1989–90

Bishinik (Choctaw Nation, Durant OK), 1985–96

Boston Globe (Boston MA), 1993

Daily Oklahoman (Oklahoma City OK), 1935

Federal Reporter (Washington DC), 1983

Hartford Courant (Hartford CT), 1982

Los Angeles Times (Los Angeles CA), 1987

McCurtain Gazette (Idabel OK), 1982–83

New York Times (New York NY), 1903–94

Talihina American (Talihina OK), 1981–90

INDEX

Act of 1908. *See* Restrictions Act of 1908
African Americans. *See* blacks
agrarian household economy, 146. *See also* households; subsistence
agriculture, 25, 29, 39, 53, 54, 79, 110. *See also* markets; mixed-bloods; slavery; slaves; subsistence
Aid to Families with Dependent Children (AFDC), 113, 164
alliances: with British, 13–15, 25; with French, 13; political, 14, 19, 219. *See also* chiefs; Euro-Americans
allotments, xxx, 6, 22, 38, 122; alienation of, 78–82, 124, 133; and land speculation, 81; and land survey, 78–80; of minor children, 79–82; in Mississippi, 19, 43; opposition to, 72–73; policy, 74; provisions, 74; removal of restrictions on, 78–83; restricted, 85; sale of, 79–80; under Atoka Allotment Agreement, 81; under Restrictions Act of 1908, 83; under Supplemental Agreement of 1902, 81–82; under Treaty of 1866, 62; unrestricted, 85; and Weyerhaeuser land, 98. *See also* Atoka Allotment Agreement; Dawes Severalty Act; "homestead"; land; Restrictions Act of 1908; Supplemental Agreement of 1902; "surplus"; timber; timberland
"amalgamation," ethnic, 218; definition of, 5
American Board of Commissioners for Foreign Missions (ABCFM), 44, 55
American Board of Indian Missions, 39–40, 43–46, 55
"annihilation," ethnic, definition of, 5
annuities, 43, 46, 53, 69
Apukshunnubbee District, 34–35, 42, 44–45, 53
Arctic Alaska Fisheries, Inc., 184
Arkansas (state), 37, 91; chicken processing in, 145, 161, 183; Dierks in, 95–96, 98–99, 172; Weyerhaeuser in, 175, 181, 195–96
Arkansas River, 37, 61; plantations along, 53
Arkansas Territory, 37
Armstrong Academy, 53
assimilation, xxix, 6, 14, 18, 39, 47–48,

198–99, 218, 223–24; and churches, 47; definition of, 5; Euro-Americans and, 14; factions, 31–33, 55; and incorporation model, xxix; and mission schools, 39; and mixed bloods, 47; traditionalist resistance to, 43; and U.S. government, 49. *See also* mixedbloods
asymmetry, xxxiii, 28
Atoka Allotment Agreement, 73–74, 78–81. *See also* Dawes Severalty Act; Supplemental Agreement of 1902

bands, indigenous, 7, 21, 26, 199, 206. *See also* clans; *iksas*
Baptists, 39, 40, 45. *See also* churches; missionaries; schools
Battiest, Oklahoma, 51
Beach community, Oklahoma, 118
beadwork, 138–40, 148, 156, 213. *See also* crafts; subsistence
Belvin, Jimmy, Chief, 205
Bethabara, Oklahoma, 44
Bethel, Oklahoma, 51, 104, 116, 207, 211
Big Lick Church, 51
big man, 8, 25, 44. *See also* chiefs; *mingoes*
bilingualism, 23, 27, 31, 114. *See also* interpreters; language
bingo. *See* Indian gaming
Bismarck, Oklahoma, 98
Bixby, Tams, 82, 87, 88
blacks, 21, 49, 65, 104, 116, 161; allotments to, 84; population of, 2, 104. *See also* freedmen; slavery; slaves
blended families, xxxi, 31, 35, 118. *See also* households; intermarried whites; mixedbloods; whites
boarding schools, 23, 40–41, 43, 47; mixedbloods and, 43. *See also* education; schools
Board of Commissioners of Indian Missions, 62. *See also* churches; missionaries
Board of Indian Commissioners, 78
Boggy Depot, 55
"boom and bust," xxvi
borderlands. *See* Mississippi "borderland"
Boserup, Ester, 29

259

Index

221; in Indian Territory, 61; land, 80, 132; on noncitizens, 69; and public welfare, 164; regional, 189; on traders, 63, 69; tribal, 66, 69–70, 72, 210; and Weyerhaeuser, 190–93, 196–97. *See also* Choctaw Nation Tax Commission

tenant labor, white, 63, 65

termination, xxx, 4–5, 55, 61, 65, 67, 73–74, 77–78, 198, 201, 204; and Choctaw progressives, 72

Territorial Ring, 78

Texas (state), 64, 76, 91, 106, 108, 129, 141, 186, 210

Texas Instruments, Inc., 210, 214

Texas, Oklahoma, and Eastern Railroad, 98, 175

Texas Trail, 58

third world, xxvi, 102, 168

"Thomas LeFlore Company," 35, 44

timber, 23, 37, 60–61, 74; clearcutting of, 2, 103, 119, 133, 180, 185, 192; cutting, 67–68, 71, 86; Dawes Commission appraisal of, 86; illegal cutting of, 90; illegal sale of, 68, 71, 76, 81–82, 85–86, 88, 94, 98; in Indian Territory, 25, 37, 60–61, 81; and land survey, 86; loblolly pine, 2, 101, 103, 175; market for, 101; monopoly of, 100–101; National Agent, 66; outside access to, 91–95; pine timber, value of, 80; and railroads, 59–60, 63, 66–68, 72, 85–86; reserves, tribal, 86; royalties from, 67; sale of by Choctaws, 67, 86; speculators in, 81, 86; standing, 101; standing timber, value of, 79, 90; as subsistence resource, 71; survey of, under Atoka Allotment Agreement, 78–80; tribal regulation of, 66–67, 70; as tribal resource, xxi, 61, 71, 86; and U.S. economic development, 75, 95, 99; used for railroad construction, 37; value of, 91; value of Choctaw, 101. *See also* clearcutting; Dierks Forests, Inc.; timber industry; timberland; Timber Law of 1871; timber region; timber workers; Weyerhaeuser

timber industry: and Choctaw allotments, 88, 98; and Choctaw surplus, 81; and Dierks, 95–99; and land fraud, 19, 38; and proposed forest reserve, 87; tribal, 59, 70–71, 92; unallotted, 85–89; 97; and

Weyerhaeuser, 95, 98–102, 132, 172–75, 181, 190–94, 196, 221. *See also* Dierks; timber; timberland; Weyerhaeuser

timberland: allotted, 98; appraisal of, 78–79; Choctaw allotments and, 88, 98; Choctaw surplus, 81; Dawes Commission appraisal of, 86; grabbing, 81; and land fraud, 19, 38; monopoly of regional, 100; outside access to, 91–95; and proposed forest reserve, 87, 98; survey of, 78–80; tribal, xxi; unallotted, 85–89, 97–98; value of, 79, 91; value of, tribal, xxi, 101; Weyerhaeuser and, 105. *See also* Dierks; timber; timber industry; timber region; timber workers; Weyerhaeuser

Timber Law of 1871, 66, 86

timber region, xxvii, 54, 60, 74, 81, 103, 108–9, 116, 119, 137, 152, 171; allotments in, 81; Choctaws in, xxix, 25, 49, 60, 71, 76, 79, 102–3, 108, 128, 136, 141, 150, 156, 164, 171, 201; employment in, 110; full-bloods in, 119, 193; full-blood subsistence in, 51; Northern counties, population of, 54; outside entry into, 92, 94, 96, 99, 101; speculators in, 81, 86; timberland in, 91, 106. *See also* Dierks; timber; timber industry; timber workers; Weyerhaeuser

timber workers, 161; Choctaw, 70, 71, 145, 155, 160; in Choctaw sample, 159; Weyerhaeuser, 196; women, 103, 181, 183, 221. *See also* Weyerhaeuser

trade, tribal regulation of, 50

traders, 11, 13–14, 21; British, 14; as change agents, 21; Euro-Americans and, 14; French, 14; and intermarriage, 30, 50; noncitizen, 63, 69; white, 13–15, 21, 25, 30, 63, 69. *See also* citizenship; "Indian factory system"; markets; trade

trading posts, 17, 55, 58

traditionalists, 18–19, 22, 27, 31–33, 38–66, 72; and removal to Indian Territory, 19. *See also* factions; full-bloods

Trail of Tears, 1, 19, 113, 206, 224

treaties, 15, 40, 55, 74, 77, 200; and mixed-bloods, 54; of removal, 18, 54, 62; whites and, 22

Treaty of 1866, 48, 55, 62–63, 69–70, 74, 106; allotment provision of, 62; railroad rights-

271

Weyerhaeuser Timber Company, 100
Weyerhaeuser Townsite Company, 175
Wheelock Academy, 41, 44
White Earth Anishinaabegs, 38, 43
whites, 21, 23, 116–17, 119, 182–83, 215, 220–21, 223; allotments of, 81, 83; Choctaw relations with, 80, 108–9, 138, 142, 144, 165–69; and citizenship, 65; as culture brokers, 23, 27–30, 36, 39, 41–42; effects of Choctaw contact with, 8, 11, 15, 17–19, 22–25, 27–32, 60, 117; as entrepreneurs, 28–29, 58–60, 64, 67–70, 72, 77; exploitation by, 131; as guardians, 81; ideology of, 27; illegal entry of, 59, 61–64, 66–69; in Indian Territory, 55; and intermarriage, xxxi, 26–28, 30, 32–33, 39, 50, 53–54, 58, 62, 84, 120, 200; and land, 16–20, 51, 72, 80–81, 83, 85, 101, 109, 122, 133; and land fraud, 90–91, 131–34; land sales to, 122, 124–25; and language, 21, 28, 49; migration to Indian Territory, 48, 50; and missionizing, 41–42, 46; in Mississippi borderlands, 29–30; population of, 2, 54, 63, 65, 84, 104; and schools, 39, 42–43; as tenant labor, 63–65; in timber region, 85; and trade, 30, 63, 70; traders, 13–15, 17, 21, 30, 50, 62–63, 69; and traditionalists, 33, 43; and tribal influence, 47; tribal regulation of, 50, 58–59, 63, 63–66, 69–70, 73–74. *See also* intermarriage; intermarried whites; mixed-bloods
Whitney, Ely, 16
Williams, Loring S., 44
Wilson, James, 88
women, 25n, 138–40; as captives, 26; as change agents, 28, 36; changing status of, 25n, 28–29; and chicken processing, 161, 183; and church gatherings, 47; and clan politics, 8, 10, 12, 25, 29; as culture conservators, 140; and division of labor, 7, 12, 24, 29, 136, 221; economic activities of, 103, 108; and economic power, 29, 36; education of, 158, 222; in formal economy, 139; household influence of, 29; and household labor, 162, 169, 188; in informal economy, 136, 138–39, 222; and intermarriage, 15, 26, 28, 30, 50; and land rights, 12, 24; and matrilineal descent/inheritance, 51; and patriarchy, 28; political participation by, 8, 10, 29; and re-

source ownership, 51; sale of, for debt, 17; as secondary labor, 196, 221–22; and subsistence, 11–12, 36, 43, 136, 138–39, 158, 162, 169, 187; status of, 12, 17, 25, 36, 221; and technological innovations, 29; and timber work, 103, 181, 183, 221; and unpaid labor, 139, 158; wage labor by, 103, 108, 136, 139, 158, 161, 169, 180–82, 187; white, 120, 138. *See also* crafts; division of labor; foraging; gardening; males; quiltmaking; subsistence
Women, Infants and Children Program (WIC), 141, 211
Woodworkers Local W15. *See* International Association of Machinists and Aerospace Workers, Local Lodge W15
Works Projects Administration (WPA), 108, 169
world system, xxiv, 3, 21, 23, 115, 136, 146; incorporation into, xxii. *See also* colony; core/periphery; global economy; incorporation; internal markets; markets; world-systems theory
world-systems theory, xix–xxi, 3, 13–14, 21, 23, 115, 136, 146; Choctaws and, 146; and colonies 3, 4; and "dependent" development, 3, 102; and dependent enclaves, 3, 4, 221; and "domestic dependent ethnicity," 6; and domestic dependent niche, 102, 171; and "domestic dependent tribes," 17, 198; and internal colonies, 4; and "periphery," 3, 4. *See also* colony; core/periphery; development; "frontier"; global economy; incorporation; internal colony; markets; periphery
Wright, Alfred (Allen), Chief, 44, 64, 66
Wright, Benjamin, 43
Wright City, Oklahoma, 41, 99, 113, 146, 174–75, 178, 180, 182, 189, 198
written code of laws, 33

younger nuclear households, 110, 120, 129; definition of, 120; family size of, Choctaw sample, 121; income of, Choctaw sample, 157, 159; landholdings of, Choctaw sample, 110, 129–30. *See also* extended families; extended households; older nuclear households